WORKING MEN'S COLLEGE.

LIBRARY REGULATIONS.

The Library is open every week-day evening (except Saturday), from 6.30 to 10 o'clock.

This book may be kept for three weeks. If not returned within that period, the borrower will be liable to a fine of one penny per week.

If lost or damaged, the borrower will be required to make good such loss or damage.

Only one book may be borrowed at a time.

A History of the
Liberal Party.   .

AUTHOR SIR HENRY SLESSER.

TITLE A HISTORY OF THE
LIBERAL PARTY.

Date	MEMBER'S NAME.
....	1
....	....

DEMCO

A History of the Liberal Party

The Right Hon. Sir Henry Slesser, P.C.

HUTCHINSON & CO. (*Publishers*) LTD.

LONDON : NEW YORK : MELBOURNE

Made and Printed in Great Britain at

Greycaines

(Taylor Garnett Evans & Co. Ltd.)
Watford, Herts

CONTENTS

A*

CHAPTER I

INTRODUCTORY

THE unique pragmatic genius of the English people to contrive working principles out of elements apparently incompatible is nowhere more clearly disclosed than in the history of the Liberal Party. There, gathered into one political unity, have been found great landowners suspicious of the new plutocracy and wealthy capitalists complaining of territorial predominance; working men in revolt against the severity of their masters, erastian defenders of the State Church and those who refused to conform to it; constitutional monarchists and extreme Radicals dabbling with Republicanism; the defenders of oppressed nations, clamouring for British intervention, and the denouncers of armament and war and, lastly, the disciples of *laissez faire*, who deplore the encroachments of the State, acting in common organization with those who see in ever-increasing collective activity the protection of the distressed and the only hope of future social development.

The Liberal, far more than his Tory opponent, is characteristically a product of English ways of thought and action. Conservative ideals of loyalty to tradition and authority, imperial expansion, toleration (where necessary) of coercive law and the maintenance of defined status, are in no sense limited to this country. Such notions are to be found in many countries at all times, and though the Continent has known of Liberal politicians, they have had about them an academic quality which, fortunately, is here wanting—invariably, owing to their divorce from the opinions and habits of their fellow citizens, they have failed; in England alone have the Liberals succeeded in accommodating their advocacy of freedom to the instinctive desires of their compatriots.

Despite all inconsistencies and antagonisms, therefore, it would appear that there has always existed in Liberalism a unanimity as to the value of liberty which made the development of the Party possible. It is not easy to summarize this fundamental libertarian idea, but perhaps it may be expressed in the conception that, to the Liberal, authority is only to be supported as a regrettable necessity; for him, individual freedom is the *summum bonum*; whereas in the Conservative case (possibly also in the Socialist) external discipline and regulation have generally been regarded as inherently unobjectionable.

Throughout the Victorian era, and for a decade after, the diverse Liberal interests were able to co-operate so successfully that during the greater part of the epoch they maintained themselves in power. Then at length the logic of fundamental disparity overtook them; the wealthy, alarmed by the growing Radicalism of their colleagues, drifted over to the Conservatives. The advanced Liberals, infected by Socialist ideas, broke away to help to found the Labour Party; the religious interests declined—in the end, it was not easy to see what would be left. For a time the compelling personality of Gladstone had arrested the coming disruption; it was left to that mysterious statesman, Joseph Chamberlain, to bring about the disintegration. Why he did so is not clear

7

—it is obvious that, had the Home Rule question never arisen, it was but a matter of time before such Whigs as Hartington and Goschen would have found the new Liberalism intolerable; but Chamberlain was a Radical, the Party was fast moving in his direction, indeed he was in command of that new social insurgence which in all probability, had he wished, would have developed on his original lines. As it is hoped to show later, his differences with the Home Rulers were at the outset negligible; yet he chose the perils of isolation and political impotence rather than attempt to accommodate the comparatively small differences which existed between his Irish self-government scheme and that of Gladstone. On this he broke his party—for no one else could have reconciled the elements which later were to find independence in the Labour Party. In the result his action was more fatal to Liberalism than the Home Rule policy of Gladstone, for in the defection of Chamberlain the fate of the Liberals was irrevocably determined.

Liberalism, whose cause is the defence of personal liberty against the coercions of authority and the State, can only arise where there has come into being a desire for the vindication of the right of personal expression and action, and an attempt to suppress it. Without the possession of an ideal of freedom Liberalism would be purposeless; in the absence of imposed restraint its appeal would be unnecessary.

In seeking therefore for the origins of the Liberal idea, we cannot disregard the time when first it was that the attempt to achieve free self-expression arose, and in this matter it is generally conceded that the Greeks have the supreme honour: it was they who first countenanced *homo sapiens*, the independent thinking man.

Impartially to ask, "What is the supreme Good?" was to enquire to what end a man voluntarily should dedicate his life. The question assumed as possible a conscious choice; a capacity in the individual, irrespective of tradition, uniquely to criticize existent morality and out of individual meditation to develop a personal method of behaviour and responsibility.

From these self-conscious efforts came the Sophists, culminating in the Socratic, Platonic and Aristotelian questionings. At Athens the art and science of Politics arose—in little more than a hundred years, the most momentous period in human history—a new culture, dependent upon free speculation, had come into being.

It was not long, however, before the second necessary condition for Liberalism, that of opposition to these bold speculations, began to develop: the need for an aggressive and protective party had come—Socrates was its first outstanding martyr.

Such freedom, however, as was claimed was admittedly regarded as the privilege of a small class. From Pericles to Cicero, the notion, now obtaining among the Germans, that "civilized" man must be supported economically by slave labour, was almost universal. The early Christians, in the political and economic spheres, also assumed it—only in the world of the Spirit was the Christian to be free; as Whitehead has put it, "For a thousand years, to be civilized was to be a slave owner." (*Adventures of Ideas*, p. 16.) Yet once Christianity had made familiar a belief in the integrity of the human soul, the question was bound to arise, how far slavery could be reconciled with the Faith? Sometimes as a result of these questionings slavery was pronounced a blessing, because, like poverty, it afforded the opportunity of practising the virtues of humility and patience. By St. Augustine slavery was justified as one of the penalties of man, incurred by his original sin in Adam. (*De. Civ. Dei.* XLX. 14.) Finally, St. Thomas, following Aristotle, declared that some men are born to command and others to obey: slavery obtains both through original sin and as a consequence of capture in War, which being necessary, is just: slavery is therefore not contrary to natural law; if used according to Christian methods, like private property, it may be justified. There is, however, both in St. Augustine, and more markedly in St. Thomas, an apologetic note which is entirely absent in Aristotle. In truth, in the Middle Ages, slavery had already given place to serfdom; the right to services had largely taken the place of control of the person and the way to the later wage contract was open.

As to liberty of the mind, it is to be noted how already the right to free opinion had come to be appreciated by the time when Cicero and Seneca wrote. The mind, says the latter, cannot be given into slavery. (*De Beneficiis*, III, 20). The Christian, Lactantius, speaks to the like effect; indeed, from the Christian recognition of personal responsibility and ultimate judgment, no other conclusion could long remain possible.

The early Church itself was constituted upon the most democratic basis. Bishops were elected on a universal suffrage and, says Lecky, "if the principles had been continued, the habits of freedom would have been so diffused among the people, that the changes our age has witnessed might have been anticipated by many centuries and might have been effected under the patronage of Catholicism". (*Rationalism in Europe*, Vol. 2, p. 141.)

The Church, however, became absorbed in theological conflicts and later, in disputes with the secular power of the Emperor, and in these and other disputes the notion of the liberty of the individual was almost ignored. Indeed, it came about that it was in the religious field that liberty was particularly menaced; the belief in the exclusive power of the Church to ensure salvation led to a hatred of the heretic comparable only to the modern nationalist attitude towards treachery in war. The converted Emperor lent his aid; Constantine persecuted pagans and heretics indifferently and he was followed, even more rigorously, by Theodosius. St. Augustine took upon himself to formulate a theology of persecution. He declared heresy to be the worst of crimes though but few were, in fact, persecuted before the days of the Albigensians. The view had come to be taken in the Church that she should never take the responsibility of blood shedding, but Pope Innocent IV enjoined heretical extermination by torture, and even Luther, the reformer, thought that heretics might be properly punished by the civil magistrate. In this country, by the statute of Henry V, "de Heretico Comburendo," the Church could consign heretics to the civil authority for death—a power not revoked until 1677.

Nevertheless, in England, the first liberal advocates of toleration were believers. As Protestants they were bound to uphold the rights of private judgment and on that basis found it increasingly difficult to support the view of exclusive ecclesiastical power compulsorily to enforce credal salvation. Although there were many who still, illogically, combined the right of private opinion with an assertion of the political and legal coercive supremacy of the Church (even the atheist Hobbes justifies religious persecution as an attribute of the strong State) yet, the notion of the fallibility of human reason to decide on ultimate beliefs displayed by such Anglicans as Hooker, Berkeley, Chillingworth and Taylor; the freedom of religious opinion accorded by Milton, Cromwell and the Independents as against the Presbyterians, and the sceptical Deism which followed the Restoration, all tended in a Liberal direction.

By Milton, the Catholics alone were to be excluded from toleration on the ground that they were idolatrous! The argument that as Catholics themselves disbelieved in toleration they would, if tolerated, work to destroy the liberty of others, is to be detected in the opposition to their emancipation which was sought to be established by James II. For a long time after, the exceptional case of the Catholic presented the Whigs with a problem which many of them answered in a manner inconsistent with their doctrine of universal religious liberty. Atheism, also, for many years stood outside the sphere of permitted opinion.

The mediæval Catholic Church had always held a critical attitude towards the secular power. The Tyrant, a sovereign who does not govern according to law, in the opinion of most of the mediæval doctors of the Church could rightly be deposed, if not killed. Revolt against him, they declare, is not sedition, and the distinction between a lawful monarch and the despot was long emphasized by the Society of Jesus. The libertarian theory (government being the result of a social contract), so important to the history of Liberalism, was supported by the Jesuit Suarez as early as the beginning of the seventeenth century. The Sovereign, he asserts, is the servant of the people; by the Pope he could be properly slain for heresy: even Catholic kings were to be regarded as subject to law and papal approval. It would have been disconcerting to the early Protestant democrats to realize that, in the age of unfettered sovereign power, the Jesuits were actively on the side of the people.

The French Gallicans, on the other hand, like the Anglicans in England, exalted the Sovereign at the expense of papal and ecclesiastical authority. Among the first reformers Luther supported the State erastian, Calvin the republican position. In Scotland the views of the Calvinist Knox also resembled in their attitude towards Kings the most extreme of the Jesuits. His follower, Buchanan, openly relied upon the principle of social contract. Regal power, he says, springs from the nation, kings otherwise have no right. The deposition of Mary of Scotland was defended upon such grounds, and the decision to execute Charles I may well have been influenced by similar considerations.

In Charles II's time, in the year of the beheading of the Whig Russell, the University of Oxford, in terms, condemned the views of Buchanan and Milton, and the Church of England broke so completely with mediæval tradition as to lead a movement in favour of absolute obedience. It was from such post-mediæval sources therefore that the Tory party was derived.

Thus, when History is dispassionately read, it will be realized that the Tories, from Wentworth and Filmer to Bolingbroke, were the party of innovation in proclaiming personal absolute sovereignty; the Whigs the party of tradition and common law—though by most people they have, uncritically, been thought to have been the Radicals of their day.

So we come to the testing time of James II, for it was in his reign that the Tory doctrine of divine right inconsistently foundered upon the rock of Roman Catholic assertion. Thereafter, for many years, the Tories were a dismembered opposition; some remaining true to their formularies (the Jacobites and non-jurors), some reluctantly supporting the Revolution Settlement—the selection of kingship by Act of Parliament and Law—essentially a mediæval and Whig conception—and some, at length, in desperation, transferring their exaltation of monarchy to the new parliamentary Hanoverian kings. It was during this period that the Whigs so triumphed that, even after their fall, their political assumptions of the rule of law and popular consent were scarcely challenged. In no other country had the same dilemma appeared—in no other did there develop anything comparable to the English Whig party.

The first attempt to use Parliament for ends which did not accord with the Sovereign will is to be detected in the petitions organized by the Puritans in the later days of Queen Elizabeth. During the Parliament of 1584, conferences of those discontented with Church government, and with the bishops in particular, were convened in London and other towns; in the session of 1586, after provincial criticism of the Church had been voiced, a synod was held in the metropolis. Supplications to the Houses were made, and outside agitation undertaken to purify the Church of the last vestiges of Catholicism was entered upon; even election campaigns were inaugurated. The Queen was driven, in terms, to forbid the discussion of religious matters in the Commons, but the complainants were not to be deterred. Bills were introduced by the bolder Puritans to substitute government by Presbyteries for that of Bishops. The Speaker vainly attempted to intervene, until the Sovereign, enraged, sequestered the Bills, and five of the party who were promoting them—including Peter Wentworth, their leader—were imprisoned in the Tower. In 1591 the Star Chamber took a hand in the attempted suppression. Again, on his release, Wentworth strove to inaugurate a Puritan movement in politics; again he was imprisoned. Though having little toleration about him, yet he may fairly be claimed as a pioneer in the assertion of parliamentary right as against the Executive —in this sense he may be called the first Liberal.

It is common knowledge how the Commons, originally summoned only to grant extraordinary sums to the Crown, had made a premature attempt to control government in the time of the later Plantagenet kings; how Parliament had been regarded by Wolsey, on the other hand, as a mere instrument of the King's will. The failure of the Cardinal in 1523 and 1525 to obtain loans from the Commons induced his successor, Cromwell, to ensure their subservience by creating new boroughs of royal influence by bribery and by direct interference with the elections. Thereafter, until the later days of Elizabeth, Parliament for the most part remained the creature of the Crown. It was the Puritans who first challenged that long royal supremacy.

In the active social legislation of Elizabeth we detect a further change. A committee of the House in November, 1597, was asked to consider "the sundry great and horrid abuses of idle and vagrant persons, and the miserable state of the godly and honest sort of the poor subjects of the realm". The Bills ensuing received such examination and criticism and were so often amended as to display the increasingly active part which the Houses were now prepared to take in domestic legislation.

Once the legislature was active, tension between the Houses grew, the Commons being affronted at their frequent discourteous reception by the Lords—their spirit was rapidly rising.

On his way from Scotland to take the Crown, James had received a petition, said to have been signed by a thousand of the Puritan clergy, that they might be excused from using the sign of the Cross in Baptism, that Saints' days be no longer observed and so forth, and in January 1604 a conference met at Hampton Court to consider the whole matter, the King, like Constantine on a former occasion, presiding. Dr. Reynolds, on behalf of the petitioners, asked that the clergy might meet in Synod— a word of hateful recollection to the King. Enraged, James dissolved the meeting with angry threats, but the majority in his first Parliament supported the Puritans; nevertheless Order was made that the clergy obey the rubric, and three hundred, being recalcitrant, were ejected from their livings. The House of Commons protested—in direct opposition to the King's will, they manifested their anger by refusing to agree to the Union of England and Scotland. In consequence of their obduracy they were dissolved.

Three years later an even more recalcitrant Commons met. It sat a month only, but during that period fearlessly had attacked the foreign policy of the King, his extravagance and favouritism, and the granting of privileges and monopolies by his ministers. There was a breakdown of responsible government; after the death of Robert Cecil, Lord Salisbury, the Privy Council almost ceased to function—the elder statesmen and peers were affronted by the ennobling of the favourites, Carr and Villiers, and refused to act, but an unpopular peace was still kept with foreign nations. Raleigh was sacrificed and, as part of the plan for the propitiation of Spain, the project of marrying Charles to the Infanta was supported in official circles. The substitution of another Catholic princess, a French one, did little to ease the growing Puritan indignation.

Under the leadership of Coke, the Judiciary also began to take an attitude less subservient than heretofore to Monarchy. Coke himself refused to advise the King in private as to the extent of his prerogative powers—these were matters, he said, to be laid down in open court. He was dismissed from the Bench and Council, to become one of the leaders of the anti-authoritarian party in Parliament, which the King, to obtain money, was at length forced to summon in 1621.

Here, in Coke's assertion of the rights of the Law and the subject, we find the juridical foundation of Liberalism. He directed the impeachment of Bacon, the supporter of prerogative, and won for Parliament the right to rid the country of unpopular ministers; a power which the Tudors had exercised through that assembly for their own ends. A fierce anti-Spaniard, Coke next led the House to demand a share in the control of foreign affairs. Following the precedent of Elizabeth, the King sought to forbid the House discussing matters relating to continental policy. They replied by entering in the Journals a protest against the royal claim. The King in his turn sent for their book and, childishly, tore out the offending resolution; in 1622 he again dissolved Parliament.

Thus, by the end of his reign, the coalition of Puritans, common lawyers and patriots had established a claim for the independence of Parliament which a quarter of a century before would have been considered highly seditious. The war which the Commons desired had started, with results so far unsatisfactory. Incited in particular by Sir Robert Phelips, the House of Commons, to manifest their want of confidence in the War Minister, the Duke of Buckingham, refused to grant supplies; this was a grievous blow to authority, for while the King had a private (and diminishing) revenue apart from Parliamentary grant, it was altogether insufficient to maintain costly hostilities. Nevertheless the Crown still thought dissolution to be the only remedy to curb the Commons' arrogance, but next year even greater financial necessity compelled the King again to summon his unruly subjects. In the words of a member, Sir Benjamin Redyard, it was "the crisis of Parliament; by this one we shall know whether Parliaments live or die". This was said in 1628, by which time the King had been told bluntly by Sir John Eliot that if he wished for supply he must first remedy grievances.

The beginning of a Conservative monarchical party is to be detected when Wentworth, who had agreed in attacking the ministers, refused to blame the King. He sought a compromise, and at last half prevailed on the new King, Charles, to consider whether the much-needed subsidies might not be receivable after the Commons had detailed their complaints in a Petition of Right. The Secretary of State, however, was more obdurate than, perhaps, was the King himself, and finally the King was made to say that the Subsidies must come first—then it was that Phelips spoke of the 'crisis'. Eliot persuaded the House to remain firm; the petition in the form of a Bill was sent up first and Wentworth now had to abandon all hope of accommodation. When the Bill was read it openly accused the King of breaches of the Law, and the King, yielding at the last, the royal assent was given to the Petition of Right. Wentworth soon went to the Lords, but his followers remained to defend the King's challenged prerogative powers; the issue between Whig and Tory had arisen.

It is now generally admitted that the dispute as to finance which now began to occupy so much of public attention—whether the King could raise moneys without the consent of Parliament—was the result not so much of royal greed as of necessity. The old feudal idea of the Crown as Supreme Estate had carried with it the royal obligation to provide for the monetary obligations of the realm out of the Sovereign's treasury. The fall in value of money had sadly reduced the regal wealth —the failure of Henry VIII to retain the fruits of the spoliation of the Church in his own hands had thrown away the last chance of monarchical solvency. Increasing expenditure and extravagance and a diminishing revenue precipitated the crisis; the King and his advisers saw that he must, at all cost, find new sources of financial supply.

B

From the earliest times it has been recognized that only grants for extraordinary necessities justified the calling of Parliaments. It was the duty of the Commons, at first their sole function, to authorize the Sheriffs of the counties to raise such abnormal revenue by taxation to supplement the King's own resources; but inevitably there was a border land where free gifts and forced loans might be attempted. The latter had been relied on in 1626; after the parliamentary refusal of a Subsidy. Commissioners for each county were appointed to collect it. Eighty men, more or less wealthy, who would not comply had been imprisoned by the Privy Council or Star Chamber for their recalcitrance. Others, less opulent, were impressed for military service. But the result was a failure, and another Parliament became necessary. Many of the gentry in opposition to these irregular proceedings were returned, to form a Liberal nucleus. That they were for the most part rich will be admitted; richer in many cases than the conservative Lords. That fact has been used in the anti-Whig reaction of recent years by such writers as Belloc, Chesterton, Taylor, and others to support the view that the revolution was but a plutocratic revolt against a benevolent monarchy.

Tonnage and Poundage, originally customs of wine and merchandise imported (save wool, ships and leather which were the King's right)—being taxation which Edward I's Parliament had declared to be illegal to be levied without their consent—were now restricted to one year instead of being granted for life as heretofore; the Customs were to come under the direct annual control of the House of Commons.

"If any merchant," they declared, "shall volun.... .ly pay subsidies of tonnage and poundage not being granted by Parliament, he shall be reputed a betrayer of the Liberty of England and an enemy of the same." (*Resolution*, March, 1629.)

Buckingham was now dead and the financial government was in the hands of Weston, the Lord Treasurer. Weston it was who, in this dilemma, found the devices for supplementing the exhausted revenue by endeavouring to resuscitate obsolete legal expedients. With the King's decision to dispense with Parliaments altogether—there was none from 1629 to 1640—other methods of finding money had become essential.

Ship money, which had been levied on seaports only, was now sought to be extended to the whole Kingdom. When the matter was ultimately litigated, on the concerted refusal of Hampden and his friends to pay, only seven judges to five supported the Crown. But one, Finch, went so far as to declare that Acts of Parliament to take away the royal power to defend the Kingdom were void, and, apparently, extended the dictum to cover the case of moneys to be raised by extra parliamentary means for that purpose.

On the ecclesiastical side also, bitterness had increased. While it is true that the great majority of the Parliamentarians were of the landed and mercantile classes, this fact—so relied upon by the modern cavalier apologists—cannot be extended to cover the religious controversy, for the most zealous of the Puritan dissenters were to be found among the humbler people.

For all his Catholicism, Laud, in the post-mediæval tradition, admitted and supported the royal supremacy. All power, spiritual as well as temporal, he said, was derived from the Crown. All important acts of

Church government were submitted by him to the King for approval. In the Star Chamber he associated himself in judgment with the secular judges and administrators. If it be not a paradox to say so, his Anglo-Catholicism was thoroughly Erastian.

It was this order of regal-ecclesiastical discipline which Laud sought to enforce upon the Scots, with results which are common history. His control of the Press by Bishop's licence was vainly used to stem the flow of Puritan pamphlets, many of them scurrilous, which nevertheless testified to the democratic nature of that rising movement. The dissenting conventicles were suppressed, but rarely were the parliamentary gentry to be found therein—to assert that the anti-Caroline agitation was composed solely of the comfortable and wealthy is to ignore that whole side of it which was based upon religion—then (unlike now) the chief common interest.

In 1637, Prynne, Bastwick, Burton and Lilburne were all sentenced to mutilation or flogging for their attack upon the Episcopacy. They were of the gentry, more or less, but the crowds which angrily gathered around the pillory and cart-wheel disclosed an increasing revolutionary and menacing aspect—it needed no financial intriguers to make them support these martyrs, as they saw them—in the cause of liberty. The religious rebellion in Scotland accentuated the trouble; finally, in despair, the King recalled Wentworth from Ireland to save the monarchical and conservative interests. The Bishop's War, as it was called, had united the democratic forces in England and Scotland and, for want of an adequate army, Charles was driven temporarily to abandon his military designs.

In September, 1639, Wentworth finally became chief adviser to the King, an office which he retained for over a year. He it was who advised the calling of a Parliament in April 1640. It sat but a month, for, on Pym proposing a resolution to oppose the Scottish War, it was dissolved, but not before he had declared that "the powers of Parliament are to the body politic as the rational faculty to the soul of man".

Thereafter the Conservatives temporarily triumphed: members of the Short Parliament were imprisoned; illegal taxation again revived and Church power was exalted in new canons. The Scottish War, against the will of all—except the courtiers—was renewed. The Train Bands, largely Puritan, would not fight. Pressing and compulsion but led to rioting and further discontent. When the Scots advanced to Ripon practically all their claims had to be conceded and the indemnity which he was forced to give them compelled the King, after long consideration, to call yet another Parliament (for he was bankrupt, both of money and of policy)—it was his last.

The position of those conservatively minded members of Parliament who advised the King, such as Portland, Colepepper and Hyde, was not made the easier by reason of the fact that the King in some of his most momentous decisions, such as the attempted arrest of the Five Members, had never consulted them. Nightly, wrote Clarendon, in his *Life*, these three met. The future Lord Chancellor was by no means an uncritical royalist—he had procured the suppression of the Earl Marshal's court, one of the many which exalted prerogative. He had been offered and declined the office of Solicitor-General—by his own account he was much distrusted by both sides—each thinking him a supporter of the other.

At length two most drastic Bills, for the removal of the Bishops from the House of Lords and the popular control of the Militia, were sent by Parliament to the King. Colepepper advised the Sovereign to agree to the former and, in the end, Charles was prevailed upon to sanction it.

Revolution was now not far off—the Parliamentary leaders, Pym, Hampden, Lord Bedford and others were determined that the Sovereign, in the coming struggle, should no longer have the monopoly of force. The abandonment of Strafford by the King, ending in his attainder and execution, was the result of the clamour of the Long Parliament. Popular agitation was deliberately fomented. The arrest of Laud deprived the Government of yet another of its chiefs. After the failure of the impeachment of Strafford and the passage of the attainder in the Commons, tumults and riots were deliberately organized and rumours of plots and revolution spread. The Lords were mobbed, they faltered, and passed the Attainder Bill. The agitation was, in part, genuine; probably no unrest can be organized without some foundation; and there is little doubt that, in London at any rate, the destruction of Strafford and Laud was exceedingly popular.

Finch and Windebank, the other principal ministers, had fled abroad. The invasion of the House by Charles in his pursuit of the Five Members followed; an act, as has been said, decided on the King's personal initiative. This was in January, 1642. On the tenth of that month the King left London and the raising of the King's forces by Commissioners of Array and the Parliament's by military ordinances proceeded, until the clash of actual war came in August.

It was during this time that the opposition of the parties became apparent. Indeed the Civil War may be said to have created the Party System. The royalist members gradually withdrew from both Houses; they constituted the majority of the Lords and a considerable number of the Commons. There remained at the seat of the legislature three hundred of the Commons and some thirty peers, for the moment all more or less of the same mind. The Conservative organization, we may say, was at Oxford; the Radical in London.

Even now the breach was not complete; Hyde, now of the Privy Council and Chancellor of the Exchequer, relates how, early in 1643, Commissioners of Parliament came to Oxford to treat with the King. Their powers were strictly limited, so much so that Charles told them that they might as well have brought the proposals as common carriers. Even Hyde, a moderate and would-be conciliator, thought the terms so unreasonable as to be impossible of acceptance. In the field the Cavalier forces were temporarily victorious, and people, even in London, were clamouring for peace. The relief of Gloucester and the Battle of Newbury, where the monarchists suffered grievously, stabilized the position; there followed a fresh invasion from Scotland and the battle of Marston Moor; thereafter compromise was impossible. In 1645 came the royal defeat at Naseby and the royal power was over.

In Parliament, after the death of Pym and Hampden, there was sad lack of leadership. No attempt at a settlement was made; instead came the intolerant exclusion of two thousand Anglican priests and the prohibition of the use of the book of Common Prayer. The estates of the Cavaliers were confiscated or compounded for at grievous rates and, even in the forces, sectaries, who did not accept the Presbyterian form of Church government, zealots, anabaptists and the like were persecuted. Laymen were forbidden to preach, and Unitarians and Atheists made liable to death penalties. In the result, the Army under Cromwell took possession. They were far more democratic and tolerant than the Presbyterians. They demanded equality of opportunity, and some, such as the Levellers, an economic equality as well.

Meanwhile, the generals, Cromwell and Ireton, were endeavouring to come to terms with Charles. From Carisbrooke he began to attempt a counter-revolution with the aid of the Royalists and even the Presbyterians, the "Grandees" as Lilburne called them. There is no doubt that by 1648 many of the Presbyterians had repented of their breach with the King. Some already were neutral—it was the Independent Army which carried on the war. The Scots were fast going over to the Crown and, had they not been defeated at Preston, it is probable that they and the wealthier classes in England would have effected a restoration. All this it is which explains that purge of Parliament, which excluded so many members that less than one hundred were left, and abolished the House of Lords. The trial and execution of Charles were now inevitable. Like Louis XVI after him, he was killed by the misdirected policies of his friends.

The most momentous constitutional decisions of the Restoration, the recognition of the validity of all Acts of the Long Parliament to which Charles I had consented, and the fictional dating of the new reign from the time of his death, undoubtedly owe their origins to the juridical genius of Clarendon. To him is due the fact that the special prerogative tribunals, the Star Chamber and the provincial royal councils and prerogative courts, were not restored. Clarendon's attitude to the religious claims of the Nonconformists has given to his memory a reputation for arbitrary government which otherwise he does not deserve. The Parliament elected in 1661 was overwhelmingly Anglican. They forced the King to repudiate his promise to the Puritans of religious toleration, but it is only fair to recognize that freedom in religion was an ideal entirely foreign to the minds of Presbyterians when they held power. The penal laws of 1661–1665 excluded from nearly every public function those who would not give "unfeigned assent" to everything in the Book of Common Prayer. The Chancellor relates in his *Life* how the Presbyterians, who were still numerous in the restored Convention Parliament, ineptly sought to prevent the Book of Common Prayer from being reintroduced and how they formed organizations to exclude the Bishops. Such conduct naturally infuriated the Royalists and Cavaliers. The King was forced to notice that the Puritans "had offered him no advice towards the composing of differences in religion—therefore he would try what he could do towards it himself".

A conference had been convoked between the ministers who were the heads of the Presbyterian party and an equal number of the orthodox Clergy—it was held at the Chancellor's lodgings, and in all probability the idea originated with him. Meanwhile, by royal command, no one was to be punished for failing to use the Book of Common Prayer, though orthodox Anglican practice was also expressly permitted. The Puritans were certainly unpopular; their discouragement of gaiety of all kinds had been resented long after the autocratic meddling with the private morals of the rich by Laud in Church courts and the Star Chamber had been forgotten. The parliamentary election of 1661 had largely been fought on the religious issue, whether Presbyterianism or Episcopacy should be the creed of the national Church; the attempt at a concord had failed completely and nothing was left but to give effect to the will of Parliament, which, far less tolerant than the King, insisted on the full enforcement of what, somewhat unfairly, has been called the "Clarendon Code".

Here, then, is to be seen the origin of the Tory Party, though the name was not generally used until 1680. It was theologically undemocratic in the sense that it wished to see Church government taken out of the hands of the congregation. On the other hand, the influence of Clarendon, trained in the Common Law, prevented the growth, at any rate while he held power, of any movement to diminish parliamentary authority. Standing armies, such as those which had ruled England under Cromwell, were abhorred; thus, unlike the later Conservatives, the first Tories were at once anti-militarist and aristocratic—the squires, the country clergy, and the Universities became their main support. The Church in particular, writes Woods (*History of the Tory Party*, p. 17) had now become a very definite vested interest within the fabric of Toryism—conversely, in the small minority in the Cavalier Parliament, the remnants of the Presbyterian and other sectarian parties came to form the rudiments of the Opposition. In their relations to the Crown, the maintenance of the supremacy of Parliament, in legislation and in the granting of supplies, in the preserving of the Common Law and in regard for the sanctity of property, they were scarcely divided from their religious opponents.

The failure of the Dutch War, following four years of peace, and the disasters of the Plague and the great Fire, strengthened the Opposition, until then concerned only for Puritan Protestantism—but the whole Parliament now united to attack Clarendon. But Clarendon, though the Cavaliers knew it not, was in essence a constitutional Tory, and his defeat proved, ultimately, to be a defeat for the Cavaliers. Thereafter, the King chose his own ministers. A close Cabinet arose, the "Cabal," of much diversity of opinion: Clifford, a Roman Catholic; Ashley, a tolerant sceptic, with whom Buckingham may be associated—there was scarce a convinced Anglican among them. Their secret relations with Louis XIV were looked upon with distrust by the Anglican patriots, and the new-formed country party of Roundheads, Presbyterians and Nonconformists was ready to support a Protestant alliance against the Catholic French despot and his English friends. It was not long before the King and his ministers found themselves in the sinister position of Charles I, opposing a united Parliament—the dismissal of Clarendon and the French intrigue had shattered the loyalty of that Cavalier Parliament which, originally, had combined to support the Crown.

Thus it came about that the underlying purpose of the King was to free himself from that very Parliament which had been elected to support him. To the Tory politician such a cleavage was fatal—the Whig "country" party alone could hope to benefit by the estrangement.

To make himself an absolute King, which was now his objective, Charles, in the Treaty of Dover, had sold himself as vassal to the King of France. He had received secret subsidies and even his religion was to be determined by that great tyrant. Despite the pleading of Bryant, in plain fact Charles II was a traitor, and had he been a subject would have been guilty of High Treason.

By the secret Treaty of Dover he was to be freed from Parliament by receiving bribes from Louis—no such device had been considered by Charles I or his father—such a policy was not Toryism but treachery. The Secretary of State, Arlington, and the Catholic, Clifford, alone were fully in the secret, for Charles descended not only to cheat his Parliament and his People, but even the majority of his own chosen ministers.

The obligation to help Louis demanded a declaration of war on the democratic Dutch. In 1673 the expenses of that contest compelled the summoning of Parliament—it had not met for two years. The recognition of Dutch gallantry could not be suppressed in England, for Holland had been saved by a fearless voluntary inundation of her borders. Before the days of the psychological treatment of the masses by a controlled Press, broadcasting or cinema, the people, it would seem, were more swift and independent in judgment than they are to-day and often expressed themselves by open violence. The Commons swung with opinion— again the country party raised its head. Shaftesbury, on the issue of religious indulgence and dispensation of penal laws (primarily designed as part of the French concordat, to help the Catholics), deserted the Cabal. The Opposition demanded the dismissal of Lauderdale, the supporter of Scottish Episcopacy, and the impeachment of Arlington. Buckingham, whose resignation was also asked, joined Shaftesbury in opposition to the King, and the exasperated Monarch, in breach of his French undertaking, was compelled to make peace with Holland and dismiss his remaining ministers. Once more Parliament had triumphed over irresponsible monarchy.

The exhibition of hatred against Catholicism (which had become so strong that even Nonconformists denounced the General Declaration of Indulgence and supported the Test Act which excluded them from office) at length persuaded Charles that, although he might still hope for a subservient Tory Parliament or, better still, by living on Louis, do without one at all, he must abandon the hope of converting England by bribery or muskets to the Roman faith. His choice of First Minister, Danby, an Anglican Tory, shows clearly the drift of his policy at the time. During the four years of Danby's rule, the reconciliation of King and Parliament was zealously attempted. The hostility of Danby to Louis disarmed suspicion. According to Burnet, Danby publicly drank "confusion to all who were not for a war with France", and the Tories, once more united, turned to attack the Whig country party again.

A Tory non-resisting Bill would have made it illegal for anyone to hold public office who did not declare that the King should never be opposed. Seeing that Danby himself had come into power by resisting and destroying the King's French alliance, the proposal had its cynical side—still, it was good enough to harass the Whigs. The only hope for them now lay in a dissolution. Shaftesbury, for impugning the legality of that Parliament which had now sat for over fifteen years, was imprisoned by the Peers, but both Houses and all parties were unanimous against the Papists. They carried with enthusiasm a resolution that there "was, and still is, a damnable and hellish plot to murder the King, subvert the Government and destroy the Protestant Religion". It was now universally believed (particularly as the result of the discovery of the letters of Coleman, once secretary to the Duke of York) that there was being concocted a design to enable James, now an avowed Roman Catholic, to introduce, sooner or later, his detested religion—the King, curiously, was still regarded as potential victim rather than as fellow-conspirator.

On November 2nd, 1678, it was moved in both Houses that James should be ejected from the King's Councils. Sacheverell, the leader of the "Exclusionists", boldly raised the question whether the King and Parliament might not control the succession to the Throne. On this issue as to the defeasible right of James, a new cleavage arose between the Royalists and Whigs; it was in this anti-papal turmoil, fed by Titus Oates, with every degree of misrepresentation (based largely on unknown but exaggerated fact), that Danby, very unwisely for his cause, to avoid impeachment advised the King to dissolve Parliament. At the ensuing elections, in February, 1679, the Protestant anti-Catholic party won a great victory. The Whigs, as they were now commonly called, compounded of malcontent nobility, small Protestant yeomen, Republicans, Dissenters and city merchants smarting from aristocratic hauteur, together with many disinterested patriots, were now organized under the skilful direction of Shaftesbury. Pageants and music, colours, pamphlets and speeches, together with the requisite financial inducements, all were employed in this, perhaps the first, electoral contest to be conducted by direct appeal to the people. Small as was the franchise the Court was greatly alarmed. Louis, secretly, to defeat Danby, exposed the solicitations of Charles for money, for which Danby, probably without justification, was held responsible. If it was thought that the election would stop the impeachment of Danby, never was there a greater miscalculation. Despite the King's pardon, the trial went on and he was imprisoned. The Tories found themselves in a dilemma. The Exclusion Bill to keep James from the Throne had passed the Commons, but in the Upper House, Halifax and Rochester, with the support of the Bishops, ensured its rejection. In March, 1681, the Parliament was dissolved. The new one had a smaller Whig majority. They were summoned to meet at Oxford and, on the Commons once more introducing the Exclusion Bill, were again dissolved. But by this time the Catholics had been excluded from all offices, save that of the Throne itself.

The cautious and wise Halifax, who had originally supported Shaftesbury, still wished to keep James as King, but under parliamentary control. Many Whigs supported him and opposed total exclusion, for as a party, on this question, they were by no means united. From Temple arose the idea of a mixed government by a reconstituted council, some Tory, some Whig, thirty in all, which proved quite unworkable. But not until the reign of George I was the idea of a government entirely of one party again acceptable to the Crown. The notion long lingered, particularly in the Lords, that each minister is entitled to advise the Sovereign according to his individual opinion. The disappearance of the principle was only possible when the King was no longer held responsible for the Crown's governmental acts.

Charles now recognized that, in ordinary circumstances, Whig majorities were almost unavoidable; the middle classes, who were mainly on that side, controlled the boroughs, and to some extent the same tendency was shown by the small landowner in the country. The King and the Tories alike realized that their only hope was to dispense, as far as possible, with Parliaments altogether. The Catholicism of James was overlooked and absolute submission to the Crown extolled, the city loans to the Crown were repudiated and local government overturned by the confiscation of charters in Whig boroughs. In the words of Trevelyan, "The second Stuart despotism had come into being. It was based, as Charles had designed in 1670, on a standing army and financial help from France." (*England under the Stuarts*, p. 425.) It remained for James, in raising universal opposition to himself, to restore the temporarily routed Whigs.

The notion of toleration of opinion, if not of complete freedom in the expression of it, which later became the basis of Liberalism, found little support among the early Whigs. It has been remarked how even their dissenting supporters refused a toleration which would have had the effect of benefiting the Roman Catholics. The release of thousands of Catholics and Nonconformists by James, one of the first acts of his reign, was more unpopular with the latitudinarian Whigs, in so far as it freed the Catholics to practise their religion, than with the orthodox Anglicans who were mostly Tory. His later attempts to suspend the penal laws against all religions met with the fiercest objection from the same quarter. Not until James directly attacked the Church in the promotion of a Papist to be President of Magdalen College, Oxford, and in the prosecution of the Bishops for refusing to read the King's toleration declarations, did the Tories join the Whigs in inviting William over. Even then, it must have been a most unpalatable decision for the advocates of non-resistance—Danby, the anti-Gallican; Trelawney, Bishop of Bristol; Shrewsbury (who had actually crossed the seas to visit William), Sunderland and others.

Though the Tories had thus reluctantly been driven to deny their own precept of the Divine Right, yet, on William's arrival, they were naturally unwilling to do more than confer on him a Regency or make him consort to Mary as reigning Queen.

William, as was expected, refused any such offers, and in the proposal of joint Sovereignty (William as elective, Mary as hereditary) the prejudices of both parties, it was hoped, would be satisfied. But the current of affairs had changed. In the past, even when the Whigs had a majority in Parliament, the Stuart Kings had never given them their confidence. With William it was otherwise—by the nature of their profession the Whigs from the first supported him *ex animo*. Himself a Calvinist, he readily obtained Puritan support and his anti-French sentiment had been expressed upon the battlefield. Though his first government was a coalition, he came inevitably in the end to repose more and more upon the Whigs, who were the first to welcome him and who, from the outset, had displayed a genuine anti-Jacobite enthusiasm. From now onwards the Whigs were no longer a semi-seditious opposition— they represented, far more completely than the hesitant and semi-

B*

treasonable Tories, the royal as well as the popular policy. Disguise it as the Tories would, the Glorious Revolution was a Whig triumph— the Toleration Act proved it. After a temporary recovery in the reign of the High Church Queen Anne, the Tories sank for many generations into supine, and sometimes disloyal, opposition.

The acerbities, which, since the failure of Tudor paternal government, had so distracted the Nation, both in religion and politics, were only in part healed by the triumph of an essentially liberal constitution in the acceptance by the Convention Parliament of the limited monarchy of William and Mary. The Tories (divided between the Jacobites, now outside the State pale, and those who reluctantly recognized the abdication of James as a final end to absolutism), though unable to enforce their reactionary principles, were sufficiently powerful to cause a breach in that unity which was so essential if the country was to cope with the aggressive and, as we should now say, totalitarian ambitions of the French King.

There can be no doubt that at this time the Tories were fundamentally unpatriotic; they grudged the King supplies to fight his enemies, and a new issue developed, not so much between the Sovereign and the Parliament (for that matter had been decided by the Bill of Rights and other legislation in favour of the Houses), but on the question which leaders in Parliament should exercise power. In the first government of William, Tories were to be found in the Ministry, for both parties had in the end combined to bring him over. Foreign matters were directed by the King himself; but at home, the Tory, Danby, became President of the Council and Nottingham, with Shrewsbury, Secretaries of State (there were then but two), while the equivocal Halifax was made Privy Seal. The Treasury, however, was in Whig hands, though the inescapable Godolphin did the business, and the Council, generally, had a Whig majority. In the Commons the Whigs were also supreme, for the Convention Parliament, elected without the menace of soldiery or threats, was composed for the most part of enthusiastic adherents of the new régime. In the Lords, the Tories were more powerful.

Notwithstanding that the Convention had not been summoned by royal writ, it declared itself, with royal approval, to be a Parliament, though already the Tories, who wished for another election, pedantically argued that it was not one. With these increasing contentions, coalition government became almost unworkable. The Whigs insisted that no one should sit without taking oaths of allegiance to the new monarchs —it was a very essential requirement—and nearly all the members of both Houses, save a few Bishops and Peers, Clarendon among them, complied. It was the first great Whig triumph. Meanwhile the Tories in the government were becoming recalcitrant, Halifax and Danby renewed their old quarrel and the two Secretaries of State were at serious odds. In ecclesiastical politics feuds soon broke out as to the toleration of Dissenters. The low Churchmen, who, with the Nonconformists, formed the backbone of the Whig party, had as their chief the King himself. Burnet, the Whig, was made a Bishop and Nottingham, a zealous High Churchman, reluctantly had to concede a Toleration Act. On the other hand the blasphemous obligation to take the Sacrament as a condition of municipal office, on the motion of the Tories, remained untouched. The Test Act was not repealed, toleration was denied to believers in Transubstantiation and disbelievers in the Trinity, and a general attempt at religious comprehension failed. These disputes and the failure of Parliament to concede the customs for more than a year or give the King more revenue than the amount levied in December, 1690, induced him to dissolve Parliament. The Whigs, to his personal chagrin, had refused to pass that General Act of Indemnity which the King thought would unify the Nation in their great struggle with France, and they had also sought, vindictively, to exclude from municipal rights those who had surrendered the Charters in Charles's time. The party value of this move was manifest. The freemen who possessed votes in many towns had been admitted by the City oligarchy, and to drive the Tories therefrom was to guarantee a permanent Whig domination. Doubtless the King became enraged at these petty factional manœuvres; for the time he gave his support to the constitutional Tories, though many of them were in correspondence with James; and in the result, in the spring of 1690 there was returned a Tory majority. Gratefully, a Tory House voted William moneys for the Irish campaign, then beginning. Nevertheless, as Woods thinks, by reason of incompetence in the Commons (*History of the Tory Party*, p. 63), in their jealousy of William's Dutch advisers and, still more, because of their refusal, whole-heartedly, to co-operate with his foreign policy of military opposition to Louis (which was the purpose of the King's coming to England), notwithstanding the apparent Tory success at the polls, the Government gradually became more Whig. The Whig leaders, the Junto, as it was called, were anti-French and patriotically Protestant; to them William became reconciled and, with patronage in their hands, enough Tories seceded once more to give the Whigs a working majority.

At first, after the election, Danby, now Carmarthen, had become in effect Prime Minister and First Lord of the Treasury. Shrewsbury resigned, but there remained as Danby's colleagues Nottingham, the other Secretary and Lowther—for the time it looked as if a Tory government might be formed. In any event, in the Council of Nine they formed a majority. On his return from Ireland William was entertained almost entirely by them—but soon, as has been said, it began to be impressed upon the King, more particularly after his discovery of the many affiliations of the Tories with the Jacobites, that the Whigs who were willing to push matters to extremes against France (though some of their supporters might seek to reduce the King to a cipher) were yet, in principle, pledged to his own purposes and that their allegiance was less qualified than that of their opponents. It is said that Sunderland, in particular, urged upon the King that a strong united government, which would support him faithfully, could only be found on the Whig side—certainly the Tories had openly said that England should leave the defence of the Netherlands to the Empire and other German powers. By 1690, the King having fully accepted this view, the Whigs again are to be found in control, and power passed to Somers, the Lord Keeper, and Montague, the financial expert, while the manipulation of the electorate was left to be controlled by the unscrupulous Wharton.

It was under Montague that the most far-reaching of financial expedients to support the War was arranged, the supplementing of tax revenue by loans provided on the security of the State itself. In return for an accommodation of over a million pounds at 8 per cent interest, a new corporation, the Bank of England, received a chartered privileged position. The East India Company granted a loan of two million pounds to the country and, in their turn, obtained substantial monopolies in the East India trade. The days of Charles's repudiation of debt were over and the Government and King eventually were driven to depend upon the wealthy lending classes for their solvency and credit. The interests of the City thus came to be closely associated with that party by whom their rights and monopolies had been secured. For many years, whatever else failed, the Whigs could always count upon the support of the moneyed classes.

War continuing, with estimates constantly growing, the dependence upon the lenders of money increased yearly. Land taxes and customs proved utterly insufficient; borrowing became a necessity. A million was raised by a lottery loan, in addition to that already mentioned. The Tories, much perturbed, in order to counteract the influence of the financiers, suggested the alternative of a bank consisting of capital raised on the security of land—the contest was passing from that of King and Parliament to a fight between Land and City. The latter, however, were victorious. Montague became Chancellor of the Exchequer, Shrewsbury returned, and all the other great offices were filled by Whigs; Carmarthen only remaining of the old Tories, together with Godolphin, who was regarded rather as an essential administrator than a politician.

It happened that in 1695 there was much concern in the public mind regarding allegations of corruption, more particularly in relation to army contracts. The three principal names mentioned were Carmarthen (now Duke of Leeds), Trevor, who was Speaker, and Seymour—all three were Tories. Seymour was said to have trafficked in saltpetre with the East India Company, and Trevor was censored for receiving money from the City in relation to the passage of one of their Bills. Leeds, for the second time, was impeached, but the accusation was put an end to by prorogation. Thereafter, though nominally President, he was not summoned to the Council, and the entire Government, save for the accommodating Godolphin, was at last Whig.

In these latter days, when Liberals have so often been taunted with lack of patriotic fervour, it is interesting to observe how entirely loyal they were to the King at a time when their opponents grudged him support in a contest as far-reaching in its consequences as the twentieth-century German wars. The consuming Whig desire for victory over the tyranny of Louis made them markedly less vindictive and petty than in the earlier years of the reign and William, in consequence, now gave them his support without reservation. Even Marlborough, the Tory, as a soldier was reconciled to Whig government. The Assassination Plot, in which no reputable member of opposition was associated, nevertheless still further strengthened the patriotic ideals of the Whigs. They seized the opportunity to inaugurate a great declaration to safeguard the Protestant Succession. Over four hundred members of the Commons subscribed, though, in the Lords, a few Peers, led by Rochester (while agreeing that William had a right to the Crown), refused to sign.

This hesitation did the Tories much injury; the concurrent failure of their Land Bank accentuated their plight.

On the other hand (though in 1696 it had suspended payment of its notes), new moneys poured into the Bank of England, and the only rival to Montague, Godolphin, on an allegation that he had knowledge of the designs of the suspected plotter, Fenwick, resigned. The Bill of Attainder directed against Fenwick was a serious error and found many opponents, but it is interesting to the historian of politics as disclosing a new method by which the Whig leaders sought to enforce discipline —the dissentient members of their party were summoned to a meeting where their duty as loyal Whigs was expounded to them; it was the beginning of the coercive Whip system.

The Treaty of Ryswick (wherein Louis acknowledged William to be King of England) was a great Whig achievement, for though the King admitted no interference in foreign matters, yet the concession was effected under Whig administration. Like all triumphs it demanded its price; the urgent need for patriotism was over, and now that the perils of war were past, the burden of taxation was not so readily acceptable and the Tories were less liable to be suspected of treachery. Moreover, the feeling of emergency dispelled, the cohesion of the Whigs was shaken and their majority began to fall away.

The King and the more far-sighted of the Whigs had no illusions— they knew that, dealing with Louis, nothing more than an armistice could be expected, but this opinion was not shared by a peace-loving people. Agitation for the reduction of the army and the taxes grew; particularly did the nation wish to see the foreign troops leave the realm. Harley, in origin a Whig, now joined the peace party. In an angry House he carried a motion with the support of many dissident Whigs, by 185 to 148 votes, that the armed forces should be reduced to the number obtaining in 1680.

The operation of the Triennial Act necessitated a general election in 1698, and it was soon evident that the new majority was critical of the policy of the King and his Government. The army was to be reduced to 7,000 men, all of whom were to be natural-born subjects; the Dutch Guards were to go. Government was changed. Montague left the Exchequer and Lowther, now Lord Lonsdale, returned. Soon Somers and Russell were succeeded by Godolphin and Rochester—the Tories were again in the saddle. At this juncture, James II dying, Louis, in breach of his word, recognized the Pretender. Back swung opinion to Whiggery; the King and his advisers had been right when they refused to trust the perfidious Frenchman! War was again declared, and when William died in 1702 the Whigs were unmistakably in possession—the more trusted because of their foresight. The settlement of 1701 accepted the House of Hanover as heirs presumptive on conditions as to Protestantism and other matters which marked the achievement of future Whig domination. They it was who had insisted on the rights of the Electress Sophia and, in the end, they were to benefit from a line of grateful dependent foreign monarchs. Meanwhile, the High Church Anne, though battling with Louis, lent a fitful support to the distracted and semi-seditious Tories.

Their difficulties were great; the war with France was at its height, and to the waging of that war the Whigs alone had ever given enthusiastic countenance: Louis in his desire to control Europe by placing the Crowns of France and Spain under the Bourbon had made all reconciliation impossible. Although in 1702 the Tories had won a majority, they were forced to continue the strife. Marlborough in the field was disgusted with their equivocation and almost was persuaded by his wife to join the Whigs. Godolphin, another Whiggish Tory, agreed with the great general. Against them stood Nottingham, the Secretary of State, Dartmouth and the quasi-Jacobite Rochester. The Government, on the most serious question of the day, resistance to Gallic aggression, was thus divided and by a cunning expedient sought to placate their differences and please the Queen by harassing Nonconformity, a policy which the Whig House of Lords deplored in its tendency to divide the Nation in the face of the enemy. Again the Tories showed themselves to be both illiberal and unpatriotic.

At length the exigencies of war compelled the expulsion of the reluctant Tories from Government—in 1702 Rochester resigned and Nottingham in 1704. It was now sought to form a war party by the introduction of Harley and St. John, both of whom at the time affected a support of Marlborough and Godolphin. The victory of Blenheim, in 1704, greatly strengthened the Whigs; even such a writer as Woods, in his *History of the Tory Party*, concedes that the Tories were thought to be tepid to the national cause. (p. 105.) In 1708 Harley and St. John, being suspected of intrigues against Godolphin, who was in effect Premier, were dismissed. The Government was now indubitably belligerent and Harley took upon himself the leadership of the opposition.

His skill in organization and the very completeness of victory operated to develop the feeling that the war had gone on long enough. The army was, at this time, mostly recruited as to its officers from the landed gentry and in the ranks from proletarians. In either case the great Whig financiers and merchants had nothing to fear; either in person or in loss of their sons or in money. As the war proceeded more loans were raised and a greater supply of commodities demanded, and the City bankers and contractors grew increasingly rich; but to others the hostilities, like all wars, brought little but hardship and sorrow. As early as 1711, St. John was in secret communication with the French, through Torcy, their Foreign Minister. The terms included the abandonment by England of the objection to a Bourbon Spanish King. The Tories, who had been in office since the summer of 1710, had not yet broken openly with Marlborough, but Godolphin, who had never been one of the Whig Junto, was forced out and the attack on the absent general began to mature—without Godolphin to protect him at home, his position was becoming precarious. His wife had lost all influence with the Queen, and the foolish prosecution of the High Churchman, Dr. Sacheverell, had already thrown his royal supporter into an ungrudging reliance upon Harley and St. John, soon to become respectively Lords Oxford and Bolingbroke.

On the last day of December, 1711, twelve new Tory peers were created to support a final peace and Marlborough's dismissal followed. There resulted the Treaty of Utrecht. On the whole, it was a good settlement for the allies—France was exhausted, Holland safe, and

Austria remained in possession of her part of the Netherlands, retaining a hegemony in Italy: the balance of power was restored and Louis frustrated. It was little recognized at that time that it was due to Whig pertinacity that he was reduced to such a condition.

So great was the desire for peace that the achievements of Marlborough were forgotten; like another great national saviour, Wellington, he was abused in the streets, and with less justification, for he had never opposed popular demands.

But soon stalked the bogey of the Succession: undoubtedly, an active minority of the Tories would have welcomed the Queen's brother. At any rate, they were sufficiently strong to prevent their party establishing contacts with Hanover; the Queen's own attitude was ambiguous and, to make matters worse, a blazing quarrel broke out between Oxford and Bolingbroke. The latter, although he afterwards denied it, was far more zealous for the succession of James than was the cautious Oxford. In December, 1713, Bolingbroke had told Gaultier, a French Jacobite priest and envoy, that he could not tolerate a German King in England and assured him that Parliament could be persuaded to repeal the Act of Settlement if James would but follow Charles II's example and dissemble his religion. On being solicited, however, the Pretender would do no more than undertake that he would not disturb Protestantism.

Meanwhile the Whigs, who were in close touch with Hanover, were vainly urging the Queen to receive the Electoral Prince. Oxford was dismissed and Bolingbroke, after vainly seeking an understanding with the Whigs, was about to fill the Government with men of marked Jacobite sympathies. On July 28th, 1714, the Treasury, now vacant, was temporarily put into commission and next day Anne was taken with a fatal seizure. The proposal that Shrewsbury, the semi-Whig, should be nominated Treasurer, was inexplicable save in Petrie's view that Bolingbroke was "at any rate temporarily off his balance". (*Bolingbroke*, p. 250.) Next day, August 1st, Anne died and the foreigner, George, who could not speak English, was declared King without overt opposition. Immediately, abroad, he nominated a council of Regency (it had long been in preparation), from which Bolingbroke and all his fellow ministers, except Shrewsbury, were omitted. The long period of Whig power, to last nearly fifty years, had begun.

CHAPTER II

OLD WHIGGERY

IN so far as the Whigs can be said to have had any formulated political principles, they are to be found principally in the works of John Locke and, particularly, in his *Essay on Civil Government*. At the outset of that treatise Locke, following Sidney, launches an attack upon the doctrine of the Divine Right of Kings, more especially as expounded by Filmer. In its place, like Hobbes, he reverted to the notion, which, as has been said, was supported by the Jesuits, of a social contract between men whereby they have mutually agreed to put themselves under government, but his reason for this surrender of individual freedom is directly opposed to that of Hobbes; the absolutist philosopher believed men to have come together because of their individual savagery, whereas Locke, following Aristotle and St. Thomas Aquinas, conceives them under the law of Nature to have possessed social qualities and thereby, from the beginning to have had a capacity for co-operation.

Thus assembled, it was through human conscious choice that government arose, and if it departs through tyranny from the assumptions of that universal concordat which gave it power it can rightly be overthrown. Although few of Locke's followers realized it, to proclaim this doctrine was to revert to the mediæval view that Princes are under the Law, in any case it was the direct contradiction of the doctrine of unlimited power and, therefore, very congenial to the Whig mind.

In pursuance of this idea of conditional obedience, Locke formulated four conditions of just government—it must be according to established laws of universal application, it must legislate for the good of the people as a whole, the legislature must not part with its power save to the electors or the people who bestowed it and, finally—and most significant for the future of Liberalism—interference with private property is only justifiable when occasioned by taxation or otherwise by the express consent of Parliament; it would seem that Locke, like the French and American revolutionaries after him, regarded private ownership as a primary condition of Liberty, not merely as the mediæval sociologists conceived in user, but also as conferring a right of almost absolute possession.

It has been remarked that Walpole, the greatest of the old leaders, rarely quoted and probably had never read Locke, yet, nevertheless, that writer's direct influence upon the more intellectual of the Whigs was considerable; indeed, it was not until the days of Bentham and the Utilitarians that any Liberal political philosopher arose to supplement him.

The rule of law and the legal limitations of kingship having been accepted in the Revolution, the original purpose of the Whigs may seem to have been achieved. The oligarchy of great landed nobility, supported by merchants and Dissenters, held an impregnable position in politics. Yet, though by the accident of Stuart folly they had come into power, it would be erroneous to think that at any time they commanded the respect or adherence of more than a moiety of the nation. Against them, unflinchingly, were set the smaller landowners (often of longer pedigree than the new peers), the bulk of the clergy other than Whig Bishops, the Universities and a large number of the agricultural poor who were still deferential tenants and devout Anglicans. The Catholics, though few in number and still in subjection, were not without reactionary influence. Among those normally Whig, many Dissenters were disappointed at the very limited amount of toleration which had been conceded to them, and the Quakers, who would not accept sacramentalism or the doctrine of the Trinity, were discontented at their ostracism.

But the official Whigs, though antagonizing the more radical elements in State and Church, had set their faces against any further electoral or religious reform: they did nothing to alleviate the conditions of the poor in town or country; they had no conception of the possibility of social legislation to improve the cities, roads or harbours of the realm, and readily left the maintenance of local amenities to the fox-hunting Justices of the Peace or to corrupt oligarchic municipal corporations. Their control of the new trading monopolies overseas was negligible, nor did they display any interest in the development of the plantations and colonies—they failed to improve the savage criminal law or to clarify the growing confusion attendant upon civil litigation—indeed, for a hundred years and more, whether the Government were Tory or Whig, it might fairly be said that, save in the conduct of foreign affairs and war, it was negative and impotent. The Kings had ceased to rule and Parliament had copied their example. Sinecures abounded and an increasing number of "Place-men", as they were called, supported indifferently any government which would guarantee them pensions, annuities and honours. Administration was in the hands of a small class in whom, it must be admitted, taste and discrimination in the Arts were most noticeable, but orthodox religion was moribund and good manners had come to be substituted for piety as the essential requirement of behaviour. It was by these aristocrats—so typified in the writings of Chesterfield, Hervey, Selwyn and Horace Walpole—that the "cits" and drinking squires, not to speak of the "mobile" in the towns, for the most part were content to be governed. The majority of the Commons were related to the Lords—indeed, it may be said that nearly all the governing families, in whichever House they sat, and on whichever side, were kinsmen.

Meanwhile, confining their civic energies to the municipalities, business men were increasing their riches. At the time of the South Sea scandal no less than a seventh of the total wealth of the country was already invested in Joint-Stock undertakings; money was clamouring for investment and the speculator had become a fashionable figure. The collapse of the South Sea Company gave to Walpole his unique opportunity, for the Chancellor of the Exchequer had himself been involved and other ministers were ruined in that adventure. This, however, did not have the effect of discouraging activity in finance; on the contrary, once Walpole had adroitly liquidated the trouble, the search for markets and commercial exploitation in India and elsewhere increased in vigour. The steadfast refusal of that Premier to involve England in continental wars nourished the rising wealth of the country. War eventually came again; but, for the most of Walpole's time, the commercial class, other than army contractors, had reason to bless that pacific Whig country gentleman who so sedulously protected their interests.

Prosperity enabled Walpole to placate even the squires by lowering the land tax. The factious opposition to Excise compelled him to modify his financial policy but did nothing to shake essential Whig power. Not only the rich but the Dissenters, who were still in a position of social and constitutional sufferance (though Walpole did next to nothing to help them) gave him their support in lack of any better hope.

"As a minister," writes Lecky (*England in the Eighteenth Century*, Vol. I, p. 400), "Walpole combined an extreme and exaggerated severity of party discipline within Parliament with the utmost deference for public opinion beyond its walls." His insistence on peace, it must not be forgotten, was alien to Whig tradition—their policy and success had long been based upon a challenge to French power.

It was in this connection that they had wished to restrict trade with that country, and argued against free trade that "mercantilism", as it was called, demanded the restriction of imports. The Tories on the other hand advocated free commerce; they saw no harm in the importation of French commodities, said by the Whigs to be "exhausting the wealth of the nation". The leading trade writer on the Tory side had been Dudley North. In his *Discourses upon Trade*, published in 1691, he states that money is a merchandise "whereof there may be a glut as well as a scarcity". The world traders should "accommodate one another". The Tory Davenant similarly declared that "Trade is by nature free, finds its own channel, and best directeth its own course". The great bankers took the same objection to the Mercantile theory. As against these advanced thinkers, Locke the Whig was an orthodox supporter of protection, yet one cannot but suspect that a political suspicion of France, rather than the logic of his individualism, went to produce his economic outlook.

However this may be, Walpole succeeded for a time in wooing the Whigs away from their belligerent past. His task was not an easy one, the dynastic disputes in Spain, involving France and Austria, had nearly caused a British intervention at the time of the Succession of George II, for Austria and Spain had entered into an understanding and the former's encouragement of their Ostend Company alarmed both English and Dutch competitors. The alliance of England, Prussia and the French, in 1725, was most unpopular—it was regarded as a device to save Hanover from the Austrians and thus angered both political parties; the Whigs because of the contact with France, their opponents on account of the succour given to the detested Hanoverians. Yet the power of Walpole, the architect of the plan, was not seriously affected. As a counterpoise, in 1731, by the Treaty of Vienna, he conciliated the Austrians and left the French to fight them, but the success of France in this contest rekindled the lurking fear of that nation in Whig hearts and the opposition within the Party to Walpole increased. The King also, who was by nature martial, added to the Premier's difficulties.

Walpole, however, had one invaluable instrument to achieve his pacific end—political corruption. George II was promised one hundred thousand pounds a year more than his father had been voted, the Queen was to have a similar jointure. Bribery, direct or concealed, was not a new thing, either of members of Parliament or other electors. In theory it was condemned; Trevor, Ranelagh, Aislabie and the Craggs were all persons of high office who had recently been politically destroyed by the exposure of their direct receipt of moneys from interested persons, but there were other methods, less blatant, to achieve the same ends, and it must be conceded that Walpole's use of public moneys was to obtain votes to maintain his policy and not for his personal enrichment. As to the elections, the Whigs did nothing as a constitutional party to purify the methods of filling Parliament, save sporadically to unseat their opponents, nor did they complain when the Prime Minister gained support by offering lucrative sinecures to the dependable—a method later improved by Bute when he granted to his friends the promotion of loans on advantageous terms. Systematic corruption, in one form or another, now that the power of monarchy was spent, was the recognized method by which both parties for many years ensured their power.

There can be no doubt that it was the un-Whiggish desire of Walpole to come to terms with France and Spain which ultimately undermined him. If the Tories had hoped to gain by his removal they were disappointed. Though Bolingbroke, their only leader of intelligence, had returned to England, he was still excluded from the Lords—Walpole had seen to that. The dissident Whigs, who complained of Walpole's want of martial patriotism, were even further removed from Tory and Jacobite French sympathy than was the Prime Minister; for with Walpole an understanding with France was sought only to preserve the peace. In Tory policy such amity was necessarily inherent.

That unimpressive nonentity, the Prince of Wales, was chosen by the "Boy Patriots", as Walpole scornfully mocked them, to be a rallying centre, and for a time it looked as if a union of the young Whigs and Tories against the Premier was possible. The restraining hand of Wyndham, the Tory leader, being removed by his death in 1740, his party again became intransigeant, and when Walpole finally resigned, in 1742, the power was still with the Whigs Pulteney and Carteret; Walpole himself, now Lord Orford, helping them to construct the new Government—the Tories had again been outwitted.

But the future lay with Pitt, the young dissentient Whig—for the moment he was refused office—he had been used by Pulteney and Carteret to exclude Walpole, but there was to be no reward. For a time he dabbled with Toryism, denouncing the Hanoverian connection as fiercely as any Jacobite—for this the Court never forgave him. At length, in 1744, Pelham succeeded Carteret, the Hanoverian, and Pitt, once more turning patriot, in 1746 became Paymaster-General.

The incapacity of the Government, displayed during the Scottish invasion of 1745, was, of course, of no assistance to embarrassed Tories suspected of Jacobitism; Carteret's ideal of a "broad-bottomed Ministry", to include the Opposition, became impossible. During the Pelham administration France was victorious in Europe. Tournay and Ostend, Mons and Namur, were theirs, and the invasion of this country was considered probable—it was under the pressure of such events that the King had been forced to accept Pitt. In April, 1748, came the Peace of Aix; it was to the disadvantage of England. "We are too weak to fight", said the Prime Minister—through necessity he was inclining to the pacific principles of Walpole.

Government proposals to naturalize foreign Protestants and the Jews were attacked both by the Anglican Tories and the Whig city magnates, who feared alien competition. In March, 1754, Pelham died and there followed a general election. Not more than one hundred and fifty were returned in Opposition; but these, significantly, were mostly from the counties where a wider franchise of small freeholders existed than in the close, doctored electoral rolls of the towns. A new war was brewing; already hostilities with the French had broken out in America. Pitt, now become an extreme Whig and patriot—he was a close student of Locke—to unify the nation began to support the long-postponed civic emancipation of Dissenters. For this and other reasons, after much intrigue, he was dismissed and the avaricious Fox became leader of the House of Commons. At length, after an alliance between Austria and France had put the country into dire jeopardy, Fox resigned, and a genuinely popular patriotic movement arose which could not be confined within official Whig fences. America, to be saved; a militia on a national scale to be raised; the foreign troops to be sent home, and the seas to be secured by a strong navy—such was the policy which Pitt, with magnificent eloquence, advocated. The French had already invaded Germany and the services of Pitt were demanded by the country. He became a hero, but on a national stage, not merely in the opinion of a few excited young men at Westminster.

Under his direction there followed the great years of victory, Pitt being now Secretary of State, and in effect Prime Minister, though the ubiquitous Newcastle controlled the votes. On the Continent, Frederick, the Prussian, was perhaps really the victor; but in Canada and in India the modern British Empire arose on the ruins of French power. Party politics were forgotten in a universal congratulation and relief and, whether he deserved it or not, Pitt emerged as undisputed national leader.

But again the very completeness of victory produced a general desire for peace, and the administration of Pitt, like that of Marlborough, fell in a vain endeavour to prolong the war. By this time the young George III was reigning, and a new Government, favouring his personal rule, had been formed—until October, 1761, Pitt and his brother-in-law, Temple, remained the only members of it who supported the pursuance of the war.

Unfortunately for the administration, a Scotsman, Lord Bute, had been chosen by the Sovereign to preside, and the feeling against that country, inflamed by the recent invasion, was so strong that his presence was enough to imperil the whole administration. "No Scotch, no foreigners", was a cry which appealed to all the people. In any case, as Fielding rightly points out (*The Second Tory Party*, p. 72), "it is a mistake to regard the new Government as a Tory one". Actually, the Tory Party "in the Parliament of 1761 was not much stronger than it had been for many years".

On October 5th, 1761, Pitt and Temple resigned on the question of extending the war to Spain, a country which had recently concluded an alliance with France. The former's acceptance of a pension temporarily lessened his popularity but soon it revived.

For the moment the war with France continued. The West Indies fell to England and Frederick regained Silesia—Bute and his friends were confronted with a nation-wide enthusiasm for Pitt; for him it "rained gold boxes" containing the freedom of cities, but the day of pacification was near—Grenville, a peace-maker, led the Commons, and Bedford in the Lords, another pacificator, became Privy Seal. On a refusal to continue further assistance to Prussia, Newcastle at length resigned—in November preliminaries for peace were signed in Paris.

The underlying purpose of the young King, however, was not so much to promote a peace policy as to encourage the ideal of the restoration of active Kingship as a factor in government. That he and his mother had absolutist ambitions cannot be doubted, but the framework of the constitution had been so established during the long Whig domination that an attack upon it could only be made by concealed and devious methods. As has been said, the foolish selection of an incompetent Scotsman as figurehead had enabled the opposition to the new régime to marshal more support than would otherwise have been possible, and the popularity of Pitt was another factor in their favour—though it can hardly be thought that the long corrupt ascendancy of Whiggery itself could appeal strongly to people other than those who had directly benefited from it. Those benefits were now to be conferred upon the King's friends and the temptation to change sides proved overpowering.

In 1763 there was launched from the Palace a general proscription of the Whigs. Not only Lords-Lieutenant but humble Customs officers were dismissed. Newcastle, Grafton and Rockingham were relieved of the headship of their counties, followers of Fox and Bute being installed in their place. Fox pressed for a general extirpation of the Whig interest, but soon he resigned with a peerage, and in the new, more tolerant, ministry of Grenville, appeared several names afterwards to become notorious: North, Sandwich and Egremont.

These in name were mostly Whig, yet they it was who broke up the Whig party and hazarded constitutional government. Grenville was a strong supporter of authority. He was a haughty, aloof man, but the King saw in him a useful instrument—he forgot that the power which Grenville sought was for himself alone; to that extent he was no Tory; the Church and King received his respect but his own office of Prime Minister was his chief concern. It was not long before the Monarch wearied of his hauteur. He had taken office to prevent "unwarrantable force being put upon the Crown", but he—and not George—was to be master. Grenville's least fortunate actions were his programme for taking the colonies and regulating their trade, a plan which included the unfortunate Stamp Act, and the prosecution of John Wilkes.

This latter disastrous act was apparently suggested by the King himself. Wilkes had committed the unpardonable offence (with intention rather to inculpate the Ministers than to belittle the King) of regarding the royal speech at the opening of Parliament as the words of the Government, George being treated as a mere mouthpiece. This, perhaps, was not unpleasing to Grenville but to the Court it was blasphemy. In his polemic journal, the *North Briton*, Wilkes had gone so far as to refer to the Sovereign as "Chief Magistrate". He had already insulted the King's mother, elliptically comparing her and Bute to Edward II's mother and her paramour Mortimer—he was a fervid patriot and supporter of Pitt. To George and his friends, this somewhat absurd demagogue soon came to be regarded as chief enemy.

There is reason to believe that the Premier was still sufficiently Whig to dislike the raising of the delicate legal and constitutional questions which an attack upon the fearless Wilkes would certainly precipitate, but he was dependent upon the Court and Tory votes; his own family, Temple, his brother and Pitt regarding him as a family traitor, were his most insatiable opponents. His position was precarious; he decided to yield to the King's insistent demands and to arrest Wilkes.

The historic importance of the imbroglio which followed cannot be over-estimated. Wilkes himself was a curious mixture of patriot, radical, adventurer and rake. From the standpoint of literature his writings are cumbrous and involved; he was a poor speaker, yet he had the fortune to be the man on whom the principles of the common law were to be tested. The Whigs were ashamed of their champion—Pitt's personal dissociation from him was accompanied by an acknowledgment of the justice of his cause—but while the opposition could have wished for a more reputable protagonist, they could not ignore his usefulness to them in their cry that the Constitution was in danger—they regarded Wilkes, more particularly after his expulsion from Parliament, as the best means of vexing and criticizing the administration and the King. The proud Temple did not hesitate openly to support the Wilkeites and their leader.

The judicial condemnation of the intrusion into Wilkes' house of the servants of the Government and his own seizure were taken by the masses, ignorant of the niceties of law—(in reality he was released by Chief Justice Pratt on the very technical ground that he had not committed a breach of the peace and so fell within the privilege of a Member of Parliament)—as a vindication of Pitt and belligerent patriotism. Riots and demonstrations broke out all over London. Wilkes was expelled the House of Commons, and in the Lords his erstwhile companion in salicity, Sandwich, further enraged the public by inaugurating an attack upon him for privately printing an indecent poem. On a vote declaring General Warrants to be illegal (it was under such a one that Wilkes had been imprisoned), the Government majority fell to fourteen; it looked as if the radical agitator had rallied the Whigs against the Court. Even now the King failed to realize the seriousness of the issue; "the impudence of Wilkes is amazing", he wrote to Grenville; "his ruin is so near".

The growing opposition in Parliament, however, made the King doubt whether Grenville was not a failure. His personal distaste for the Court circle made accommodation to the King's will the more difficult. Reading George's letters it is not difficult to detect that he soon came to think that the Premier had mismanaged the Wilkes affair. Vindictively he writes to that harassed statesman: "The defection (on the General Warrant question) is undoubtedly very great. I hope those who have deserted may feel that I am not to be neglected unpunished".

The King was as good as his threat—in April, 1764, Conway, Lord Hertford's brother, was deprived of his regiment and a similar course was taken with many other independent Members of Parliament. The device to coerce the House had been used by Governments before, but the personal intervention of the Sovereign without the approval of his Government was now carried to lengths which made things unbearable even for such a mild Whig as Grenville.

The final breach came over the first Regency Bill, necessitated by the King's mental derangement. Grenville and his friends decided that the King's mother was not eligible to be appointed to the Council of Regency, as "not being of the Royal family". On his recovery, the King took this as a personal insult. Temple and Grenville, now in their common opposition to the new personal rule, were reconciled. They demanded the dismissal of Bute's brother and wished the Duke of Cumberland to be made to yield up his office of Commander-in-Chief; some even of the more independent Tories supported the Prime Minister. In the end, the King, saying that "necessity not choice" compelled him, with grief entrusted the Government to the orthodox Whig, Lord Rockingham.

Pitt had attempted to form a Ministry, but the obduracy of Temple made it impossible; the Tories were still too weak in the House to take office, and in the end the Duke of Newcastle agreed to help Rockingham. The King was compelled to take back Conway, whom he had recently dismissed from the army, as Secretary of State; as a solatium, Mackenzie, the brother of Bute, was restored to the insignificant office of Lord Privy Seal for Scotland.

The Rockingham administration succeeded in repealing the Stamp Act which had caused such friction in America, but it was really to conciliate Pitt that the Stamp Act was repealed: an accompanying measure was passed declaring that Parliament had the right to enact laws binding the colonies "in all cases whatsoever". This was a compromise, but, even so, most of the Scots, the Tories, and the Bishops voted against it. In the Government were now nearly all the leading Whigs except Pitt and Shelburne, but all the praise from the merchants who had lost so heavily by the interference of trade caused by the Act went to Pitt. The demand to bring back Pitt into the Government grew, and his refusal to co-operate with Rockingham ultimately brought down the Government. In July, 1766, Pitt, as Lord Chatham, accepted the Privy Seal, Rockingham was dismissed and a new Ministry formed by the new Earl and Grafton, the erratic young Townshend being Chancellor of the Exchequer. From the outset, however, the warring Whig groups, the Bedford, Rockingham and Grenville factions, all made difficulties. Meanwhile, Chatham being ill, the irrepressible Wilkes, who had received a temporary pension from the Rockingham Whigs, returned to London. "Wilkes and Liberty are everything", wrote a contemporary diarist. To shout and riot for him and to chalk up the figures "45" everywhere was the means whereby the disfranchised masses began to show their restlessness at all these aristocratic intrigues and governmental indifference to their lot.

The usual aftermath of long war had come; wages were falling, and the obsolescence of the old statute powers of the Justices to fix minimum wages had deprived the operatives, in the absence of effective powers of combination, of their last protection. A few favoured older trades—curriers, hatters, wool-staplers and calico printers—still limited their numbers by apprenticeship systems and occasionally succeeded in getting through Parliament some special Act to protect their remuneration; but prices were rising and in the new industries developing under primitive machinery, in the spinning and weaving trades, in the expanding coal and iron industries, and in the pottery trades, the operatives for the most part were without any means, industrial or political, to improve their condition. As Adam Smith pointed out, the masters had all the advantage; there were Statutes against combining to raise wages, none against combining to lower them. The masters could generally starve the men into submission, the men's agitations "generally end in nothing but the punishment or ruin of the ring-leaders".

It is not suggested that the agitation which centred round Wilkes was directly connected with this economic servitude; on the contrary, nothing is more noticeable than the absence of all reference to social amelioration in Wilkes' speeches, but the terrible conditions of the poor in London and other growing towns may well have furnished the ground-swell of that discontent which so rapidly developed. After scenes of great disorder, on March 29th, 1768, Wilkes was returned with popular acclamation as Member for Middlesex.

The burden of coping with this democratic agitation fell upon the new leader of the House of Commons, North, rather than on the indolent Grafton. North had obtained the ear of the House and was himself conspicuously free from that corrupt ambition which had disfigured the careers of so many of his contemporaries. He was a good and skilful debater and of placid temperament—no better man could be found to ride out a storm, and storm there certainly was.

The election of Wilkes had taken place amid riots and confusion in London, exceptional even in the days when the police did not function, and the intervention of the military was entirely casual and ill-directed. The houses of the wealthy were attacked and the great assaulted. Meanwhile, the sailors in the docks had struck for higher wages and were marching on the King's palace, and other working men were following their example. Horne Tooke, a radical clergyman, and the Dissenters saw a means to raise their grievances and, more alarming to the Government, the City of London magnates proved to be largely on Wilkes' side. In the Lords, Chatham and Shelburne supported the constitutional protest; nor did the condemnation of Wilkes, after his outlawry had been reversed, help his opponents. On the contrary, his prison became a centre of political agitation. Outside, the great journalist known as Junius, fed the fire. Law suits against Ministers for illegal practices were started or re-opened by Wilkes, no longer an outlaw; in some cases, such as that of Halifax, resulting in large damages for the aggrieved Radical. After the domestic contentions of the Whig oligarchy, which had for so long filled the political stage, it was obvious that something bigger and more sinister was afoot. The troops in quelling one of the riots unfortunately had killed some people, and Lord Barrington, the Secretary for War, had the folly to congratulate them just at the time when those responsible were being charged by a Middlesex grand jury with murder.

The King was now determined that Wilkes should be expelled the House. On February 4th, 1769, this was accomplished, but only by a majority of eighty-two. A new by-election was held on February 16th and Wilkes was again returned, almost unanimously. Again, on March 16th, after a further expulsion, the same result occurred. The position was becoming serious: cries of "Wilkes and no King" were heard. Merchants pledging support to the King were rabbled, and London, at any rate, was in a revolutionary condition. On the fourth occasion of Wilkes' election, the House declared the minority candidate, Luttrell, elected, though he had received under three hundred votes. Petitions for the dissolution of Parliament flowed in. In the Lords, Chatham moved for enquiry into the Middlesex election, and the Chancellor, Camden, for supporting him, was dismissed. Thereupon Grafton resigned on January 27th: Wilkes and Junius had overthrown the Government!

The new Prime Minister, North, was not officially a Tory. He himself would never use the word. He had served under the Whigs, Newcastle and Chatham, and had few affiliations with Bute and the Palace party. He favoured further relief to Dissenters, which was emphatically not a Tory position, and during the whole of his administration displayed no sign of High Churchmanship. On the other hand, undoubtedly, he was a supporter of the King.

Most of the old Whig leaders had died or were aged. Until Fox passed over to the Opposition, Burke was nearly the only strong man left among the official Whigs. Grenville, Bedford, Egremont and Beck-ford, one of the few sitting Wilkeites, who never numbered half a dozen in the House, were all gone, and North proceeded to try to eliminate what hostile influence was left by dealing with specific grievances in a manner novel to the legislature. Thus, in 1770, the wages of coal-hewers were stabilized by Statute and, later, journeymen and weavers had their wages similarly improved.

• Parish reform was undertaken, naval pensioners helped—for the first time since Elizabeth's day Parliament was used, though sparingly, for the conscious betterment of social conditions.

In Canada, the Catholic priesthood was recognized, together with the maintenance of French Civil Law. The old Corn Law was repealed and importation allowed when wheat was forty-eight shillings, and in India the East India Company was put under some governmental control, Warren Hastings being nominated Governor-General.

The Royal Marriage Act, passed on the personal insistence of the King, lost the Government the powerful support of Charles Fox. As a poor exchange, George Germaine and the Tory, Meredith, joined the Government ranks. A general election in 1774 gave North a majority of nearly three-to-one; exceptionally, the City of London went Radical and Wilkes, unmolested and unopposed, sat for Middlesex. Fortunately for the administration, he had now turned his attention almost exclusively to municipal affairs, seeking to be Lord Mayor of London.

The American problem now emerged, rapidly passing into a warlike stage, and in that contention new issues arose and new reputations were to be made. Broadly speaking, three solutions had been advocated; the first, the King's, which North reluctantly supported, was to treat the Americans as rebels outside the law—the men who took this view, the King above all, regretted the repeal of the Stamp Act, declaring that the token exception of tea as an affirmation of principle had but been used to cause the Boston demonstration in 1774 or had, at least, been an excuse for it. In 1775, North had proposed that each colony might be exempted from Imperial taxation as regards the cost of its own defence, but such a remedy was then too late.

The second suggestion, that of Chatham, was to allow the Americans, through Congress, generally to tax themselves, a plan which Franklin had for a time supported—the third view was that taken by the advanced Whigs in England—that the Americans were entitled to a Bill of Rights which would give to their Congress complete self-government.

Largely through the influence of Chatham, support of the colonists became an essential part of the Whig programme; one result was to produce a new body of Court Whigs who, once war had started, agreed with the Government that before any further discussion could be con-sidered, the war must be won. The fact that Wilkes and his friends protested against the treatment of the Americans did not ease the fears of the more timorous of the Opposition. On the Government side, the leader was probably the most eager of his party for reconciliation, but the King and his friends were of a different opinion and every failure in the field made them the more stubborn. Although Fox and Burke were vehement in opposition, the support they obtained was poor, nor is there any reason to suppose that the country was substantially behind them—on the American matter there is no sign of any public animation comparable to the excitement roused by Wilkes. In the House, Burke's plea for conciliation had been dismissed by a majority of nearly two hundred votes, and although Grafton resigned—he had taken office under North—Burke and Fox were systematically voted down, while promises of royal victory receded and ultimate defeat became the more certain.

The dilemma which inexorably pursues statesmen who continue to oppose a war after it has started confronted Fox on two occasions in his life. In the midst of hostilities, more particularly if unsuccessful, antagonism is not only unpopular but distasteful to a patriotic opponent. In these circumstances, two courses are open to the subject who wishes to remain loyal: the one is to withdraw from public life altogether; the other, to criticize the conduct of the war itself: in 1776 Rockingham and Burke chose the method of secession—Fox determined to remain and fight.

In December, 1777, came the news of the surrender of Burgoyne at Saratoga. Fox concentrated his fury upon Germaine, the Secretary for War, and found ample material for his attack. Back came the Whigs, some to suggest a settlement, others to urge further and more efficient warfare; for the time being, the pertinacity of Fox had saved the party.

All his hesitations, however, were ended when France joined the Americans in 1778. Fox had early private news of the fact and exposed the weakness and folly of the Government. Again a cry arose for the old veteran, Chatham—North would have been only too willing to hand over the direction of so terrible a situation to him; Fox would have served— the Rockingham group, alone, raised difficulties. But Chatham soon died and the last possibility of accommodation with the States, now "United", was gone. Richmond, who led the Opposition in the Lords, had been half-hearted, but the fight against France had resolved his doubts also—of that war he was without hesitation a keen supporter. The Whig anti-Gallican past sustained the Party—France was ever the foe, cried Fox; "the war against America is against your own countrymen, France is an inveterate enemy". He demanded that the navy, the militia and the army should all be strengthened. From 1778, the Whigs became critical but enthusiastic patriots—many of them, Grafton, Richmond and Devonshire, left London to command the militia in their respective counties.

In June, 1779, Spain joined the enemy, but George, against the private protests of North, still clamoured to destroy the Americans. The recognition that the King's infatuation was ruining the country was fast spreading. In the Commons in April, 1780, a motion by Dunning, the Whig, that "the influence of the Crown has increased, is increasing and ought to be diminished", to the horror of the Monarch and the Court, was carried against the Government by eighteen votes. An attack on the Civil List revenues, the principal source of royal patronage, followed, and without a division an enquiry was ordered. The utter incapacity of the Government to cope with the riots organized by Lord George Gordon as a protest against the relief of Catholic disabilities—a measure promoted not only by the Whigs but by North himself—showed the administration to be as feeble in domestic as in foreign affairs. In October, 1781, Cornwallis surrendered at Yorktown: as North truly said:

"It is all over". In December he had to tell the House that it "is not the intention of the Government to reduce America by force". This admission was followed by a motion of Conway in February, 1782, to abandon the American War, to be lost by only one vote. On March 20th, North, braving the King's anger, found courage sufficient to resign.

The unscrupulous Chancellor, Thurlow, was employed by the King to find him a new government and Rockingham entered on his second administration, the terms being the Independence of America and the abolition of those sinecure offices by which, in the past, George had systematically corrupted Parliament—together with the retention upon the Woolsack of Thurlow himself.

The new Cabinet, with the exception of the inescapable Chancellor, was Whig, though from the outset there was friction between the Rockingham and Shelburne groups. The latter supported electoral reform; Burke, the mentor of Rockingham, relied upon the exclusion from Parliament of royal influence. The two ideals were not inconsistent, but Burke had an irrational objection to tampering with the existing franchise in any way. It is interesting to note that the young Pitt, though he would not join the Government, favoured franchise reform, as did the Duke of Richmond in the Lords.

In 1782 Rockingham publicly declared that there were 11,500 revenue officers and that 70 elections were decided by their votes. Borough jobbers assessed the average value of seats at, at least, £3,000. Some contests had risen in cost to over £30,000 (according to Horace Walpole). In 1761, Sudbury advertised itself for sale, he writes, and at length a few brokers in borough seats actually had to stand their trial (*Memoirs of Geo. III*. pp. 129–135). As to the House itself, in 1774, 254 members in England and Wales represented 11,500 voters and 56 had constituencies of 38 electors, while six members had only three electors each. In Scotland the matter was even worse. Political reform societies were fast rising, but all they could do was to make speeches and petition. Pitt had inherited his early desire for reform from his father. Chatham's chief interest had been in cautious redistribution—he would have increased the county representation (he was hesitant about destroying the rotten boroughs), and so by increasing the shire's vote would have diminished the influence of the "mercenary borough".

It was not so much Pitt's particular proposals, however, but the fact that so important a statesman thought franchise reform necessary at all which makes his opinion significant. He by no means accepted the new fashionable view of Horne and his supporters that a member of Parliament should be but a delegate, but Chatham was of opinion that "there should be a permanent relation between the constituent and representative body of the people." (*Chatham Correspondence*, III, 457.) In the words of Johnson, "Chatham was a Minister given to the King by the people"—he had the support of the unenfranchised, and once a minister got into such a position, it was natural that he should wish his followers to be able to give legal expression to their enthusiasm.

The objection of Burke to parliamentary reform is not easy to understand. Personally he disliked Chatham. He thought he was an "ambitious man of light and no principles". (*Correspondence*, II, 276.) Burke had a far greater fear of the public than had the Great Commoner;

the Legislature was a trustee for the people, he wrote. He went as far with the reformers as to approve the reporting of debates and divisions, but of the new idea that members were mere delegates, as he told his Bristol electors in 1774, he would have nothing; "your representative owes you his judgment and he betrays you if he sacrifices it to your opinion—Parliament is a deliberative assembly of one nation with one interest, that of the whole—not local prejudice ought to guide but the general good". That was very noble and very wise, but its connection with the perpetuation of the right of very rich men to buy parliamentary seats is not very easy to discover. He thought that "the machine itself is well enough to answer any good purpose provided the materials were sound". (*Correspondence*, II, 383.) On this basis he and his friends opposed all attempts to redistribute seats or enlarge the franchise; he denounced the societies who urged these reforms and objected to any attack upon "the tried usages of the Constitution", even going so far as to say that "our representation is as nearly perfect as the necessary imperfection of human affairs will suffer it to be". (*Works*, x, 92–108.)

Thus, through Burke's efforts, the young Pitt's motion in 1782 for enquiry into parliamentary representation was defeated by twenty votes, for while Fox and Sheridan supported his demand, not only did Burke denounce the very moderate request for investigation as "revolutionary", but many less important Whigs and Tories also, fearful of losing both their seats and financial electoral assets, were unsympathetic to any change. Ten days later, Pitt asked for shorter Parliaments. Here, it is true, he was seeking to amend the Whig expedient of William III's time when the Septennial Act was passed, but in truth he was a better Liberal than those who opposed him. Not until 1910 was the period of Parliament lowered from the undemocratic length of seven years— but in 1782 it was Burke, the real Tory, who led the Opposition. In the Lords, on the other hand, that early noble Radical, the Duke of Richmond, moved for manhood suffrage. The difference of opinion on this matter provided the comic spectacle of Pitt and Wilkes serving on the same reform committee.

Although Fox was now joint Foreign Secretary, America, still in law a colony, fell under the jurisdiction of Shelburne. It was that states-man's object to promote a peace simultaneously with France and the United States, while Fox wished without any delay to acknowledge the independence of the American colonies. Shelburne began negotiations with Franklin, who asked for the yielding of Canada—this was refused, and the Cabinet was inclining to Fox's view of a separate peace, apart from France, when, on July 1, 1782, Rockingham died.

The King sent for Shelburne, but Fox, Burke and others, to avoid serving under him, demanded that a comparative nonentity, the Duke of Portland, should become titular head. The King, as he was entitled constitutionally to do, declined the dictation, and thereupon Fox resigned, Burke with him. The Duke of Richmond, however, disapproved the secession and remained in the Cabinet.

In the Cabinet, Lord John Cavendish alone had followed Fox, and Pitt, at the age of twenty-three, became Chancellor of the Exchequer. It was in December that Shelburne had to announce that in the end he had been compelled to sign preliminary articles of peace with America before all the outstanding French problems had been solved. Feeling his weakness, he desired to strengthen his position by bringing in North, but Pitt refused to agree.

It was clear that Fox's desire for peace with America first had been satisfied, and he generously admitted it in a speech in the House. He wished, however, to be further assured. Was the treaty with America dependent upon an agreement with France? Pitt said it was irrevocable, but the foolish King thought otherwise. He would not, he said, recognize American independence unless the French pacification went through; Pitt had spoken without authority. In January of 1783, however, the preliminary treaty with France and Spain was signed. By nineteen votes it was carried in the Commons that the concessions to France were unjustified and Shelburne was thereupon compelled to resign. At last Pitt was given permission to endeavour to bring Fox into the Government, but that fiery politician refused to come unless Shelburne went out and the negotiations broke down on the personal hatred of Fox and Burke to the Prime Minister, who certainly had treated Fox with great equivocation over the American negotiations when they were both Secretaries of State.

The King long struggled to keep Fox out of the Government. It was suggested that Pitt should be Premier, but he refused. North, being asked to come in without Fox, declined, and, in the end, on April 2nd, the Duke of Portland, Fox's former nominee, became First Lord of the Treasury; North and Fox to be Secretaries of State.

Much criticism had been directed against Fox because in this ministry Lord North found a place. It cannot be suggested that Fox was not entitled to join his own nominee, Portland, and therefore the condemnation of the coalition must rest primarily upon North. Yet North had never been a Tory, his own inclinations, as has been shown, on the whole were Liberal—now that the American war was over there was little to divide him from the Whigs if but he would abandon his subservience to the royal will. By this time the King had come to regard his erstwhile servant as a deserter—he was almost as uncongenial to George as was the detested Fox. North now declared to Fox that he had come to believe in united Cabinet control; he abandoned the Tory doctrine that each minister was responsible only to the King. As Fox said: "The American war was the cause of enmity between myself and the noble Lord. The American war and the American question is at an end".

Socially, Fox and North were in the same jovial circle. Shelburne was a frigid and exclusive man who stood aloof, a fact which counted for much in the days of select aristocratic government. Horace Walpole, usually so censorious a critic of Fox and his friends, to judge from his contemporary letters was not much shocked at the alliance. Perhaps the best test of opinion is afforded by the re-election of Fox without opposition for that democratic and intractable constituency, Westminster.

A much more serious difficulty was the difference among ministers on such fundamental matters as that shown by the rejection of Pitt's renewed demand for electoral reform. The endorsement by the Government of that treaty of peace with France which they had condemned when Shelburne introduced it was probably inescapable and wise, but their tolerance of Burke's retrograde refusal to consider the franchise question—an inaction which postponed all adjustment of an indefensible mode of representation for fifty years—shows how far they were from achieving any higher notion of Government than the maintenance of a perpetual freehold for the Whig oligarchy.

The major problem which concerned the Government was the future of India. Wealth from that country was now affecting public life, as did the incursion of moneyed interests from South Africa at the end of the Victorian era. The new Governor-General, Hastings, was at odds with the Directors; the majority of the Court of Proprietors were on his side. Fox and North determined to overthrow the vested interests which had collected round the Nabobs and adventurers who were now living on India and buying influence at home. Here Burke was whole-heartedly with them; he had, he believed, discovered grave injustices, if not cruelties, perpetrated in the administration of that great country. The Government, for once united, suggested that the sovereign control should be taken from the Company and vested in Commissioners to be nominated by the Government and subsequently appointed by the Crown, while an executive in India should work under them. This scheme was necessarily regarded as an invasion of their chartered monopoly rights by the proprietors and it is not difficult to foresee that from the outset interested persons would seek to wreck it. All other holders of charters were alarmed; for the first time the City turned against the Whigs, even Wilkes supported the Opposition; Plutocracy was showing its teeth. By a great folly, Lord North's son appeared among the proposed commissioners—it was one of those acts which make the historian doubt the political intelligence of public men. The capitalists organized a campaign, directed against Fox in particular. The King, who had no love for City opinion, saw in this agitation a means of overthrowing the Ministry. He declared in his old style that "whoever voted for the India Bill would be considered by him as an enemy". The Lords, persuaded both by Court and City, deserted, and on March 17th, 1783, the Bill was rejected there by nineteeen votes. Next day the King took the seals from his Whig opponents and Pitt became Prime Minister.

Apart from the India matter, the record of the Coalition was a poor one. They had refused, as has been said, to help Pitt to eradicate corrupt boroughs or lessen election expenses; they declined to introduce much-needed parliamentary reforms in Ireland; they had proposed to grant the Prince of Wales, their friend, £100,000 a year. A Bill to prevent waste in Government offices, another scheme of Pitt's, was rejected, and they continued the bad old system of giving preferences in the floating of national loans to their supporters. Until the split on the India question, the City had given the Government their support—their chief claim to honour is that they had not feared to make the moneyed interests break with them by their advocacy of a progressive Indian policy.

The new Premier at first sought another Coalition—North to retire and a compromise on the Indian question to be attempted. This failed, and soon, of the great Whigs, only the Radical Richmond supported Pitt. Temple, his relation, left him at an early stage and Shelburne was not invited to join. Against the young Prime Minister stood the great Coalition majority; what the Foxites chiefly feared was a dissolution—

their leaders went so far as publicly to deny to the Crown the right to call a new Parliament during a session. Fox did not hesitate to hold up the Mutiny Bill, which annually legalized the Army, and in other ways encouraged his followers to practise every possible obstruction.

Pitt, on the other hand, demanded an election—let the country (or such small part of it as had votes) decide. For four years Fox had supported motions for annual Parliaments. Why, asked Pitt, this cynical change of front? At this time, undoubtedly, Fox had lost much of his popularity—whatever may have been the excuses for the alliance with North, though the governing class took it calmly—the unfranchised people as a whole were astonished that the leader should so soon join hands with the man whom he had so vilified for so long a period. In the House the usual Government inducements and threats were brought to bear upon the members and the Whig majorities steadily fell until, finally, in a division against the Government, they had a majority of but one. Then Pitt struck; he dissolved, went to the country, and was returned with a two-hundred majority—the rule of the Whigs was over.

One effect of Pitt's triumph was to kill reform. Though he still appealed for it (he would have enfranchised London and County areas by destroying thirty-six small borough franchises, a turn-over of seventy-two seats), North and Burke both opposed him, though Fox was on his side. It speaks for the utter confusion of party labels at this time that even on so vital a matter as fair representation there was no clear cleavage. Pitt was defeated by seventy-four votes and Reform ceased to be a live issue. The reason is obvious. It was the Tories who in early days had pressed for a more equitable distribution of seats, for most of the small boroughs were then Whig. No member with vested personal interests of great social and financial value was readily going to throw away his status and property. The holders of the impeached seats, whether Tory or Whig, would naturally vote for their retention, but such an attitude deprived such of them as were Whigs of their last justification to be a progressive party.

Another cleavage to be deplored arose over the fiscal treatment of Ireland. Pitt was for low mutual tariffs—a proposal most unpopular with the English manufacturers. Indeed Fox, by taking a strong protectionist line, almost won back the industrialists of the north. Finance and Commerce were becoming very powerful in politics and Pitt was forced by his own Cabinet to withdraw. His attempt at Irish conciliation failed; the menace of disharmony within the United Kingdom remained undispelled.

Money had also influenced the making of the French commercial treaty of 1787. Fox, as usual, opposed all contacts with France—it was the old Whig tradition, but the business interests of Manchester merchants, ironmasters, manufacturers generally, and bankers in search of new markets were vocal in the House and out of it—they insisted on trade arrangements and obtained what they desired. No longer were financiers exclusively Whig; a vast creation of new peers, some forty-eight in all during Pitt's administrations before 1790, included many representatives of finance and commerce (among them the first of Jewish descent, Gideon, Lord Eardly), Robert Smith, banker, and others.

But the support of Pitt was not limited to the City. Men of all kinds of belief, tired of Whig faction fights, acknowledged his leadership. The representation of Middlesex—now shared by Wilkes, the erstwhile Radical, and Mainwaring, a King's friend—was typical. Those who wished to see the Court restored to power and those who favoured parliamentary reform alike trusted Pitt; nevertheless, he himself was an isolated and often thwarted statesman—the very multitude and incompatibility of his supporters was a weakness, for there was scarcely anything that some of them wanted which another group would not oppose. In the field of finance alone, the City insisted that he be given a free hand. He abolished many futile and vexatious duties, instituted the Sinking Fund and laid the foundations for the great Victorian budgets. In this department he was well served by Jenkinson at the restored Board of Trade and by Grenville, Pitt's cousin, who, with Eden, piloted through the difficult Anglo-French commercial treaty.

In all this Pitt was in constant consultation with the moneyed interests —they it was who constituted his chief support, but like many another minister who depends upon commercial men, he had to pay for their concurrence.

Despite Pitt's associations, he himself—at any rate in his early days— was a reformer, indeed a more consistent one than Fox; but, as he used sadly to say, "Fox and Coalition had destroyed the Whig Party for ever". In the absence of any strong party organization Pitt, in his dependence on King and City, was never a free agent.

His advocacy of the reform of the Slave Trade, then a test question for religious and progressive minds, exhibited the weakness of his position. Only by two votes and a threat of resignation could he get a very mild measure curtailing the worst excesses of slave dealers through the Lords. It was a Bill, he said, which he wondered that "any human being could resist". In 1791 the House of Commons rejected a motion for the total abolition of the slave trade by nearly a hundred votes, though the promoter was Wilberforce, Pitt's especial friend, and Pitt had supported him. All the Cabinet would do was to say that the slave trade must remain an open question.

When, therefore, the matter is carefully examined it appears that Pitt's very success and general support, while keeping him in office, by no means gave him complete personal power. He was continually beset by obstruction from his own side. On the prosecution of Hastings the Cabinet was divided, though he, the Prime Minister himself, supported the impeachment; only in the regularization of finance, in simplifying the tariff, instituting assessed taxes and inaugurating the office of Comptroller and Auditor-General and in making loans a matter of public tender, was he allowed a free hand.

As to the Indian question, in 1784 a compromise was reached by setting up a Board of Control ruling through the Company, but in 1786 the Governor-General was given civil and military sovereignty. In effect, therefore, Pitt had followed Fox and defeated the East India Company —as Erskine May writes, "the Company were now accountable to Ministers, in their rule . . . the administration of Indian affairs came . . . under the review of Parliament". (*Constitutional History of England*, p. 381.)

But soon followed one of those domestic crises which are so much more interesting to the political world than social amelioration—in the autumn of 1788 it was evident that the King's reason was once again deranged and a Regency of some sort had become necessary.

To the Whigs, this was expected to result in the bestowal of power on their patron, the Prince of Wales. Pitt and his friends were not willing to admit that the King's illness was permanent, they wished for delay. It was moved by Pitt to appoint a committee to seek for precedents. Fox, unwisely, opposed this, uttering the most unwhiggish doctrine that the Prince was in law already Regent and that no parliamentary authority was required. The proclamation of this extreme Tory view alarmed the Whigs, and Pitt was quick to satirize them, saying that he would "unwhig Fox"; he certainly did so. He pointed out that the Bill of Rights, the Revolution, the Balance of Power and all the Whig armoury were against Fox's contention. Needless to say the Committee was appointed; it recommended the Regency of the Prince and gave him the power to choose ministers, though not to make life appointments or create peers. Here, it might be thought, the Whigs had gained their point; but Fox elected to fight again, declaring for the Prince's unrestricted power. All this was to deny the rights of Parliament; if Fox were reinstated it would only be as the Prince's nominee—once more circumstances had tempted him to advocate high Tory doctrine. The conduct of Burke was even worse—he mocked at the King and cried that God had hurled him from his throne. Thurlow, as usual, played a double part. On February 19th the King, by recovering, confounded the whole intrigue.

Never had Whig opportunism sunk so low, never had Pitt been so respected; the antics of Burke and the inconsistencies of Fox had raised general disgust. The Prince of Wales, at best, was not a figure likely to command public approval and some of Pitt's supporters, to show the liberality of their minds, were willing to concede a measure of relief to the Dissenters who were now, particularly when wealthy, drifting away from Whiggery.

In 1787 a proposal to repeal the Test and Corporation Acts, surprisingly, came from the Government side of the House to be defeated by eighty votes, and in 1789 the Bill only failed by twenty. Next year, however, it would appear that the French Revolution had inflamed feeling against the Nonconformists, who were still regarded in many quarters as Radical. This time the proposal was attacked not only by nervous Tories but also by Burke. At the General Election in 1790 there was little change in the distribution of parties, but Burke had already begun to disagree with the Foxite opposition on the question of the French Revolution. Hearing of the fall of the Bastille, Burke denounced France as a nation who had "thrown off the yoke of laws and morals". To contrast this with Fox's famous "how much the greatest event which has happened in the world and how much the best", discloses the fissure which was developing in the Opposition.

In February, 1790, Burke, while agreeing with Fox that France was no longer to be feared, deplored his exaltation of the Revolution. Burke's critical *Reflections* on the Revolution sold to the extent of thirty-two thousand copies in a year—it was violently hostile to the new ideas. Fox, on the other hand, still maintained that the French had erected "a glorious edifice of Liberty". Finally, on the Quebec Bill, Burke took

c

of it, he would not employ him. Fox's past visit to Napoleon, "a damned imprudent act" as Creevy commented, had also annoyed many of his former supporters, now enemies of French aggression, such as Coleridge. "Mr. Fox is excluded by the express command of the King", wrote the Sovereign to Addington. Pitt, promising to drop Catholic relief, became Prime Minister again in May, 1804, but as the military situation deteriorated Pitt again asked for a coalition; again the King refused, when Trafalgar saved the Government. At last, after Austerlitz, Pitt died, and the King sent for Portland, who was still sufficiently a Whig to say that he would not serve without Fox. This time the King yielded; the Ministry of all the Talents, as it was called, was formed with Fox as *de facto* leader—his office being that of Foreign Secretary. Immediately his Liberal influence was felt and he was pressing for Catholic emancipation and the abolition of the slave trade when he died. "At this time", writes Lord Holland (*Memoirs*, II, p. 75), "we might have had a separate peace, but it would have been of short duration"; in the event negotiations failed and the Government were censured by Whitebread, a brother-in-law of Grey, for their failure.

Whitebread was one of the first Radicals to censure his more conservative colleagues, but Holland, Fox's devoted nephew, and many other of the young men were also out of sympathy with the elder Whigs; to strengthen himself, Grenville approached Canning, a "left wing Tory". The Catholic question was again insistent, and the young reformers wished to give to the Papists who had the right in Ireland, a power to hold the King's commission everywhere. Howick introduced a Bill to this effect, the King saying "not one step further". On the other side Addington, now Lord Sidmouth, opposed all Catholic liberation—he was also against the emancipation of the slaves and had the support generally of the more obdurate Tories. Lord Eldon, a close friend of the King, was also of this way of thinking—indeed at all times he was against all change whatever. These reactionaries and their associates forced the Cabinet to withdraw the measure enabling Catholics generally to hold commissions, but the younger men, led by Canning, were becoming restless. His rival, Castlereagh, had taken office under Addington, but both were now back in Portland's government, the former being Treasurer of the Navy, Castlereagh President of the Board of Control. As their policies diverged, their personal relations became more strained, and when Canning sought to have Castlereagh removed from the War Office his action resulted in a duel. Before this, in March, 1809, Canning had tendered his resignation, and now it was found that the whole Ministry had been jeopardized by the scandal; Portland, who was infirm, retired, and a dispute arose between Perceval—who led the Commons—and Canning who should be the chief. Canning, disappointed at not receiving first place, withdrew from the Government, to be out of office for seven years; not until 1816 did he accept the comparatively lowly position of President of the Board of Trade. Meanwhile Perceval, after suggesting that he was willing to serve under a peer, Grenville or Grey, was appointed Premier. Canning was altogether excluded and Wellesley followed him at the Foreign Office. Canning was suspected of favouring Catholic emancipation, and although he had proved of great value by discovering the designs of Napoleon on Denmark and perhaps first saw the advantage of attacking the French in the Peninsula, he had aimed too high. When Perceval was assassinated in 1812, Liverpool became Premier, Castlereagh being willing to yield it to him, Canning being again offered the Foreign Office. Once more he refused unless he might lead the House as well—a proposal which was not entertained. His extreme ambition seemed for the time to have destroyed his chances.

Whatever may be thought of the character of Canning, there can be no doubt that his retirement from Government on the death of Portland removed from the administration its last liberalizing element. The general situation was deplorable. Napoleon was still master of Europe. At home, after debate on the Walcheron disaster, Gale Jones of the Corresponding Society, against the will of Canning, had been imprisoned for placarding London in protest against the exclusion of Press and Public; and Burdett followed this up by an attack on the House —he called it a "Whited wall"—to his electors in Westminster. The Government decided to send him to the Tower, but he entrenched himself in his house and was ultimately seized, to the great advertisement of Radicalism. Many towns petitioned for his release; another Wilkes' movement seemed on its way, and this time in the midst of a great war in which the country was in extreme peril. In these circumstances, Canning again was offered employment; again he declined anything but the Foreign Office, together with the restoration of his friend, Huskisson, also an "advanced" Tory.

The Combination Acts of 1800 had made it criminal for working people to combine in Unions—at the same time the old Elizabethan method of fixing minimum wages by the Justices had become obsolete and attempts in Parliament generally to restore statutory wages had been defeated. Despite the efforts of Brougham, in the 1807 election, to fill "every bookseller's shop with pamphlets and provide copy for all the newspapers to enforce the measures of or expose the adversaries of the Whigs" (Holland, *Memoirs*, II, p. 227), the active opposition returned numbered only some twenty, over whom the very timorous "Grenvillite", Ponsonby, had no control at all. Brougham and his friends (he had been returned in 1810) argued for an early peace, universal education, reform of law and of prisons, and for the abolition of the Slave Trade and flogging in the Army. They had abandoned the old protectionist "Mercantile System" and, under the influence of Adam Smith and Bentham, were now rapidly passing to a belief in Individualism. Burdett and Cochrane had been returned for Westminster and were ready for any innovation. Wardle, who had made it his particular business to attack the Duke of York as Commander-in-Chief, especially for granting army commissions on the solicitation of his mistress, succeeded in forcing the Duke to resign his office. The "Mountain", as the advanced Whigs were called, included Whitebread, Mackintosh, Weston and Creevy—they were the only Whigs who received any support from the Radicals outside the House. Despite the paucity of their numbers, Brougham and his colleagues managed to get a Bill through making Slave Trading criminal. Moreover, by his eloquence that fiery lawyer had forced the Government to withdraw the "Orders in Council" which provided, in his words, "that no vessel should enter a French port without having touched at one in Great Britain". By this achievement he pleased the merchants and

hoped as a consequence to be returned for Liverpool. Other influences
there, however, were too strong and from 1812 to 1815 he was without
a seat in Parliament.

In 1811 the King had become permanently insane and the Prince
of Wales, by statute, was appointed Regent. Perceval had wished to
impose the restrictions on him which had been suggested in 1788.
Sheridan, the only Whig with whom the Prince had remained in contact,
was for taking the same attitude as Fox had formerly held and, in the
end, as the Whig Lords would not give him that support which he
expected, the Regent decided to make no change in Government. He
would have welcomed a coalition, but the Whigs would not join the
Administration unless Ireland were granted Catholic relief. Castlereagh
became Foreign Secretary, and the reactionary Sidmouth was soon made
Secretary of Home Affairs. On the death of Perceval, Lord Liverpool—
the negotiator of the Treaty of Amiens—was appointed Prime Minister,
an office he held for fifteen years.

During the earlier part of this period the industries of the country
were at a standstill. America had declared war and there was practically
no international trade. Riots of unemployed and starving people were
endemic. Wellesley, before resigning, had complained that his brother
was insufficiently supported in Spain, and the Whigs and Radicals, in
despair of any constructive betterment, came to concentrate on the
alleged grievances of the Princess Caroline as a means to attack the
Regent and discredit the Government. A scandal with regard to the
custody of the Princess Charlotte added to the excitement. Even the
abdication of Napoleon did nothing to restore the popularity of George,
who was hooted in the streets, and the Administration was nearly as
distracted as the Opposition.

From the end of the war, for some eight years the country was in
a state of unprecedented distress for which the reactionary Government
of Lord Liverpool had no remedy except to attempt to allay discontent
by suppression. The middle classes took alarm at the destruction of
machinery and the burning of ricks by the under-paid and unemployed
labourers. Those who supported any claim for social improvement were
stigmatized as Radicals—their position was possibly worse in the estimation of the respectable than that of the Communists between the two
Great Wars. "It was an awful period", says Sidney Smith, "for those
who ventured to maintain Liberal opinions." The reformers, in their
defence, formed societies and clubs, lawful and illicit, under the leadership
of Owen, Spence, Cobbett, Hunt, Thistlewood and others.

Notwithstanding the fact that the country was at peace, the Government sought in their notorious "Six Mile Acts" to crush all reformative
movements. The time was "like a history of civil war". (*The Skilled
Labourer*, Hammond, Introduction.) The garden, ale and Sunday
leisure which the workman had formerly enjoyed were threatened by the
new factory system. His wife now had to work in the mills, his children
also. Long working days and night toil were becoming general. Industries which had been artificially stimulated during the long hostilities
were collapsing and few new ones were to be found. For all this the
Government had no remedy but further prosecution and repressive law.
Grenville and the old Whigs on the whole supported the Prime Minister;

even Tierney and Brougham had to walk with care, for, as Sidney Smith wrote, "it was safer to be a felon than a reformer". Nevertheless, though he might deny that he was one, Brougham, on his return to Parliament, of necessity became the real leader of the Parliamentary Radicals. He protested against the passage of the Act preventing public meetings not controlled by magistrates or Lords-Lieutenant. This measure was calculated to deprive the people of their last redress, as Lord Holland vainly protested in the Lords; in the result came the crowd of fifty thousand demonstrators at Manchester with its Yeomanry charges and Thistlewood's plot to assassinate the Cabinet. Brougham saw clearly that the only hope to avoid general violence lay in the revival of a Whig party with a progressive programme.

The times were not propitious; in the absence of franchise reform it was scarcely possible to bring new blood into the House. An attempt to establish connection between the discordant Whig elements was made through Lambton (later Lord Durham), who shared Brougham's opinions, and had married Lord Grey's daughter. To placate the centre Whigs, Brougham now very definitely dissociated himself from the intransigents of the left. It is curious to note that the first Whig victory, in 1816, was to throw out an income tax as "inquisitorial".

Next year the fight against the Government prosecutions of reformers brought Grey, Tierney, Lambton and Holland to Brougham's side, and the secession of so many of the Whig magnates under Grenville to the Government helped Brougham to form—out of the remainder—the elements of a Liberal Party. On the death of the ineffectual Ponsonby, Tierney, with the support of Romilly and Brougham, had been chosen to be Leader, but he proved useless as a means to co-ordinate the remaining Whigs and the "Mountain". The more conservative Whigs hoped, without further reform, for office through Tory divisions, while the Radicals, now fully persuaded of the need for a progressive programme, pressed for the abolition of trade restrictions and thus had succeeded in enlisting the sympathy of the manufacturers and merchants, who, now that agitation was dying down, were beginning once more to take a liberal view of affairs. The Radical policy of reduction of expenditure was another "plank" which appealed to the City; but, above all things, their scheme for providing the middle classes with votes, and so of control of Parliament, had the most unifying effect. It would curb aristocratic privilege while giving no power to the labouring classes; it was inexpensive, and gratifying in its promise of increased power to the growing great "respectable" bourgeois class which for a century was to determine public opinion.

But politics are ever the sport of the unexpected. In January, 1820, the old King died, and almost at once, on the insistence of George IV, came the Bill, introduced in the Lords, to deprive the Queen of her position as Consort. Canning, one of the most potent of the progressive Tories, resigned in order to dissociate himself from the Divorce Bill. Again the people, excited by the Radicals and the speeches of Brougham before the Lords, rallied round the somewhat sordid figure of the Queen, as their only means of expressing discontent. This uninteresting, foolish woman had proved the means which brought Whigs, Liberals and Radicals into one fold. In the Lords, a third reading only obtaining a very small

C*

majority, the Government, not unwillingly, abandoned the Bill and the King was reduced to the petty expedient of refusing his spouse admission to his Coronation. But the work had been done; an unfortunate foreign woman's matrimonial troubles had united those political elements which the skill and intelligence of Brougham had for so long vainly been seeking to reconcile.

In August, 1822, Castlereagh, one of the most hated of the Government, killed himself. The King was angry with Liverpool for his failure in the Divorce matter and the Administration was visibly weakening. Again the obliging Grenville was called in for consultation and talk of Canning being used to renew a coalition was bruited.

But the Catholic question, which had upset so many plans, was at length arising in inescapable form. In 1821, Plunket had moved for Emancipation, Canning supporting him, though Peel, who had moved into Canning's place, opposed. Nevertheless, the third reading was carried. In the Lords the Bill was only rejected by thirty-one votes. Clearly the question demanded solution.

By this time trade was recovering and a general easing of tension was evident in which a mild Liberalism might hope to thrive. The return of Canning to the leadership of the House after the death of Castlereagh inaugurated a new policy. Huskisson at the Board of Trade, and Robinson at the Exchequer, provided the Government with great financial ability of that new mentality which accepted the principles of Adam Smith. Ricardo, the economist, who had entered Parliament in 1819, had now great influence. He had even suggested, capitalist as he was, the paying off of the war debt by a Property Tax and had formulated a law of rent, critical of land holding, which had the result of drawing attention to the enrichment of the great estate owners caused by heavy corn duties. Rent, he declared, was only the surplus profit which any given land, either from the convenience of situation or from the fertility of the soil, yields over the worst land in cultivation. The landlords, in other words, appropriated the surplus profits—a very congenial doctrine for tenant manufacturers and shop people. It is not suggested that the full import of these ideas was understood, even by advanced Radicals, but their very appearance in print pointed to a new outlook in economic affairs. A middle class policy, hostile to the pretensions of the old landlords, concerned for the removal of restrictions in trade, tolerant of variety of religious belief, and, to a point, desirous even of smoother relations with labour, is discernible. In 1824 and 1825 the Combination Laws were amended and workmen's associations became lawful. In 1824 there arose disputes whether the statutory wage-fixing powers for the Spitalfield weavers and other craftsmen should be repealed. It is to be noted that the Radical individualists, such as Ricardo and Hume, were for depriving the workmen of statutory protection, and the whole question of the legality of Trade and Labour combinations came up for review. Huskisson, for the Government, supported Hume's proposal for a general enquiry. Chiefly as the result of the labour of Place, the Commission recommended the repeal of the Combination Laws; only where threats of violence existed should either employer or workman be deprived of the right to "employ his labour or capital as he may deem most advantageous". After the passing of the Bill there were many strikes and the total repeal was modified the next year. Threats to induce a workman to leave his employment were now made specifically illegal and the Courts and lawyers, not for the last time, settled down to a long argument as to the extent of the legalizations and prohibitions; still, the old general veto against workmen's combinations was gone and Trade Unions rapidly increased in numbers and membership. Under the influence of the new philosophy, voluntary association came to be preferred to State activity.

Meetings in general were once more made lawful, and restriction in trade discouraged; duties on importation were reduced in number, and raw material allowed in many cases to enter free of tax. The Corn Law of 1815 had, in effect, prohibited all importation and a new duty decreasing as the price rose was recommended—a sliding scale. This method was carried, despite the insistence of Ricardo on a fixed small duty; if the price rose to eighty-five shillings a quarter the duty was only to be a shilling.

Next was undertaken the question of retrenchment. In this, the Radical Hume was the pioneer: he obtained a reduction of the number of receivers of land tax and their remuneration by fixed salary and not by poundage; he pressed successfully for the reduction of the service and other votes. The malt and agricultural horse tax were repealed on the motion of Western, in both cases against the wish of the Government; the Ministry was again in difficulties and was subject to constant reverses.

One cause of their difficulties was that both Canning and Peel were now outside the Government. On the retirement of Sidmouth, Peel went to the Home Office and a small group of the old Whigs came in with Lord Buckingham, created a Duke for his services in the matter. When Parliament met in 1822, the Opposition still clamoured for economies and in several cases defeated the Government. Both in the demand for reduction of taxation and for economy the Ministry had to yield to public opinion. Yet one thing was needed, the presence in Government of the brilliant Canning. The King, who had before refused him office, was reconciled—to Canning's annoyance he said that he would forgive him for his sympathy for the Queen. Canning at length consented to become Foreign Secretary and brought Huskisson to the Board of Trade and Robinson to the Exchequer—the Government had been greatly strengthened; the days of Eldonian Toryism were over.

Reforms followed fast; capital punishment was abolished save for murder and a few treasonable offences. Romilly's long advocacy had been rewarded though he did not look to see its consummation; but Mackintosh, an old law reformer, with the support of Peel in 1823 carried through both Houses four statutes "exempting from capital punishment about an hundred felonies". Eldon, though still on the Woolsack, was ignored. Other legislation of 1823 included the reform of the marriage law, the substitution of Reciprocity for Protection in Navigation, and the reorganization of the Sinking Fund—all these reforms being due to the activity of Canning, Peel and Huskisson in Government and to the disinterested support of the progressive Whigs; it was the old Tories who had most reason to complain.

The year 1824 was one of trade revival; cash payments were resumed and, as is so often the case, an era of reckless speculation followed. The Bank of England was reduced to very small reserves of bullion and asked to be allowed again to suspend cash payments; all the relief they could obtain was leave to issue £1 notes—in all, seventy-four banks failed and thousands of gamblers were ruined. Yet, under the new libertarian economic theory, the Government, influenced by Huskisson, refused to take any active part in the salvage.

By now, only one-third of the population were working on the land and the commercial influence was ever strengthening. The manufacturers persuaded Huskisson and Canning again to attempt to lower the corn law duties, but in the midst of this dispute with the landed interest the Prime Minister was incapacitated by a stroke—for a time the Government went on without him, and on Canning's suggestion corn was to be imported free when it was at seventy shillings. Tory and Radical proposals respectively to raise and lower this standard were both defeated; all this time the country was without a Prime Minister.

The delay was due to the fact that the King wanted Canning, but did not want to emancipate the Catholics—it was a dilemma; during the interregnum Burdett had only failed by four votes in the Commons to carry a Catholic resolution—on Parliamentary reform, on the other hand, Canning was an irreconcilable opponent and this prevented him from obtaining the support of Grey and the Whigs. There was talk of some alternative Tory government which alarmed both Whigs and Radicals; they saw a return of the old gang—Eldon, Wellington and their school.

At length, on April 10, 1827, Canning was appointed to be Premier; at once Peel resigned, together with Eldon, both ostensibly on the Catholic question. There followed Wellington, Bathurst, Melville, Westmoreland and Bexley—almost the whole Government. Harrowby, Wynn and the two financial experts, Huskisson and Robinson, remained loyal to Canning.

Many of the Whigs, on the other hand, were willing to give him support. They agreed with him on Catholic relief, they approved his general attitude at home and abroad; only on electoral reform were they seriously divided—indeed, even then Grey alone was seriously opposed to an alliance; Lansdowne, Tierney, Holland and last, but most important, Brougham, supported some understanding. Robinson went to the Lords as Gooderich and became leader, Sturges Bourne was appointed Home Secretary, Canning himself taking the Exchequer, while Palmerston went to the War, Lord Dudley to the Foreign Office. Copley was made Lord Chancellor—taking the title of Lyndhurst.

A fierce Tory attack when Parliament met induced some Whigs to go to Canning's assistance; Lansdowne and Tierney both joined him, but Grey was still obdurate—a crisis soon came over the Corn Bill. This measure passed the Commons, but Wellington in the Lords had carried an amendment raising the minimum price for free foreign importation. On this Canning withdrew the whole Bill and shortly afterwards, on August 8th, died. What was feared by the Progressives had come about; after Gooderich had vainly sought to form a Government, the Duke of Wellington succeeded as Prime Minister.

It was the expressed desire of the Duke, who was wholly unacquainted with all the literary and speculative ferment which divided the times from those of his youth, that "Liberalism should be got rid of forever"; unfortunately for his desire, Peel told him at their first interview that the Canningites at least must be invited to come in if a stable government was to be formed. The key man was Huskisson; the Whigs implored him to go into Opposition, but he was induced to take the Colonial Office. The other leading friends of Canning, Palmerston, Dudley and Lamb, also came into Government; Peel returned to the Home Office and Aberdeen appears as Chancellor of the Duchy of Lancaster. Some old Tories complained, the Duke of Newcastle objected to the omission of Eldon, but for the most part they were jubilant. Huskisson's statement that Wellington would tread in the "footsteps of Canning" was interpreted as a pledge that free trade should be continued, but Wellington denied any such undertaking. The position from the outset was unstable. In the Commons a motion to emancipate Dissenters by repealing the now obsolete Test and Corporation Acts was carried against the Government by 237 to 193, and a compromise amendment, asking that a declaration should be made not to subvert the Protestant Established Church, was added to the Bill. In the Lords the words "on the faith of a Christian" were added to the declaration. The effect was to exclude the Jews and atheists, though it is doubtful if such a consequence was thought of at that time.

Ten days after, Burdett again brought the Catholic relief question before the Commons; this time he had a majority in his favour of six. After a conference between the Houses, in the Lords the hostile majority fell to forty-four, but what was more significant, instead of vehement opposition, both the Prime Minister and the Chancellor spoke in compromising terms. On the disfranchisement of East Retford for bribery, disputes broke out in the Cabinet as to what should be done with the seat. The old Tories were for throwing the electors into the adjacent county, the Canningites wished to give the constituency to a large town. On this, in the Commons Huskisson and Palmerston voted with the Liberals and Peel was defeated.

Thereafter Huskisson offered his resignation; to his surprise it was promptly accepted. The effect was momentous for later political history in that Palmerston, Lamb (afterwards Lord Melbourne) and the other Canningites followed him into Opposition. Aberdeen became Foreign Secretary in place of Dudley.

But the Catholic question would not rest; in Ireland after great disorders the Catholic Association had practically taken control of the country. The Duke's scheme was to suppress it and to enfranchise the Catholics simultaneously. He prevailed on Peel to support emancipation and in the end even persuaded the King. In February 1828 it was known that emancipation was in the Government programme. The Tories were disheartened and inclined to be mutinous, but after threats of abdication by the King and resignation by the Duke, the Bill came before the Lords, where the Prime Minister commended it as a means of staving off civil war. This was after a committee had recommended that only the offices of Lord Chancellor and Lord Lieutenant of Ireland should still be withheld. The former great office, despite recent protests

in Parliament, is still denied to those who will not take oaths against
Transubstantiation, the Invocation of Saints and the sacrifice of the
Mass. (*Judgment Reserved*, Slesser, p. 194.)

The change-over was very sudden. On December 11th the Duke,
addressing the Catholic Archbishop of Armagh as "Dear Sir", had
said that he "saw no prospect of a settlement—Party had been so
mixed up with it". A month later Peel told Croker, a subordinate
member of the Government, that he was converted.

The majority in favour in the Commons on third reading was one
hundred and seventy-eight; in the Lords, the Anglican Eldon, already
infuriated by the Repeal of the Test and Corporation Acts, indicated
his intention of undertaking even more vehement opposition to the
Catholic Bill; he was as good as his word—he presented many hostile
petitions; on every line he fought Lyndhurst and Wellington. Nevertheless, on April 2nd, on second reading, he was defeated by one hundred
and five; on the third reading the voting was two hundred and thirteen
to one hundred. Next day Eldon wrote to his daughter: "The fatal
Bills received the Royal Assent yesterday afternoon. God Bless us and
His Church!" So ended an age-long dispute. The Irish had saved
their co-religionists from further unjust discrimination, but the general
growing approval of toleration had done its part. The only criticism
was, as Lord Shaftesbury said of the Ministry, "We are not the men
to do it".

The real victory lay with the Radicals, who were now a force to be
reckoned with, more particularly in the bad times which were approaching.
Both manufacture and agriculture were again smitten. Great talk of
Unions for labourers alarmed the middle classes, who, none the less, were
pressing to take part in government. The death of Canning had made the
position of his followers very unsatisfactory; like the Whigs, they had
seen their policy of Catholic Emancipation carried by one whom everybody had regarded as a reactionary—Wellington—but until the King
died in June no one seemed very anxious to displace him. Meanwhile,
under Brougham's direction, the Whigs and Radicals were busy organizing
themselves for battle. On the death of Tierney, forty of them had asked
the moderate Althorp to be their leader in the Commons and Brougham
and Lord John Russell had agreed.

In the absence of any other immediate policy, it became the desire
of the Opposition to seek to introduce Canningites and Whigs into
Government. Catholic Emancipation had lost the Prime Minister the
support of the old Tories and it was thought that he might look with
more favour on a centre party. The excitement caused by the attack
of the King of France and Polignac on the constitution in France had
helped the Whigs. Brougham himself, at the General Election, was
returned as a Knight of the Shire for the county of York—a great victory,
and, in the Lords, the French King's plot having been defeated, Grey
spoke of "our duty to secure our institutions by introducing a temperate
Parliamentary Reform". To the general surprise the Duke was obdurate,
saying that "the representation of the people at present contains a large
body of the property of the country in which the landed interests have a
preponderating influence. Under the circumstances, I am not prepared
to bring forward a measure of this nature, but will at once declare that,

so far as I am concerned, I shall feel it my duty to resist such measures when proposed by others".

This unqualified refusal made all further co-operation between Tory and Whig impossible, and the Opposition in the Commons from this time onwards set out to remove the Prime Minister. On November 15th, a motion for a committee on the Civil List was carried against the Government by twenty-nine votes—next day they resigned and the new King sent for Grey, who took office on condition only that Electoral Reform should be a Cabinet question. The Sovereign agreed, and a new era in politics began.

It is essential, if subsequent developments are to be understood, that it should be realized that, at this time, outside the circle of Radicalism, the idea of general democracy formed no part of prevailing progressive opinion. What rather was sought was an harmonious balance of conflicting interests—a notion which early instruction in the *Politics* of Aristotle would make very familiar to the educated, who alone had charge of affairs. To accomplish this end, both Whigs and Tories bent their minds for many years. To enfranchise the illiterate masses, it was generally thought, would be to overthrow the political equilibrium and give to the class least fit to exercise it a preponderating power. It is not necessary, here, to quote the many opinions from all quarters which gave expression to this idea. Not until the later Liberal days of Gladstone was any other outlook accepted, even by many who called themselves advanced. The long opposition by some Liberals to the enfranchisement of women show how late they were to accept the prevailing modern idea of equal electoral rights.

The view, however, that Parliament should be controlled in one form or another by external opinion was, perhaps, the strongest feature of eighteenth-century Radicalism; a name, according to Harriet Martineau, first definitely assumed in 1819. In 1830 there had been constituted in Birmingham, one of the large cities which had no representation, a Political Union, in the words of Huskisson, "with subscriptions, funds, meetings, discussions and its great agitator". The agitator he mentioned was Attwood, who subsequently became the City's first member. Their proceedings were imitated in other large towns, and in October, 1831, in the middle of the fight in Parliament, there was formed a National Political Union with its headquarters in London. The Union passed into the hands of extremists who demanded universal suffrage, but this was what the respectable classes would never concede. In the end, when the fight was won, the 1832 Act had only added about half a million electors in a population of over sixteen millions. As Sir John Marriott has said, "the Reform Act broke the principle of aristocracy without admitting that of democracy". (*England since Waterloo*, p. 101.) "The general result was to place the borough representation in the hands of shopkeepers, and the county representation into those of landlords and farmers." (*Political History of England*, Brodrick, 1801--1837, p. 306.) Even such Radicals as James Mill would have limited the franchise to men with £100 a year. He argued that working men (who rarely then earned that sum) would follow "the intelligence of that virtuous rank with which they come most immediately in contact". (*Essay on Government*, p. 32.)

What really was affected was the character of the representative the new electorate favoured. Brilliant clubmen, young aristocrats and, above all, ambitious statesmen found it more difficult to be returned. Members were now required, to quote Spender, "to be of character and solid worth, sober, judging, sound men, trained in Quarter Sessions, men who knew all about money and credit, who were sufficiently well endowed to be removed from temptation, and had enough other employments to render them free from all suspicion of being professional politicians". (*The Public Life*, I, p. 27.) As Bagehot declared, "The object of the 1832 Bill was to transfer the predominant influence in the State from special classes to the general aggregate of fairly instructed men" (*Parliamentary Reform*); even as late as 1859 Bagehot wrote that Liberals "would have been shocked to hear themselves called democrats"—in 1832 the objection would have been even greater.

To pass to the actual reform proceedings, it has been shown how, both before and after the long Tory reaction, proposals had been brought before Parliament for the redistribution of constituencies and enlargement of the franchise. Lord John Russell, who subsequently piloted the Reform Act through the Commons, had raised the matter in 1820, moderately asking that towns found guilty of corruption should have their seats transferred to larger cities, and in 1821 he renewed the motion. Next year he suggested the addition of a hundred members for the counties and big towns, each of a hundred small boroughs to lose one member. He was defeated by one hundred and five votes, but nevertheless received the largest support which Reformers had obtained for a long time.

In 1826, Russell, who had now made the subject his own, again pressed for Reform, and in 1830 a direct proposal to enfranchise Leeds, Manchester and Birmingham was only lost by forty-eight votes. At the same time the limit of his ambition was shown when he and Brougham alike opposed a motion of O'Connell for Universal Male Suffrage and the Ballot, in which that Radical could only get thirteen members to support him.

So stood the matter at the time of the dissolution. Lord John was now in office and, as the Cabinet were in disagreement as to details, a small committee of Graham, Durham, Duncannon and himself was appointed to report upon the whole matter.

This Committee proposed the disfranchisement of all boroughs with less than two thousand inhabitants and some disenfranchisement for those with less than four thousand. They suggested members for towns with ten thousand and additional members for counties with one hundred and fifty thousand population. One of their proposals, the adoption of the Ballot, was objected to by Grey and dropped—why it should have been so treated is not clear. The Cabinet reduced the proposed qualification in boroughs to a ten-pound rating and agreed to the Committee's report for the enfranchisement of fifty-pound leaseholders and ten-pound copyholders in the counties.

In this form the Bill was approved by the King—the effect was to eliminate sixty boroughs and halve the membership in forty-six, giving a hundred and sixty-seven seats (including Weymouth, which had previously returned four!) for redistribution. Of these forty-four were to go to the big unrepresented towns, fifty-five to the English counties and the remaining eleven to Scotland, Ireland and Wales. On March 1st, 1831, the first reading took place without a division and on the 22nd the second reading was carried by one vote. A resolution that the number of representatives in England and Wales should not be diminished was conceded, but certain members now deserting, the Government were defeated by seven votes and dissolution resolved upon.

The excitement was now very great; all the streets were illuminated, and the windows of the Tories broken. On June 24th, Russell introduced the second Bill into the new Parliament; he made practically no concessions, and after many debates and divisions, on September 21st the measure was passed by three hundred and forty-five votes to two hundred and thirty-six. In the Lords, on October 8th, the second reading was rejected by forty-one votes.

The news of this defeat was followed by general rioting. Nottingham Castle, the property of Newcastle, was burned; and at Bristol, where a leading opponent, Wetherell, was Recorder, the town was set on fire.

On December 12th Russell introduced a third Reform Bill. In this proposal fifty-six boroughs were to be wholly disfranchised and another thirty deprived of half their members. The total number of members in the House was maintained at the old level. The amendment enabled more boroughs to be saved and also a greater number to be enfranchised. On March 23rd the Bill passed the Commons. It was now that the King consented to the creation of new peerages to carry the Bill and, largely through the mediation of the diarist, Greville, a second reading was carried in the Lords. In committee, however, difficulties were raised, but a change had come over the Court. The King now declined to create sufficient peers to "ensure the success of the Bill in all its essential principles". He was told that at least fifty would be required. On his refusal, the Government resigned.

Lyndhurst now suggested to the King an administration to carry a moderate Reform Bill and Wellington, ever the servant of the Crown, was not unwilling to serve. Peel, however, vehemently refused. Meanwhile, on May 9th, Grey and Althorp publicly announced their resignation, which so far was known to few people. The House of Commons thereupon by a majority of eighty expressed their confidence in the Government. It was suggested that all supplies should be refused until the Reform Bill became law. Another device advocated by the less responsible was to organize a run upon the Bank of England. By Monday, May 14th, Wellington saw that his position had become impossible, and advised the King to recall Grey. Thereafter the Tories in the Lords gradually withdrew their opposition. The King at last gave his authority that peers to an unlimited number should be created to carry the Bill. This decided the matter, and on June 4th, 1842, the Bill was read in the Lords a third time, to receive the Royal Assent on the 7th.

An important consequence followed; in the heat of the contest, Whigs, Canningites and Radicals had been fused into that great Liberal Party which was to dominate English politics for three-quarters of a century.

CHAPTER IV

'LAISSEZ-FAIRE'

IF the proletarian enthusiasts for electoral reform thought to receive some immediate result from the victory, they must soon have become disappointed. The Government remained practically unchanged in composition, it was "perhaps the most aristocratic of the century— only four of its members sat in the House of Commons", comments Spencer Walpole (*History of England*, v. III, p. 195). It had already shown, in dealing with industrial disturbances, that it had no more sympathy with the malcontents than had its predecessors; new proclamations against disturbances and special commissions to try rioters had been issued in 1830. At Winchester alone over one thousand people were prosecuted, Carlile and Cobbett were tried for incitement: the latter called as witnesses Brougham (Chancellor) and Melbourne (Home Secretary), and in the result the jury failed to agree. Though the total wealth of the country as measured by money was rapidly increasing, the condition of the labouring people, now promiscuously collected in insanitary towns, over-worked or unemployed, was becoming intolerable. Forty-one thousand people in Lancashire, it was said in Parliament, in one small district were each subsisting on two pence a day. A penny an hour was normal remuneration. The position in rural areas was little better; the threshing-machine had deprived the labourers of their winter work, the commons on which they had grazed their cattle were being enclosed, arable land was becoming pasture and many demobilized sailors and soldiers competed for what little employment existed. For long it had been necessary to supplement wages out of the rates in many parishes. Emigration alone seemed likely to ease the problem; in 1832 over one hundred thousand people left their native land, driven out by necessity. In Ireland, if anything, conditions were even worse. On January 18th, 1832, O'Connell, the leader of the agitation, was arrested. At the trial he allowed judgment to be entered against him by default, but it was rumoured that a compromise had been reached between him and the Government; O'Connell had supported the Reform Bill and was useful to them. At the general election, in the midst of the Reform excitement, no further proceedings were taken; the whole matter did nothing to strengthen authority, rather the reverse.

By the peasants, the Protestant Church was sought to be made responsible for all the misfortune of the Irish people. An agitation about tithe resulted in refusals to pay; in the end, after many disorderly districts had been proclaimed, £60,000 was advanced to distressed incumbents, and eventually the whole tithe was put under a scheme, to be redeemed for some £10,000,000.

Many Liberals objected; they declared that the established Irish Church was indefensible in a Catholic country and objected to its rehabilitation. The Bill for tithe composition, however, passed, and dissolution followed on December 3rd, 1832, the last day of the unreformed Parliament.

Though the new House was composed primarily of two parties, the presence of such men as Attwood, Pease the Quaker, Jeffrey and Cobbett brought a type into the House which was formerly absent. The Radicals, however, did not number in all more than fifty. They wished to amend or abolish Tithe, the Corn Laws, the Game Laws; sought Church disestablishment, and the reform of municipal corporations and the poor law. In economic matters, under the influence of their individualistic theories, they favoured free labour; all Governmental interference even to protect the labourer they suspected as interfering with that beneficent struggle of "enlightened self interests" out of which, they believed, the finest results would come.

Had they been moved merely by economic abstractions, it is doubtful whether they would not have realized the more obvious ill-effects of unfettered industrialism—unfortunately, their material interests coincided with their opinions. Most of them were more or less wealthy, for until 1858 men who could not show that they had an established income were excluded from the House of Commons. Moreover, since the early eighteenth century, custom had gradually placed the expenses of election upon the candidate. After 1832 this was fully recognized by statute; the present expectation that a member should subscribe to charity then extended to a demand that the municipality should receive assistance from him. They sought to have their roads repaired and other public services paid out of the successful candidate's purse, nor did this expectation die out directly Parliament was reformed.

After 1832, the prescribed qualification remained as it had been since 1760—members must either own land or have it transferred to them by their supporters. In either case, the requirement closed the doors of the House to poor men. Not until 1858 were the property qualification Acts finally repealed, though they had long been an obstacle to free selection. Even in that year there was opposition, among the objectors being the son of that Lord Grey who had carried the Reform Act. It was the borough members who experienced most difficulty, for those who sought election in the counties were normally landed people. The boroughs, in any case, demanded more money from their members than the shires, and so came even more largely to be the seats of very rich men. The patronage system was encouraged, for a wealthy supporter could always finance his nominee—it was the independent man of small means and no influence who tended to be excluded.

All these factors continued to operate after 1832, and they may explain in part the small change of personnel which was brought about at that election.

Such Radicals as there were, immediately on Parliament meeting fell foul of the Whigs. The Government favoured the continuation of the Tory, Manners Sutton, as Speaker; in disgust the Radicals nominated a Whig. The votes in support of their candidate, Littleton, only thirty-one in all, disclosed their numerical weakness. Yet on the other side, the Conservatives, as they were now beginning to be called, were also divided. Peel, their leader, had broken with the old Tory tradition—in 1834 he was to declare that he accepted the Reform Bill "as a final and irrevocable settlement" and to go on to say that he would not oppose "the correction of proved abuses and the redress of real grievances". This was all in the

Though most of the attacks on the mill system of labour came from the Tories, when the poor law came up for consideration they showed themselves as enthusiastic to abolish outdoor relief and to force destitute families inside workhouses as were their political opponents; nor had they displayed any sympathy for the agriculture poor when they pressed for the Enclosure Acts which, in the alleged interest of scientific farming, deprived the labourer of his pasturage or garden without compensation. Only on the Slavery question had either party shown any sign of humanitarian feeling. Indeed it is remarkable, having regard to the plutocratic outlook which prevailed almost universally at the time, that the emancipation measure ever passed.

No interest, territorial or monetary, was benefited by the emancipation. The compensation, considering all the interests at stake, was not unreasonable, and the Government had every reason to fear disturbances by the Colonial owners. The Abolition Act stands out in the legislation of the time as an example of disinterested philanthropy—not particularly popular with the mass of people, themselves in a state of semi-servitude for whom next to nothing had been done, and certainly not popular with the landed gentry.

In 1834, the Poor Law Commission, which had been sitting for two years, reported. It had been concerned chiefly with the able-bodied poor who, particularly in rural areas, had for some time been relieved out of the rates by additions to their miserable wages. The core of the report, which was accepted by the Government with enthusiasm, was the recommendation of the almost complete abolition of outdoor relief. In future the paupers and their families were to be relieved only in the Workhouse, in which already were crowded promiscuously the aged, the sick, the mentally infirm, old and young women and children. Now it was suggested that the able-bodied and their families were to join them.

That the policy might be consistently severe, a strong central authority (itself a novelty in constitutional structure) was to be set up with almost mandatory powers over the new local Boards of Guardians. By 1862, Nassau Senior, was a Commissioner of the 1834 enquiry, was condemning the general mixed workhouse. "We never contemplated having children under the same roof with the adults", he protested. "We recommended that in every Union there should be a building for the able-bodied males, one for the able-bodied females and another for the sick." For nearly a century nothing effectual was done to alter this disgraceful condition—"unique", wrote the authors of the Minority Poor Law Report in 1909, "in Europe". For the continuance of the protracted iniquity no party can take exclusive blame, for all were equally responsible.

The opposition was vehement but helpless. In Parliament, only twenty votes in the Commons were cast against the Bill, among them the young Disraeli and his "Young England" group. The Radicals, led by Grote, supported the measure, Peel and Wellington agreed with it. Cobbett, it is true, denounced the "Bastille"; Disraeli at Maidstone condemned the "flagitious statute" and declared that "poverty was now treated as a crime"; and Dickens and *The Times* added their protest. In five years £3,000,000 was saved to the rates. An Act which enshrined the principle that no one was eligible for relief who was not actually in a state of destitution effectually prevented recourse to the Guardians except in the most desperate cases. It was designed to relieve the rates of the cost of pauperism and in this sense was most successful. Spencer Walpole, a writer typical of mid-Victorian times, says complacently, "A reform of so vast a character, suddenly introduced into every parish in England, could not but be attended with some inconvenience". (*History of England*, Vol. 3, p. 448.) Yet it must be admitted that the poor law reformers thought that they were acting according to the best principles of economics; it was essential that those who for one reason or another did not earn wages should be more uncomfortable than those who worked—the difficulty was to find means to make them so.

Out of the rage of the working people against the "Workhouse test" came the more militant Chartist movement. The class without votes came slowly to realize that they had been abandoned by the Whigs, and, for the matter of that, by the Radicals. Riots broke out, to be suppressed by Melbourne, the Home Secretary. Some labourers who had bound themselves by oath not to work for less than six shillings a week were prosecuted under an old Act because of their swearing; had they merely combined, they would now be acting lawfully! They were transported to Australia. Though the trade unions were impotent in the face of capital, a charter of their new grievances was drafted, and there was talk of a National Convention. In 1839 a monster petition was presented, but the Chartists were not in agreement; some were for seeking electoral enfranchisement; others advocated physical force—in either case nothing came of it. The demand for Free Trade and cheap bread took the place of the far more fundamental social and political criticisms of the Chartists. The riots at Birmingham and Newport alienated the more moderate reformers and greatly injured the whole movement. Though later there was a revival, from now onwards the Government treated the whole agitation with contempt.

In truth the Government were more concerned with O'Connell and his demand for an independent Irish Parliament than they were for the condition of the poor. The King's speech in 1834 had declared that he would maintain the Union. O'Connell's resolution to appoint a Committee to investigate the working of the Union was rejected by 523 to 38 votes after a six days' debate, 57 Irish members voting against him. The Government made itself responsible for the collection of tithes in Ireland under the recent legislation, and out of this obligation arose the refusal of Russell to maintain the Irish Church funds undiminished; he said, supported by the Radicals and repealers, "they were larger than was necessary". In the end, Stanley, Graham and Richmond resigned on a subject which it would seem was very capable of adjustment, the efforts of Brougham for a *modus vivendi* having failed. A misunderstanding about the dropping of the Coercion Act made the position worse, and on an intimation from Althorp that he would resign over this matter the Prime Minister himself, wearied by these foolish factional disputes, retired.

The King sent for Melbourne, and Althorp was persuaded to return. Radicals such as Grote and Hume and even O'Connell himself were conciliated.   A Coercion Bill, but without the court-martial clauses, was introduced and passed; it was only to last till August, 1835.

The Tithe Bill, which left the Church four-fifths of its revenues, on the suggestion of O'Connell was amended and had been rejected in the Lords, when, in November, 1834, Althorp, the Leader in the Commons, through the death of his father, was called up to the Lords.   Thereupon the King intimated that he thought he would have to dismiss the Government, saying that they had no one fit to lead in the Commons.   Brougham apparently told the Press of this communication, and the enraged King demanded the prompt resignation of the whole Government.

For the time, Wellington agreed solely to constitute the Government. Peel was in Italy, but, on returning, became Prime Minister and Chancellor of the Exchequer—it was now that the Tamworth manifesto, to which reference has been made, was issued.   Directly Parliament met after a general election he was defeated, both on the election of the Speaker and on the Address.   Again the temporalities of the Church of Ireland came under consideration, when Peel was in a minority. Eventually, on April 7th, he resigned.   The King had lost, his chosen ministry had only been able to hold office for four months.

If the consequences of the dismissal of the Duke of Portland by George III be compared with that of Melbourne, it will be realized how great, during the half-century, had been the decline in the power of the Crown.   In the former case, the King was able, by the lavish bestowal of places and money and the use of threats, to support Pitt until such time as he could win for himself a majority in the Commons; Peel, on the other hand, after vainly struggling against a hostile Parliament, had to submit to its wishes.   In both cases the Government which had been superseded was comparatively progressive, but had outstayed its popularity.   In the earlier instance, the Fox–North coalition was broken for ever, Peel's failure gave to the Whigs another seven years of power.

The re-installation of Melbourne, however, on Grey's refusal to return, very definitely weakened the Radical element.   The new Prime Minister was an erudite student of theology, though himself by no means what can be called a religious man.   He was of serene temperament and much disliked any disturbance of his peace.   As David Cecil writes, "He was terrified of revolution".   Reading *Oliver Twist*, he once remarked: "It is all among workhouses and pickpockets—I don't like these things; I wish to avoid them".   (*The Young Melbourne*, p. 266.)   It is not surprising that such a man did not object to the new poor law, nor to the prosecution of the Dorchester labourers—certainly he was no Radical.

The jettison of Brougham removed the last forcible protagonist of progress in the Cabinet.   During his tenure of the office of Chancellor that erratic genius had done much to reform the law.   He had succeeded in establishing a unity of process in the Common Law courts and in setting up a new court of Bankruptcy.   Other measures he proposed, to institute local county courts and improve Chancery procedure were temporarily lost, but he managed nevertheless to lay down new rules which much expedited and improved the Chancery practice.   He abolished many sinecure offices there, the conveyance of land was simplified and, most important of all, he was able to institute a Judicial Committee of the Privy Council.   According to Greville, "he smuggled the Privy

Council Bill through the Lords without the slightest notice or remark".
(*Journal*, II, pp. 365, 370.) At first used primarily for ecclesiastical
appeals, it gradually developed into a great Imperial Court of Appeal.
Brougham's scheme for County Courts became law in 1846.

From now onwards, all legislative change, save in one important
instance, was discounted by the Government—the exception was the
drastic reorganization of the municipalities, the condition of which was
certainly confused, corrupt and deplorable.

The municipal corporation had been the subject of study by a Royal
Commission appointed in 1833. They had returned that there were no
less than three hundred and two cities, boroughs and bodies corporate, of
which a third had no governing bodies; it was not possible adequately to
classify them, so various were their constitutions. Most relied upon
Charters, real or spurious; some existed by prescription (such as London
and Oxford), claiming to have had mayors, aldermen and burgesses
before they had received any charter. The possession of its own Hundred
Court was not a conclusive test of origin. As Maitland said, "Some had
received a few chartered privileges from a mediæval baron" (*Township
and Borough*, p. 17), some had received direct grants from the King.

Many charters had been surrendered; some boroughs held contra-
dictory titles—the whole disclosed an inextricable medley of anomalous
constitutions. There were those who held considerable real estate, others
had only market rights. The majority, but not all, returned burgesses,
elected on differing franchises, to represent the borough in Parliament.
Many had their own Justices of the Peace, sometimes with separate
commissions, but frequently their right to quarter sessions had not been
exercised. In thirty-five cases the Borough Justices exercised a concurrent jurisdiction with the county; there was not infrequently a power
to hold quarter sessions for misdemeanours and even for felonies. There
were instances, such as Exeter and Bristol, of boroughs with their own
sessions of Oyer and Gaol Delivery. (*Webb, the Manor and the Borough*,
v. 2, p. 282.)

The powers which were possessed showed great variations. There were
boroughs possessed of considerable rights to regulate trade, prices, wages
and tolls. Others had built and maintained bridges, roads and hospitals
—in yet others these functions were performed by special *ad hoc* bodies,
or not attended to at all. Again, in the matter of selection of government, some mayors and councillors were elected by freemen; in other
cases the mayor was chosen by a very limited group of aldermen; sometimes he was elected by the burgesses at large. He also had differing
duties; sometimes he was not only Chief Magistrate, but also Coroner,
and the Recorder was often, though not always, subordinate to him.
The Mayor was often controller of all civic activities and frequently
appointed the town's officers. In forty boroughs, bailiffs exercised all
or some of the powers of mayors; in some towns they were under the
direction of the mayor himself. The principal officers, Chamberlain,
Town Clerk and Coroner, had varying powers and duties, as also did the
humbler officers, the Serjeant, overseers and constables.

In the absence of effective control, the funds were often spent on enter-
tainment or the remuneration of sinecure offices—the public had little
control. In Liverpool, out of 165,000 inhabitants in 1834, but 5,000

were freemen—in Portsmouth there were only 102. Even then, although
the freemen enjoyed privileges such as a right of free pasturage or
exemption from borough tolls, in many cases they had no share in local
government.

The unreformed Parliament had, of course, a vested interest in
maintaining unreformed boroughs, but once the one had been
reorganized it was impossible long to deny popular election to the
other. In the case of Scotland, in 1833, Jeffreys, the Lord Advocate,
carried a Bill to ensure a general electorate of £10 householders without
much opposition. The English Bill, owing to the greater labours of the
Commissioners, was not introduced until 1835. This time the enthusiasm
for reform was spent and the objectors were more vocal.

Under Russell's Municipal Bill, based on the commission's report, all
governing bodies were uniformly to consist of mayor and council, the
councillors to be elected by resident ratepayers. In the larger boroughs
they were to be elected by wards. The quarter sessions, if continued,
were to be presided over by a barrister Recorder. If the Tories thought
to make much out of their obstruction they were disappointed; to their
chagrin, Peel, their Leader, declared that he was in favour of the reform.
An attempt to save the franchise for freemen was defeated in committee,
and Stanley failed to carry an amendment that a third of the council
should retire biennially, the Government majorities, in most cases,
being over fifty. The Lords, however, under Lyndhurst's influence,
threw over Peel. They decided to preserve the freeman's rights, and to
have the Council elected only by the wealthier ratepayers. They provided for Aldermen to be elected for life. The Bill thus amended, said
Ellenborough, was now "a full, consistent and constitutional reform".
(*Hansard*, xxx, p. 1034.)

When it returned to the Commons, Peel found himself in a dilemma—
it was known that Lyndhurst had ignored him—"What is Peel to me?"
he had said, and used other wounding expressions. For once the Whigs
were resolute, a great Liberal meeting was held and Russell explained to
the House that they would only agree to a few minor modifications.
Aldermen were conceded, to be elected for six years, but any modification
of the electoral rights of the £10 ratepayers was rejected. Peel, who
followed, in substance agreed with Russell—an open division between
the "old" and "new" Tories had been displayed—later to come to a head
in the Free Trade debates. As usual, Wellington, the peace-maker,
advised the Lords to yield, and the Bill, with a few amendments, became
law.

The Municipal Reform Act, to those whose minds are not entirely
centred on electoral machinery, was indeed a far more important measure
than the Reform Bill, though that Act had made the local government
measure possible. Then, as now, the greater part of such social legislation
as existed was carried out by the local authorities. In the boroughs as
now constituted they were ready to receive such powers as formerly had
been given to special *ad hoc* authorities—Turn-Pike Trusts, Highway
Boards, Burial Boards, Town Improvement Commissioners and, eventually, were to become the sole authority for education, public health
and the poor law. Indeed the history of local Government, after the
1835 Act, displays an increasing tendency to transfer all hitherto isolated

powers and duties from special bodies to the municipal authority or to the other general administrative bodies subsequently created, such as the County and District Councils, which were modelled in substance upon the pattern of the reformed municipalities.

In 1835 there was no conception of any national control over the local authorities: as has been said, only in the recent case of the Poor Law had such means of enforcing national requirements been attempted. Gradually, by giving grants in aid and subventions to the financially embarrassed local bodies, the national Government acquired a degree of supervision, but general concern at local incompetence was of slow growth; as against it, the characteristic English tradition of local privilege, nurtured in the common law, regarded with healthy suspicion all encroachments from Whitehall.

As regards Ireland, the Lords were more successful—a fear of giving to Catholics a majority enabled them there to retard municipal reorganization; so also they rejected the attempt to settle the Tithe question, the Government feebly acquiescing in its defeat. Indeed, now that the municipal fight was over, Melbourne in effect refused to legislate any further. The Whigs under his direction now set out to defeat nearly all further Radical measures, and when they failed the Lords could be relied upon to destroy them. Motions for a ballot at elections, shortening of the life of Parliaments, and household suffrage were all successfully opposed by the Government, Whigs and the Tory Opposition. A Radical motion on the state of the Nation, in effect one of censure, disclosed how Melbourne had broken up the Liberal Party. Roebuck, in moving, declared that the Government was as bad as Peel—indeed, now that Melbourne had shown himself as good as a Conservative, many Tories were asking themselves what justification there was for his remaining in office. The Radicals would probably have revolted and formed a separate party, with consequences difficult to foretell, had it not been that at this juncture the King died, and at the consequent dissolution several of the leading Radicals—Roebuck, Thompson and Ewart—lost their seats. The total number was not materially lessened, but the movement towards independence experienced a set-back; the new men were nervous of destroying the Government and, fearful of losing their newly won seats, they sought to use persuasion rather than menace.

Their decision to remain within the Liberal Party was of supreme importance. Until the formation of the Labour Party in the last years of the nineteenth century there was no force, save Tory democracy (an uncertain and weak movement), to compete with Liberalism for the suffrages of Progressives. However cautious might be the Whigs, however truculent the Radicals, never again were they openly to menace one another—the gradations of opinion between the two extremes was calculated to obscure their differences. Whether the right or left on balance had its way it is difficult to determine, and in matters affecting business interests, as has already been indicated, the Radicals and Whigs were of one mind—neither cared to interfere with the free competition of capital or of labour.

As has been said, the Government had anticipated trouble in Jamaica, and they were right. The local legislature refused to assist the emancipation of the negroes or to give any protection to the freed apprentices. Indeed, they used apprenticeship as a means of continuing the young blacks in servitude. Sir George Strickland, in the place of Buxton, moved to abolish the system, and Government tried to placate all parties by introducing a Bill merely to improve conditions. Later, however, though the betterment Bill was given a second reading, a further motion was carried in favour of total emancipation. Nevertheless, the earlier measure was carried, the result of which was that apprenticeship would continue until August, 1840.

In many islands the apprentices were at once freed, but in Jamaica, though the House of Assembly had agreed to the Government Bill, they only represented a minority of the planters, and matters became so troubled there that the Government finally had to ask Parliament to suspend the Jamaican constitution for five years. This was more than the Radicals could stand, and the second reading for suspension was carried by only five votes.

The Government resigned but, on a disagreement between Peel and the Queen with regard to the appointment of her Ladies of the Bedchamber, Melbourne returned, and a second Jamaica Bill was introduced, which owing to its drastic amendment in the Lords, also failed to pass.

In 1839, Russell made his famous declaration as to the finality of the Reform Act. This was in answer to the Radicals and Chartists who were showing great discontent at the inadequacy of past electoral reform. In 1839, a national convention of Chartists' delegates, the "People's Parliament", as it was called, met in London, and an immense petition, said to have been signed by a million and a half people, was carried down to the House. It was evident that the Chartists' leaders had discovered how great had become the power of the middle classes. The petition was of course rejected, but the social conditions were becoming so serious that economic solutions were beginning to interest the people more than political ones. It was not fully understood that the miserable conditions of the poor might as readily be ascribed to low wages as to dear food, and the Chartists openly declared that the demand for cheap bread was a manufacturers' device to keep down wages. Nevertheless, the Anti-Corn Law League, which had been founded in 1838, through the skilful and tireless propaganda of Cobden and Bright, soon took the place of the Chartists in popular estimation. From now onward the repeal of the Corn Laws was the cry which united all save the most suspicious or extreme of the progressives.

In the Government, Melbourne was a pronounced protectionist. Indeed, in 1837, only three ministers had supported Villiers in his annual motion to repeal the Corn Duties; in 1839, however, their number rose to ten—it was clear by now that the Anti-Corn Law League had become the rallying-point of Radicalism.

Attacked on two fronts, the Whigs could not hope long to survive. To please the Radicals, in 1841 the Government proposed to substitute a duty of one shilling a bushel on corn for the sliding scale and to reduce the duties on foreign sugar. This latter proposal was thought by Radicals to help the slave owners, and a consequent combination of the Protectionists and the Abolitionists against the proposal resulted in a defeat of the Government by thirty-six votes.

Soon afterwards the Government was again defeated on a direct vote of censure. This was the end. In June, 1841, there was a General Election which gave the Conservatives a majority of over seventy, and on August 30th, Peel became Prime Minister. Next year, there being a large deficit, he suggested a revival of the Income Tax, together with a reduction of the Corn Duties. On the latter proposal, Villiers' amendment for repeal was rejected by four to one, and Russell's Whig alternative of a fixed duty of eight shillings was also rejected by one hundred and twenty votes—in Gladstone's phrase, "it was a table-land ending in a precipice". But though the Government carried their sliding scale, the removal of 750 out of 1,200 articles in the tariff, including a reduction of duties on imported cattle, meat and vegetables, already alarmed the Tory Protectionists, who later were to become so obstreperous.

The principal opposition to Income Tax arose, as usual, from the Liberal side. They regarded it as an impost upon commerce rather than upon land—Cobden, in particular, led the attack, but the Income Tax had come to stay. From the beginning it was a success; in the first year it yielded over a million pounds more than had been anticipated.

In 1844 came the famous Bank Charter Act, which had for its purpose the control of paper currency. In effect the Bank was authorized to issue paper to the extent of fourteen million pounds on the security of Government debt, but all issues above that required the holding of an equal amount of bullion, three-quarters of which must be gold—it was a first effort to restrain inflation.

In 1840, Ashley, who, as has been shown, was far more concerned with social improvement than were most of the Radicals, had introduced a Bill to exclude women from mines and to prevent children under thirteen being employed there. The Radicals, who had already fought for the factory owners, now tried to defend the owners of collieries—so great was their prejudice that all Ashley could obtain was a law that children of ten should not be employed more than three days a week. But his protest, as usual, was fruitful. In 1844, the Home Secretary, Graham, introduced a Bill to raise the minimum age from eight to nine in factories, but even now Ashley's desire for a general ten-hour day for women and young persons was defeated. The Prime Minister and Graham joined hands with the Liberal manufacturers to prevent any further protection of labour, though Russell and Palmerston and the Young England Tories—the "Socialist fools", as Cobden called them—supported Ashley's general Bill. So great was the power of the moneyed interest by this time that even Graham's compromise of a twelve-hour limit of labour was not allowed to pass.

A new measure was now introduced and Ashley again attempted to limit the hours of labour for women and young persons to ten. Macaulay declared himself converted but, on Peel's personal intervention that he would resign if the clause were carried, Ashley was again defeated. Not until 1847, when the Whigs were back in power, was the ten-hour limitation made law. Even then, Brougham attacked it on the ground that it must lower wages. In 1845, however, Ashley succeeded in reforming the lunacy laws. He was chairman of the Lunacy Commission from 1834 to the time of his death in 1885.

Meanwhile, the Anti-Corn Law League was growing in strength.

In the House, in 1841, Villiers had received ninety votes for abolition; in 1843 the number had risen to one hundred and thirty-five—many of the Whigs had come over; and at length, in 1844, Russell abstained from voting against total repeal. Next year he declared Protection to be the bane of Agriculture and moved against protective duties generally, in particular against the Corn Law. In the next critical year he openly supported Villiers' motion for repeal; from now onward it may be said that the whole Liberal Party was for Free Trade.

It has been stated that the potato famine in Ireland finally drove Peel to advocate abolition of the duties—however that may be, Russell was first in the field. On November 22nd, 1845, he told his electors in the City of London that he favoured immediate repeal. But before this, unknown to the public, many Cabinets had considered the matter: Peel had expressed his sympathy and Stanley, in protest, had resigned, whereupon Peel resigned also. Russell was asked to form a government, but on Grey refusing to help him, Peel resumed and, with Gladstone in the place of Stanley, on January 27th, 1846, he announced a total repeal of the Corn Laws to be completed within three years.

As is well known, the majority of the Tories, led by Stanley and Bentinck, broke with him, but with Liberal support he was, for the time being, invincible. Majorities of about a hundred carried the Bill through the Commons and in the Lords the decision of the lower House was accepted.

But the position of Peel, without an organized party, was too unstable to last. On a refusal to postpone Free Trade until another Irish Coercion Bill was passed, he was defeated. The way was now open for united Liberalism—for a time, the followers of Peel, though they gave a general support to Russell, who had become Prime Minister, remained a separate party (the Peelites), and Russell constructed his ministry on a strictly Whig basis. But although the Free Traders had been victorious, the Chartists were not reconciled. Under the leadership of O'Connor another convention was collected in London, a fresh petition organized, and an attempt made to assemble a great crowd on Kennington Common. One thousand seven hundred special constables were sworn in, secret military preparation was made, and, in the end, instead of a great procession, O'Connor and his executive committee had to carry the petition in three cabs to Westminster—the agitation had ended in general derision.

Apart from the Chartist disturbance, the year 1848 is remarkable for the passage of the first Public Health Act. This measure, from which London was excluded to receive special treatment, set up a central authority, the General Board of Health, consisting of the Commissioner of Woods and Forests and two other members; in boroughs the Town Council became the Health authority; in other places needing sanitary provision, special boards were set up. The boards were made responsible for drainage, water, streets and burial grounds, and gradually acquired many other powers. They had authority to levy rates. The Bill was opposed by many individualistic Radicals, by romantic individualists who objected to centralization—such as Toulmin Smith (though there was hardly any in the Bill)—and by most of the protectionist leaders, other than Disraeli. Bright boasted that he would always oppose such Smoke

Abatement Acts as interfered with trade. Ashley, who was made a Commissioner with Chadwick, was an enthusiastic supporter; he had long advocated sanitary reform. In 1851 he introduced and carried Bills which made the inspection of common lodging-houses compulsory and gave powers to local authorities to build them. Schemes for a water supply for London and for drainage were also devised by him and the Board.

In 1858 the Board was dissolved, but by then two hundred local boards had been set up outside the boroughs. Palmerston's scheme to place the Central Board under the Home Office was temporarily defeated, and an opportunity to enforce a coherent standard of sanitation lost. Finally, in 1875, the Public Health Act of that year consolidated over a hundred measures which had been passed as occasion arose without any relation to one another.

In 1858 also the functions of the General Board of Health as central authority were transferred, notwithstanding earlier opposition, in part to the Home Office, in part to the Privy Council, and in 1871 the central powers both as to Health and Poor Law were assigned to a new authority —the Local Government Board. Next year the country was divided into rural and urban sanitary districts—the latter being the old Borough Improvement Act and local government districts; they are now known generally as Urban Districts. In London, outside the city, the vestries became the sanitary authorities. Nearly all this legislation, it must be conceded, was carried by Conservatives.

The era in which the Liberal Pary was in process of formation is remarkable for the unusual absence of political interest in foreign affairs. From the end of the Walpole period until the Treaty of Vienna, Europe had been constantly in a state of belligerence; a condition from which this country could not escape. The effect in politics was both to stimulate patriotic enthusiasm and to strengthen the power of whatever Government was responsible for the defence of the realm.

Since Waterloo, such an attitude was less necessary. The growth of the peace movement, fostered by the advocates of Free Trade, at first met with little opposition. It followed upon the triumph of the Corn Law repeal, but the fact of the need for its existence showed how the times were again becoming disturbed.

Those very dynamic elements in Europe which created Western civilization have stimulated also a constant belligerency in conflicting national ideals. Never since the failure of the Roman Empire, save perhaps in the short-lived experiment of Charlemagne, not even when the Catholic Church had universal influence, have European Christians for long abstained from killing one another, or from glorifying war and its practitioners. Regarding the history of Europe for the last fifteen hundred years, it would be fair to say that, throughout that period, war has been endemic, cessation from hostilities occasional and precarious.

It was but natural, therefore, once the exhaustion caused by the Napoleonic struggle was over and a new generation had arisen, that the countries of Europe should again become aggressive and restless. After 1840, a renewal of Chauvinism and unrest are again to be detected in France. Nevertheless, Guizot, to arrest the tendency to new conflagration, succeeded in establishing an *entente* with England, notwithstanding the temporary disturbance caused by Palmerston's suggestion of a Coburg candidate to be Prince Consort in Spain. A treaty between England and France in 1845 had abolished the unlimited right to search each other's vessels, but in 1846 the Spanish marriages of Isabella to the French nominee and of the Infanta to the Duc de Montpensier were regarded in England as a breach of mutual understanding. To Palmerston's satisfaction, the precarious *entente* broke down. He had never accepted Aberdeen's policy of *rapprochement*, and even the Court supported the Foreign Secretary in his indignation at being tricked. To the Prime Minister's more pacific temperament Palmerston's plain speaking to France was disquieting, nor did the trouble end there. Since 1845, Italy had been in a revolutionary condition. In Naples the Austrians still held a police control, but France had warned Metternich that any further intervention would be opposed. Popular excitement was rising in all the Italian States—even the Papal See was affected, where it was believed that the new Pope, Pius IX, was a Liberal. The King of Naples, in particular, was assailed for his cruelties, and when the Crown of France fell, in 1848, the Radical movement in Italy was greatly heartened. A revolution broke out in Milan in March, and at the same time Venice proclaimed a Republic; a revolution in Vienna caused the flight of Metternich, and the whole system which had existed since the great Treaty of Vienna was in ruins. In the German States also revolutions took place. Hungary was in ferment—such was the state of Europe which confronted England in that most significant of years, 1848.

The failure of the Chartists in England, as we have seen, showed more clearly than anything else could how this country, with a very moderate Liberal administration, was determined to give no support to extreme actions. The middle classes, which abroad so often formed the nucleus of revolution, had here acquired political and economic rights. In Parliament, apart from Palmerston, the Prime Minister had the support of few men of ability in the Cabinet—Morpeth, Hobhouse and Labouchere rarely spoke and in 1847 Macaulay lost his seat—the burden of the day fell on Russell himself. Outside his own department, Palmerston rarely intervened, and even then he was more of an embarrassment than an assistance to the peace-loving Russell.

Although Palmerston was inclined to follow his master, Canning, in helping "small nations struggling to be free" and encouraging the development of Liberal institutions abroad, the fear of foreign complication and war compelled the Manchester men to condemn him and to oppose his policy—what Cobden called the "Palmerston system". In Parliament, Cobden wrote, in 1848, "three Coercion Bills for Ireland, and the rest talk!"; he complains that all the debates are on the subject of Protection, for which the Tories continued, intermittently, to fight until 1852. Little direct criticism of foreign policy can be detected.

Nevertheless, the Foreign Minister, Palmerston, however little appreciated by the Court or Russell, had become the leading national figure. "There was a comfortable impression in the public mind", writes Guedalla, "that Palmerston was generally inclined to put down the Mighty from their seats". (*Palmerston*, p. 253.) Cobden had suggested a general recourse to international arbitration but had received little popular support—the possibility of England being summoned before a foreign tribunal was generally distasteful. The new Prince-President of France had suggested a mutual reduction of naval armament, but Palmerston would have none of it, nor would he even agree to an international congress. "Sovereigns nowadays count for little", exclaimed this militarist democrat—with psychological insight he saw that the new nations "will submit to no external dictation". He was the first English statesman to realize that popular government does not necessarily involve pacific sentiment. Moreover, he believed in the rising nationalism in Europe. He helped the Sicilians, defied the rulers of Austria and Russia —only in the matter of adequate armament to support his policy was he inconsistent. It must be admitted, apart from naval preparation, that the truculence of the Foreign Minister was largely bluff. In any event, he was too impatient to await that sanction for his activities which could only be achieved by converting the Prime Minister and the Treasury to an expenditure compatible with his demands on foreign nations.

The effect of this ultra patriotic policy on the Radicals was disastrous. Bright, Cobden and their school would have none of it. They instituted Peace Societies, which had none of the success of their Corn Law League. Though Cobden and Bright had joined in the reception of Kossuth, they were both opposed to military intervention on behalf of continental Liberalism. The Conservatives of that time also supported a peaceful foreign policy—the Peelites in particular; Graham, Aberdeen and Gladstone were against increased armaments and international provocation, and neither Stanley nor Disraeli seriously differed from them.

On the other hand, there was a large, perhaps the greater, section of the Radicals and the great unfranchised public who, notwithstanding that Palmerston obstructed further electoral reform, enthusiastically welcomed his foreign policy. They refused to support the Peace Society, which at that time was trying to lessen the growth of anti-French policy. They regarded Napoleon as a dictator, the Tsar as a tyrant and, paradoxically, the despotic Turkish Sultan as an oppressed victim of Russia.

In 1850, in answer to an attack for threatening the Greeks over the treatment of a British subject, Palmerston defended his whole policy. He declared that all British subjects of whatever origin had the like right to be protected; he asserted that every nation should be free; in Belgium, Spain, Italy and Hungary; he defended the assistance he had given to freedom against tyranny. On a division many Radicals supported him, and, later, gave him a congratulatory dinner, at which he repeated his sentiments in fiery language; he proclaimed that he believed it to be the mission of this country, not only to secure Liberty at home, but throughout the world. When it is considered how nearly all the Governing Class, from the Queen downwards, were opposed to him, it is seen how dependent he was upon that Radicalism which, for the first time since the days of Wilkes, had become aggressively patriotic.

Cobden's method to help the foreign Liberal, with whom he had great sympathy, would have been to prevent the granting of loans to reactionary countries. This departure from the commercial ethics of laissez-faire—to lend money in the dearest market and borrow in the cheapest—illustrates how even the most obdurate of theories will break against elementary humanity, but to him and his pacific party war was an unthinkable remedy.

He and his friends were probably unaware that ever since 1845 the Duke of Wellington had been urging an extension of the Forces—at the time there were only five thousand regular soldiers in England and a hundred and fifty thousand militia. The Duke wished the latter to be a "trained and disciplined force", seventy-two thousand to be raised by "beat of drum" or from the Poor Law Unions. When Russell came into office, Palmerston demanded one hundred and forty thousand men to be enrolled, if necessary by ballot. Russell wrote confidentially to the Cabinet that "we are in considerable danger of sudden hostilities"; he suggested one hundred and fifty thousand men, but when he spoke in the House it became evident that the prospect of an additional fivepenny Income Tax was more alarming to the commercially-minded Commons that the fear of invasion. While the whole matter was under debate, the French Government collapsed and the scheme was abandoned; but to the historian the incident is interesting as illustrating the reviving interest in, and apprehension of, continental military activities.

Ever since Peel had resigned, the Government had been dependent upon the support of his hundred-odd followers. Both before and after his death, this, for the most part, was ungrudgingly given. There was, however, as yet no coalition, and many of the Peelite Tories were still opposed to much Liberal legislation.

The active part taken by Russell in the protest against what he called "Papal Aggression" (the Pope had created thirteen bishoprics in England with Wiseman as Archbishop of Westminster), calculated to foment a new anti-Catholic agitation, was condemned, not only by Radicals such as Roebuck, as contrary to religious toleration, but also gave offence to Anglo-Catholics who were strong among the Peelites. On the resignation of Russell, Aberdeen and Graham both refused to enter a coalition with him because of his promotion of the Ecclesiastical Titles Bill, which (although the Law Officers had already said that such a course was not illegal) sought to prohibit the assumption of hierarchic styles in the Roman Catholic Church in England. Russell offered to amend the Bill, but he had raised such an agitation that complete withdrawal was impossible, and less Aberdeen would not accept. It is curious to observe that the Pope unwittingly had made possible the return of the Conservatives in England by producing an insuperable disagreement between their common opponents.

In any case the whole position of Russell was unstable—for the need to placate the Peelites had made it most difficult for him to satisfy his own advanced supporters. On a division on further Franchise Reform the Prime Minister had said that he was prepared to lay proposals before Parliament in the next session; but the Radicals pressed for an immediate Bill, and the Government, who had internal budgetary difficulties on the Income Tax question, were defeated by four votes.

On February 21st, 1851, Russell resigned, and Lord Derby declining to form a government, advised the Queen to attempt a coalition between the Whigs and the Peelites. As has been said, the behaviour of Russell on the Ecclesiastical Titles Bill for the moment made coalition impossible, and in the end he returned again, still Prime Minister of a purely Liberal Government.

But soon Palmerston was once more in trouble; by the Court he had for a long time been regarded with aversion; it was said that he acted without consulting either his leader or the Queen. In 1849 and 1850 the Court had complained to Russell about this, and in 1851 the relations were strained to breaking-point by the reception accorded to Kossuth, the Hungarian patriot, by the Foreign Minister. He had received a deputation from Finsbury Radicals in which the Emperors of Russia and Austria were described as "despots, traitors and assassins," and Palmerston, instead of rebuking their enthusiasm, declared that he was gratified at the demonstration. In January, 1852, there followed the *coup d'état* in Paris. The President arrested many of the leading statesmen, and great excitement prevailed. Palmerston, while the Queen was urging neutrality, had told the French Ambassador, Walewski, in London, that he thought that what had been done by the President was to the "advantage of France and Europe". Normanby, the British Ambassador in Paris, complained of his inconsistent instructions, and, the whole Cabinet supporting Russell in the policy of neutrality, she wrote to Palmerston that "no other course is left than to ask the Queen to appoint a successor to you in the Foreign Office".

In less than three weeks Palmerston had his revenge. Russell had at last introduced his Militia Bill, now made necessary by the deterioration in the foreign situation. The Bill would only have reorganized the local forces, but Palmerston suggested that the whole regular militia should be reconstituted. By a majority of Peelites, Conservatives and others opposed to the Government, Palmerston's amendment to leave out "local" in Russell's resolution was carried by five votes and, again, Russell resigned.

During the period of his ministry, although the Radicals disagreed fundamentally on foreign affairs, they had all united to press for an enlarged electorate, and, just before he fell, the Prime Minister had introduced a Bill to lower the borough franchise to a £5-rating qualification and in the counties to £10-rated occupiers; he also proposed to complete the Toleration Acts by allowing Jews to omit the words "on the true Faith of a Christian", which then debarred them from sitting in Parliament, though not from being elected. This measure, however, got no further than its introduction.

There is little doubt that the victory of Free Trade, by bringing many Conservatives over to the Government, had temporarily weakened the Radical element. The division to which we have referred between Bright, Cobden, Gibson and the militants was another source of weakness. In any case, from the point of view of the condition of the great number of the workers, it mattered not whether the Radicals were powerful or weak; their best friends in practical affairs had been Tories such as Ashley, Sadler and Disraeli. By now, the old Chartist enthusiasm itself, principally political, was spent. It has been said how Ashley, in 1847, at last was able to limit the labour of women and young persons in textile factories to ten hours a day, and the comments on his Radical opponents at the time are revealing. "Bright", he wrote, "was ever my most malignant opponent, Cobden bitterly hostile"; so also the old Brougham in the Lords was among his "most heated opponents". Gladstone voted to rescind the division in favour of the Ten Hours Bill, as did Peel—both were of commercial ancestry and outlook. The revolutionary O'Connell was "a bitter opponent". Perhaps the most telling revelation of the mind of Victorian Radical Commercialism is to be found in Bright's speech on the Ten Hours Bill: "If this machinery Bill passes", he said, "I have advised my partners to set the example of turning the keys on our mills and to throw upon the legislators the responsibility of feeding the millions whom they will not allow us to employ at a profit". This was declared as late as September, 1865.

Miss Martineau, the Radical historian, according to Ashley, also gave "her voice and strength in opposition to the factory measures". As Disraeli said: "If a rapacious covetousness desecrating all the sanctities of human life has been the besetting sin of the last generation, in our time the altar of Mammon has flamed with a triple flare". His small band of young Tory democrats and philanthropists, whenever any social issue came before Parliament, were to be found in opposition to the official Whigs, manufacturers and official Tories; a few socialistic Liberals supporting them. Only in a demand for educational provision did the Radicals as a whole show any enthusiasm for social improvement, and in that subject, curiously, Ashley was not very interested.

As an old man he was by no means enthusiastic about the 1870 measure; indeed he said, "I do not expect much from it". He wished to reduce the age limit for compulsory education to ten, so fearful was he of what he called "idleness".

In 1850 the Amalgamated Society of Engineers had been founded and other unions were active, but none of them looked to Parliament for assistance in their work of raising the level of wages and conditions; yet in 1848, unknown to most of them, had been published the famous *Communist Manifesto* of Marx and Engels, in which the whole individualistic theory of betterment, which for the most part the Trade Unionists accepted, was denounced as a bourgeois mystification, and the inevitability of a class struggle was envisaged. But even when the new outlook had been transplanted to England, the "Working Men's International Association", which was addressed by Marx in 1864, was more concerned with revolutionary possibilities and the trade unions with immediate disputes about wages than were either with parliamentary action.

Apart, however, from the avowed Socialists, the departure from the tenets of economic individualism in the middle of the nineteenth century is well illustrated in the later works of John Stuart Mill, once an individualist, the political philosopher of the mid-Victorian Radical Movement.

The ideal improvement of mankind took the place in his mind of that merely negative conception of happiness which had possessed Bentham and Mill's father. Though most concerned to defend the liberty of minorities (which he saw might be challenged as well by a democracy as by a king), in his later books he became increasingly socialistic. In his autobiography he declares that he looks forward to "a time when the rule that they who do not work shall not eat, will be applied not to paupers only, but impartially to all". In earlier years he had been content to found himself upon Ricardo and Malthus, the latter of whom was even against all assistance to the poor in whatever form; now, however, writing in the 'sixties, he welcomes "socialistic experiments". "Before 1860," says Dicey, "in general, political economy was little more than a branch of utilitarianism." (*Law and Opinion in England*, p. 411.)

Thus, in the absence of all considered protest, if we except the writings of Carlisle, Ruskin, Dickens and Disraeli, it is not surprising that the mass of the people should have accepted the arid notion of a universal competitive struggle. The clergy, save in exceptional instances such as Maurice and Kingsley, did little to correct this impression, and concentrated on voluntary charity or personal salvation. The doctrines contained in such works as *Social Statics* of Herbert Spencer (an author who doubted whether even the police had not been given too much power) even in advanced circles remained almost unchallenged.

In all these circumstances, with philosophers, politicians, churchmen and men of literature all of one mind that capitalist competition was not only inevitable but desirable, it is not surprising to find the illiterate labourers for a long time hesitated to accept the alluring temptations of the new socialistic ideas.

CHAPTER V

FOREIGN AFFAIRS

FROM time to time the English people, who as a rule are concerned only with their own affairs, become conscious of the Continent. Sometimes this notice has been forced upon them by the jealousy or aggression of other nations—instances of such enforced interest may be found in the periods when Louis XIV or Napoleon I, the Emperor William II or Hitler were dominant, but there have been other occasions when it is less easy to account for that sudden popular regard for foreign affairs which has often proved so disconcerting to English statesmen.

As in the days of Walpole, the gentry at the time of Russell's Government were entirely pacific in intention and had been so ever since the fall of Napoleon. The most disingenuous democrat must admit, if he is honest, that the war fever which seized the nation in the fifties, with its accompaniment of alternate truculence and panic, was the direct fruit of popular emancipation. What is peculiar in the years preceding the Crimean War is the sudden change in the personality of the public enemy. When Russell fell, on the plea that he had not provided sufficiently for national defence, the person most feared in England was Napoleon III. The Press was full of alarming matter about him—a French fleet was being built in secret at Cherbourg. Now that steamships existed, the Emperor "could easily land 50,000 or 60,000 troops on the south coast in a single night". In reality, steam having rendered the Navy far more mobile, had made the prospects of invasion much less favourable than they were in the uncertain sailing days of George III.

The Peace Societies and "false economy" were denounced in *The Times*, other less responsible journals were more violent; the attitude of young Beauchamp, as portrayed by Meredith, is typical of the new patriotic Radicalism. The death of the Duke of Wellington, in November, reminded thousands of people of the hated Napoleon, and there were not wanting many to recall the fact that the present Emperor was his nephew.

Meanwhile, Cobden laboured to improve Anglo-French relations. At his side stood Bright, and, less publicly, the new Conservative Government and the Sovereign herself. But a new spirit was abroad, incited by Palmerston. Such Chartists, as still remained, and the patriotic Radicals interpreted their Liberalism as a crusade—if their duty to free the oppressed involved war, that circumstance must be faced; in the exigencies of the time their interest in domestic reform seemed to take a second place.

The first session of Derby's administration was occupied by the majority Opposition in making Disraeli forswear Protection, and this he did, adroitly, with the aid of Palmerston, though old Tories murmured. As regards positive legislation, a strong Militia Bill was passed and a new force of eighty thousand men, to receive at least three weeks' training, constituted. The nationalist Radicals and Liberals, supported by Palmerston, helped to carry the measure, Russell and the pacifists alone objecting. The social interest of Disraeli produced a new Public Health measure, and the Empire was strengthened by the granting of a constitution to New Zealand. These and some legal reforms had all been achieved by the minority Conservative Government when Parliament was dissolved in July, 1852.

Protection found no place in the electoral appeal of the Government. To the dismay of some Protectionists, Disraeli admitted the success of Free Trade—he conciliated his followers by promising some alternative benefit to Agriculture. In the event the Tories were found to be the largest party in the new House, some three hundred strong. The Peelites had fallen to forty; and several important Liberals, such as Sir George Grey and Cornwall Lewis, were defeated; nevertheless the mixed opposition of Liberals, Radicals of every kind, Peelites and the Irish, had a majority over the Government of about forty.

When Parliament met it was made clear that the official policy was to abandon Protection. Again it was sought to embarrass the Government by the passing of academic resolutions on Free Trade. Far more important was the Administration's success in abating the friction with France. Malmesbury, the Foreign Minister, had for long been of opinion that a *rapprochement* was possible. He was a friend of Louis Napoleon, and the Government started to negotiate a commercial treaty. There was no time to complete the matter, but despite the belligerent tone of the newspapers, the work continued and, officially at any rate, good relations were restored before the Tories were defeated on their second Budget in December.

In this final division Palmerston abstained, but Whigs, Radicals, Peelites and Irish, all combined to defeat by nineteen votes the Derby administration. In reality many of the financial proposals of the Tories were of a surprisingly advanced nature; the Conservatives were defeated on the very principles which later Liberal and Labour were to make their own—the increase of direct taxation, and, even more remarkable, discrimination between earned and unearned income. Never did a government fall more gallantly fighting its opponents' cause!

There followed the usual manœuvres incident to a period when there exists no strong party government. For some time the Peelites had been divided as to whether they should support Derby or the Liberals— Graham favoured the latter, but Aberdeen, Herbert and Gladstone, now that the Tories had dropped Protection, were inclined to join the Conservatives. Most improperly, Prince Albert had secretly written to Derby encouraging a coalition and suggesting that Gladstone should take the place of Disraeli in the Commons—how far Gladstone knew of this is not clear. Some decision had become essential—first it was hoped that Lord Lansdowne, a veteran Whig, would form a government. The refusal of Palmerston to serve made Russell's resumption as Prime Minister impossible, and finally Lord Aberdeen, the leader of the Peelites, consented to preside over a coalition of his own party and the Whigs.

Russell, from the outset, made difficulties. The proposal to give seven seats in the Cabinet and the Leadership to a party some forty strong as against the Liberal two hundred and seventy, seemed to him unfair, and so it was, if mere numbers and not capacity were to be considered. Moreover, to assimilate the discordant Whigs and Radicals was artificial. Many of the former were much nearer the Peelites than they were to their own advanced party colleagues; the followers of Palmerston were alienated from those of Russell—the Radicals were deeply divided. Once the Peelites had decided to join their fellow Free-Traders, of all the Coalition their small group was probably the most homogeneous, and certainly contained, in proportion to its numbers, the greatest talent.

Another difficulty was that Palmerston had at first refused to join on the ground that he and Aberdeen had always fundamentally disagreed on foreign affairs. At length, however, though he would much rather have supported Derby, he was persuaded to come in. He took the office of Home Secretary, thus saving his political consistency and gratifying the Court by his necessary abstention from a direct control of foreign matters. One Radical, Molesworth, was included in the Cabinet in the subordinate Office of Works and another, Villiers, was in the Ministry. Of the Peelites there were included Aberdeen, Herbert, Graham, Cranworth, Newcastle and Argyle, with Gladstone as Chancellor of the Exchequer.

Russell, temporarily, went to the Foreign Office, and the other Whigs in addition to Palmerston were Granville, Wood and Lansdowne. It was a coalition of all the talents; but, like most gifted Cabinets, its strength was impaired by the vigorous personalities of its opinionated members. From the beginning there was trouble. Russell wished to combine the offices of Leader of the House and Foreign Secretary. This failing, he would continue to lead, but without office, and Clarendon should become Foreign Secretary. Next, he insisted that the Government should introduce a reform of the Franchise to which both Whigs and Peelites in the Government had pledged themselves. Most surprising of all, he insisted that he should have the *spes successionis* of the office of Prime Minister.

At the Home Office, Palmerston, in the words of the critical Shaftesbury, was ready "to undertake any good work of kindness for humanity
and the social good, especially to the child and the working class". In
1853 Palmerston introduced and got passed a measure to include all
children in the limitation of twelve hours' factory labour. For men and
women, however, he would do nothing; he declared in the House that
"it was a matter of considerable delicacy to interfere by legislation with
the employment of those who, being of age, were to be considered as
free agents, and therefore, ought to be at liberty to work as long or as
little as they should think fit to do".

In 1853 he also was responsible for an Act dealing with youthful
offenders and at the Home Office instituted a ticket-of-leave system for
convicts. His views on public health were in advance of his times and
against Bright he supported proposals for smoke abatement.

The Government decided, principally owing to the opposition of
Palmerston, to delay their Reform Bill until the next session. There were
now over a hundred and fifty advanced Liberals and Radicals in the House
and their desires could no longer be ignored; the most they would concede
was a postponement. Had it not been for the outbreak of war, there is
little doubt that the Government would have been persuaded to inaugurate
considerable reforms, both political and economic.

It was not to be; already the foreign situation, which had been eased
by the *rapprochement* with France, was worsening in another quarter.
Although Napoleon was denounced by Cabinet Ministers as a despot as
late as 1853, the Tsar it was who now came to be substituted by almost
the whole Press, save *The Times*, for Napoleon as the great menace to
England and Liberty. The real question which perplexed all Europe
arose out of the future of Turkey. In 1844 the Tsar had been in England
and had discussed with Aberdeen and Peel what was to happen when,
as everybody anticipated, the Turkish state "must crumble to pieces".
In 1853 the Ambassador in St. Petersburgh, Sir George Seymour, renewed
the conversation on the basis of a secret memorandum as to the partition
of Turkey which had been drawn up during the Tsar's visit in 1844.
A dispute had arisen about the respective rights of Greek and Roman
Catholics to the Holy Places in Jerusalem, and it was said that the Sultan
had favoured the Roman Catholics, who were normally protected by France.
Lord Stratford de Redcliffe, the Ambassador to the Porte, was able to
persuade the Turk to give the Greek Christians equal rights, but he
dissented from the Russian view that they should have protective powers
over Greek Christians such, as it was said, the French had over Roman
Catholics. The Turks, thus encouraged, refused the Russian demand and
received an ultimatum; the Tsar marched into Waldachia and Moldavia,
threatening to hold them as hostages; already as a gesture the French
had sent their fleet to Salamis, but England for the time refused to
co-operate with them.

Nevertheless, while the Russians were crossing the Pruth to occupy
the provinces by way of protest, the English Navy had proceeded to the
Dardanelles. Austria and Prussia became concerned, and in July all
Four Powers sent a joint Note to Russia to provide for the integrity of
the Sultan, while conceding some of the Russian claims. In September
the basis of the Note was abandoned, the Turks being dissatisfied, as the

Tsar would concede no more than an admission that he would not interfere at large with Turkey.

Disturbances broke out at Constantinople. The British Navy, to protect British subjects violated the neutrality of the Dardanelles as provided by treaty. Next, the Turks sent an ultimatum to the Russians demanding the evacuation of the occupied provinces and, on a refusal, declared war. Even now, though the English newspapers raved against him, the Tsar strove for peace; after long negotiation he agreed that if England and France would withdraw their navies, he would call back his troops; meanwhile there should be an armistice. Only two matters remained for settlement—whether the Tsar should withdraw before he negotiated, and whether he would abstain from dealing with Turkey direct—to neither of these requirements would he agree.

In reply, England and France in their turn sent an ultimatum demanding that the Russians should evacuate the provinces at once; Austria and Prussia associated themselves in an evasive manner, but on war being declared by England and France, neither of the German countries would take an action.

These facts, and the further one that the Russians had already succeeded in November, 1853, in destroying the Turkish fleet at Sinope, following a consistent agitation by the public journals which had excited even the Queen and her Consort, were the actual reasons for the war which broke out at the end of March, 1854—it remains to examine its reaction on English politics.

Whatever may have been the deficiencies of Cobden and Bright in domestic politics, there is no doubt that they raised an issue of supreme importance to England and the world when they declared that it was impossible, without imposing conscription and accepting the sacrifice of all hope of plenty at home, for Britain to go crusading abroad against every Government or Monarch whom the Liberal-minded thought to be reactionary. Their opposition to Palmerstonian Liberalism, which had first engendered this chivalrous if impracticable desire, was maintained boldly when the country was at peace, and even more courageously when at last it was at war. They were without a Press, they fought against every natural prejudice arising from pride, fear or honest indignation; they braved extreme unpopularity and political annihilation. They were prepared to be burned in effigy or to be howled down at meetings, they faced every kind of misrepresentation and obloquy for what they thought to be right and, hardest of all, had to bear the taunt that they were deserting their fellow Radicals abroad. In the case of the Crimean War that particular consideration scarcely existed. The most ardent Radical had difficulty in representing the Turkish Sultan as a Liberal ruler; from a Christian point of view, it was the enemy Russia which was within the fold. Yet all this did nothing to abate the insane war fever which Radicals like Layard, Roebuck and Lindsay, together with anti-Russians, such as Urquhart, encouraged—for the moment all these vigorous protesters could do was furiously to assert their opinions.

Some weeks before the actual declaration of war, a banquet had been given by the Liberals to the Commander of the Baltic fleet, Sir Charles Napier. Graham, the First Lord, who was present, said that he would

D*

neutral flags, was not liable to capture, and blockades to be binding were required to be effective. By this treaty the ancient right of search was abandoned, but it was not to be expected that in the increasing tension of later years maritime Powers, such as England, would allow her power to be thus restricted.

At home, the advanced Liberals were still divided, for Bright was prepared to support Palmerston if he would but obtain an early peace, while Layard still wished the war not only to continue but to be extended to cover all oppressed peoples. Soon another cause for hostilities arose— in the autumn of 1856 England went to war with Persia, and a combined naval and military force defeating that country, peace was signed in March, 1857, the Persians agreeing not to interfere with Afghanistan, which had been the principal subject of dispute.

The Income Tax had now reached 1s. 4d. in the pound and it became necessary to reduce the army estimates; but once more Palmerston could not keep out of war. His new quarrel was with the Chinese over a vessel flying the British flag which had been boarded by a mandarin. The admiral seized the ports at Canton and bombarded the city, the Chinese in their turn murdered several Europeans, and on the matter being raised in the House, Derby in the Lords and Cobden in the Commons —an unusual combination—censured the Government. In the Lower House, Palmerston was defeated by sixteen votes and promptly appealed to the nation.

It was a typical "Jingo" election. He claimed the right to oppose the "insolent barbarian at Canton, who had violated the British flag, broken the engagements of treaties, offered rewards for the heads of British subjects in China, and planned their destruction by murder, assassinations and poisons". The sole question for the country was whether they approved of Palmerston and his policy, and the answer admitted of no doubt. The Radicals suffered grievously; Cobden, Bright, Gibson, Fox and Miall all lost their seats; the Peelites also fared very badly, and Palmerston was returned with a majority, pledged personally to him, of over seventy.

In the new House, although the Manchester school Radicals had been defeated, yet there were many advanced Liberals pledged to Electoral Reform and the Ballot. Palmerston, however, was not inter- ested—the most he would concede, to the great indignation of Gladstone, was the secularization of Divorce procedure, which he described as "practical reform". A Royal Commission had suggested Radical changes in the marriage laws. The theological Gladstone wearied a sceptical House with Canon Law and long quotations from the Council of Trent, but the Archbishop of Canterbury and nine of his suffragans supported the measure, and this ecclesiastical dispute and problems arising from the mutiny in India entirely absorbed the time of Parliament. The sup- pression of the Mutiny by such drastic measures as the blowing of sepoys from guns and the denunciations of Indians as "semi-maniac human beings" and similar cries for "blood, fire, fury and destruction" (*Scottish Review*, April, 1858, p. 125) showed that the long epoch of militant vain- glory was even yet not spent. When, unexpectedly, Palmerston fell, it was upon just one of those nationalistic appeals to what Mussolini has called "Sacred Egoism".

Although the actual defeat of Palmerston arose upon a subordinate matter—the desire of the Prime Minister that conspiracies in England to commit murder abroad should be made a felony—there is little doubt that several other factors had contributed to swell the Opposition vote. At the close of 1857 there had been a serious financial crisis which, like later ones, had its origin in America, where there had been a great over-issue of paper. In the autumn the banks of Liverpool, Glasgow, and the Western Bank of Scotland had all suspended payment. The Bank of England was compelled to raise its rate to ten per cent and, owing to the general position, had to issue two million pounds' worth of notes; to do this involved the suspension of the Bank Charter Act of 1844. At the same time fighting continued in India, and it was generally felt that both the Government and the East India Company had shown themselves incompetent.

To meet general criticism, the Government, in February, 1858, had introduced a Bill to abolish that system of dual government Pitt had framed in 1784, which had so lamentably failed. They proposed to abolish the old Board of Control and transfer all the powers of the Company to a new Council for India, the President to be a member of the Government. This measure might have placated Parliament, but Palmerston failed to realize the disquiet which, caused by his levity and insolence in the face of the terrible news through from India. Moreover, according to Greville, nothing had damaged him more than the appointment at the end of 1857 of Clanricarde, who was generally reputed to be a roué, to the Privy Seal.

It was in these circumstances that England was truculently asked by Count Walewski, the French Foreign Minister, to refuse asylum to criminal refugees. The Orsini conspiracy to murder the French Emperor had undoubtedly been arranged in London and bombs had been made here at the request of the plotters. It appears that Palmerston for once failed to satisfy English patriotic sentiment in not answering the insulting letter of the French minister. His Bill was thought to be a servile compliance with French dictation and, as in the case of the Crimean enquiry, again it was a bellicose Radical, this time Milner Gibson, who moved the rejection.

In the debate on the first reading most of the Conservatives voted with the Government, and they obtained a majority of two hundred. But in the ten days which elapsed before the second reading on February 19th, the Press and the Radicals had been at work: the question was now not so much whether the Bill was right as whether the country should remain silent when the French had affronted her. Gibson's amendment was, in effect, a vote of censure, and this time Disraeli persuaded the Conservatives to vote for it. With them were combined eighty-four Liberals, including Russell, and the Peelites, Gladstone, Graham and the malcontent Radicals. By 234 votes to 215 they decided that the Government had lost their confidence and thereupon Palmerston resigned.

This time Derby did not hesitate to take office. He tried to include Gladstone and Grey, but they both declined, and a wholly Conservative Ministry was formed.

Derby soon announced that an India Bill would be proceeded with at once, that Walewski's despatch should be answered, and also promised a Reform Bill for the next session. The relations with France were again very strained, but Walewski replied temperately to Malmesbury, saying that the French government would "place its reliance on the loyalty of the English people", and Disraeli was able to announce to the House that the "painful misconceptions had entirely terminated".

As to the India Bill, that country being yet in disorder, the Government frankly invited the co-operation of the whole House to devise a way out. Both Palmerston's proposed measure and that of the Government were dropped and a basis for a new Act found in a series of non-party resolutions. Russell, Roebuck, Graham and Bright (who had been chosen for Birmingham, after his defeat at Manchester) assisted, and a new agreed Government of India Act was passed with a responsible Secretary of State for India to be advised by an expert Council, another council to be appointed to assist the Viceroy in India: the long rule of the East India Company was over, it had been killed by the Mutiny. The hitherto divided authority of the Board of Control and the Company had been transferred to the new Secretary of State in Council. In India the Viceroy continued to represent the Crown. A settlement had been reached which lasted for over half a century.

This solution was not one peculiarly raising Liberal principles, for few, even of the Radicals, ever thought that the natives, who were still largely in revolt, were entitled to any degree of self-government. But at home the failure to make any advance for a quarter of a century on the electoral settlement of 1832 in certain quarters was once more causing some discontent. It has been recorded how Russell, in 1854, had been compelled to withdraw his Reform Bill. He had then proposed to transfer sixty-six seats from the small boroughs to the large towns. He would have given votes to lodgers and have enfranchised occupiers of £6 rateable value in the Boroughs and £10 in the Counties.

The Radicals had decided to support the second reading, though the Chartists still maintained that the Bill would leave the "aristocracy of labour" without votes. On the whole, however, Labour was more concerned to secure a ten-hour day in factories and an inspection of coal-mines, than to agitate for votes. Russell, as is known, in April withdrew his Bill, and thereafter most Radicals, in the comparative failure of the Crimean operations, concentrated on what was called "administrative reform"—it was, in the words of an association established for that object, to "destroy the aristocratical monopoly of Power and Place". Not only the democratic *Morning Advertiser* but even *The Times* attacked the "incompetency, aristocratic hauteur and official indifference, favour and routine" of the administrative departments. A great meeting was held in Drury Lane in June, 1855, with Charles Dickens as principal speaker, and a strong demand for the complete reform of the Civil Service arose which ultimately induced Palmerston to set up a Civil Service Commission. At the time open competitive examination was not conceded, but the more glaring effects of patronage were restrained by an examination of nominated candidates.

John Stuart Mill had already advocated throwing open the Civil Service to competition, and in 1853 a report by Northcote and Trevelyan had urged this reform. Russell disliked the idea. He did not see how it could be effected without "at last the aristocracy being altogether dissociated from the permanent Civil Service". But in January, 1854, the Cabinet was converted to Gladstone's view of open opportunity—even then the progress to open competition was slow. Not until 1860 was a system inaugurated for a limited competition among nominated candidates, and in 1870 it was agreed that a minister might, if he wished, throw open his department to general competition.

Having disposed of India, the next work of the Government was to inaugurate a general scheme of drainage for London, and, for the first time, a general authority, the Metropolitan Board of Works, was constituted for the whole Metropolis which so far had been administered, apart from the City, by vestries (of which there were no less than twenty-three) and district boards. The Metropolis Local Management Act of 1855, it was later said, had "put a virtual monopoly into the hands of the corruptest shop-keeping class in the world". The powers of the Metropolitan Board of Works were limited, and Government by Vestry was increasingly attacked until the Acts setting up the London County Council and Metropolitan Boroughs were passed in the later years of the nineteenth century.

As to Reform, Disraeli, unlike Russell (who for so long had taken 1832 as a final concession), as early as 1848 had spoken of "a larger representation of the industrial class". His organ *The Press*, had made franchise reform a part of the Conservative policy, and the carrying of a Radical motion to assimilate the County and Borough franchise, in 1851, had actually brought about the defeat of the Whig Government. The Bill of 1852 had perished with the administration, and that of 1854, as has been said, was withdrawn. Palmerston's reluctant proposals had never been introduced, and now it remained for the Conservatives to deal with the matter. Their Bill was introduced in February, 1859—it would have reduced the occupation franchise in Counties from £50 to £10, the Borough one at £10 remaining untouched; what came to be called "fancy franchise votes" to owners of £60 in the savings bank, lodgers in part of a £20 house, and graduates, lawyers, doctors and schoolmasters, were suggested. Disraeli also asked that seats taken from fifteen small boroughs should be given to industrial counties and towns.

His insistence that representation should be given to interest and not to numbers was emphatic. Whigs and Radicals pointed out that the new proposals would do nothing to bring in the working people, and Russell, Roebuck and Bright made mock of the "fancy franchises". In the opinion of the Queen, the Whigs as a whole, however, did not take this view. In writing to King Leopold she said that Russell had allied himself with Bright and Roebuck and had no other followers. She was mistaken, as a motion of Russell that "no readjustment of the franchise will satisfy the country which does not provide for a greater extension of the suffrage than is contemplated in the present measure" was carried by 330 against 291. There followed a General Election, and on June 7th, in the new Parliament, the Government were defeated by a majority of thirteen and resigned.

Lord Palmerston again became Prime Minister, an office which he continued to hold until his death. Again the Queen tried avoiding the necessity of his employment; she sent for Granville without result, but after Russell had agreed to become Foreign Secretary and work under his old rival—Gladstone also consenting to take office—there was nothing left but to entrust the premiership to Palmerston.

Once more the country was excited by foreign events—the French Empire was now at the height of its power and was beginning, at the price of obtaining Savoy and Nice, to support Cavour in an effort to throw off the Austrian yoke. In March, 1860, Victor Emmanuel annexed central Italy to Piedmont and Lombardy, which he already had won, and in April he entered Florence. Garibaldi sailed to Sicily and thence triumphantly marched north. The effect of his entry into Naples and the support which England gave to the Italians indirectly made Louis Napoleon, the friend of Italy, less unpopular in England. On October 27th, 1860, Russell declared the Government were bound to admit that the Italians were the best judges of their own interests, and that the Pope and the king of the two Sicilies had provided so ill for the welfare of their people that their subjects looked to their overthrow as a necessary preliminary to any improvement. In February, 1861, amidst universal enthusiasm in England, particularly of the Radicals, the first Parliament of United Italy was convoked. The excitement, more particularly on behalf of Garibaldi, had much weakened what small interest still existed outside political circles in the Reform Bills. In March, Russell had introduced such Bills for England, Scotland and Ireland, suggesting a £6 householder franchise, twenty-five seats to be taken from boroughs and given to large towns and provincial universal representation, only to withdraw the proposals on Whig and Tory objection in June. In 1861 Radical motions for a £10 householder franchise in the counties and £6 in the boroughs were both defeated, and it seemed for the time as if all enthusiasm had disappeared—the zeal for Garibaldi was more evident than concern for domestic political improvement. As Cobden sadly wrote, "When will the masses of this country begin to think of home politics"; and Bright lamented, when he saw so many working men cheering Garibaldi, "If the people would only make a few such demonstrations for themselves, we could do something for them".

By far the most important circumstance connected with the last government of Palmerston as it affected the Liberal Party was the remarkable rise during this period of Gladstone to celebrity. He had taken office as Chancellor of the Exchequer for the second time with much misgiving. His relations with Palmerston had always been difficult; but the old statesman at least agreed with Gladstone about the emancipation of Italy—there he discovered "real and close harmony". "The overwhelming interest and weight of the Italian question" reconciled him to differences upon electoral reform, expenditure upon fortifications and armaments and many other matters.

The Prime Minister in 1859 was again possessed by his recurrent fear of the French. He pressed for further increases in the armed services and for elaborate strengthening of the coast defences. Volunteers, as an auxiliary force, were encouraged, and Gladstone ruefully saw a constantly increasing expenditure for which he, as Chancellor, would be responsible. The settlement between the Austrian and French Emperors in July, 1859, had ended the Italian war, but the incorporation of Savoy and Nice in

March, 1860, by the French, was intensely unpopular in England, and there is no doubt that, generally, the behaviour of Napoleon did little to ease the position.

In the midst of these alarms, Gladstone conceived the idea of using his office to dissipate suspicion. He persuaded the Government to allow Cobden to interview the Emperor in December, 1859, and ask him whether the French would agree to a commercial treaty. Negotiations followed, and finally Lord Russell was persuaded to give to Cobden an official position. The protectionists in France had made every difficulty, but Cobden persisted and, in the end, an agreement was reached, to be signed in January, 1860. It was a triumph for Gladstone and the pacific school over the Jingoes, who had for so long inflamed public opinion, and it was achieved not by any emotional appeal, but by the more subtle argument of commercial advantage.

From now onwards it was recognized that the future of Liberalism lay with Gladstone. His reputation, already considerable, both with moderate business men, with the middle classes, and the manual operatives, was enhanced by his financial success as Chancellor of the Exchequer. As Morley writes, "Out of the commercial treaty with France grew the whole of the great financial scheme of 1860". (*Gladstone*, Vol. I, p. 657.) The engagement of France to reduce many duties, such as that on iron, enabled the Chancellor to withdraw from customs duty, reciprocally, over three hundred and fifty articles—as the Chancellor said, "Free Trade has reached its zenith". A great dispute arose out of the abolition of excise on paper, which was rejected in the Lords. This raised that long contention with the Upper House which continued for the rest of Gladstone's political life.

He persuaded the aged Palmerston, unwillingly, to attack the Lords, and the House of Commons by a majority of over thirty supported him. For the moment the Government accepted the position; but in 1861, Gladstone, with that ingenuity of mind which his opponents called "jesuitical", tacked the repeal of the Paper Duty to the general Finance Act, and so threw upon the Lords the responsibility of rejecting the whole Budget. For this device, in the Commons he obtained a majority of fifteen—the whole question of cheap newspapers was at stake, and for many years afterwards the Press acclaimed him as their liberator. The Lords surrendered, and, until the Budget of 1910, abstained from interference in matters of finance.

Gladstone, was still, however, in combat with many of the Cabinet on the question of the expense and expedience of great military and naval estimates—he endeavoured to show, on information received from Cobden in Paris, that the fears of French aggression were exaggerated. It is from this time that the growth of friendship between him and John Bright became very noticeable. Bright realized that, at last, his views had obtained a powerful influence in the Cabinet. Russell, despite his earlier promises, had thrown over Reform. Palmerston had tried to betray Gladstone in the earlier stages of the dispute with the Lords— it was evident that the future of progressive Liberalism must depend upon the union of Gladstone and Bright.

At this stage a new conflict, the American Civil War, temporarily disturbed the new nascent Liberalism. There was undoubtedly a Liberal feeling for the South, based upon the ground that the secessionists should be entitled to become free if they do so desire. This was the opinion both of Gladstone and his friend Acton—the Southern states to them were a nation; like the Italians, the Hungarians or the Poles, they were conceived as "rightly struggling to be free". The Conservatives (who were of opinion that the only gentlemen in America were to be found in the South) had the same sympathies. They were alarmed to think that the North, who represented the new democracy, might be victorious. On the other hand, the old dislike of slave owners was still strong in Radical and Evangelical circles, and after Lincoln had declared freedom for the slaves, the Evangelicals, Friends and many Radicals had no doubt which side was right. Bright, addressing the Trade Unions in March, 1863, eloquently pleaded for the abolition of servitude. The Government, on the other hand, by proclaiming British neutrality, had gone far to recognize the Southern States as a separate entity, and Gladstone, who in his early days had defended his father in the House as a slave owner, did not take an active position against slavery, a failure which, at a later date, he frankly regretted. Palmerston and most of his class secretly welcomed any division which would weaken the growing power of the Americans, and for the time a complete accord between Bright and Gladstone was delayed.

By February, 1863, Bright was able to write to an American friend that opinion had greatly changed and that in almost every town great meetings were held to pass resolutions in favour of the North. Nevertheless in June, Roebuck proposed in the House an alliance with Napoleon to aid the Southern States; the Emperor had already suggested mediation. In 1864 the North took the offensive and in the spring of the next year the war was at an end. It was soon after this that Bright was able to declare to his constituents that his preaching "on Foreign Policy and non-intervention had not been without effect"; and although excitement had been aroused by the cruel suppression by the Russians of the Polish rising in 1863, Palmerston no longer actively sought to intervene. Russell was zealous for Poland, it was an old Whiggish cause; he it was, the Queen thought, who now needed restraint, rather than Palmerston. A general Congress, suggested by the French, was not encouraged; the Queen was alarmed that the matter might end with a war between England and France against Germany. In the end the Poles were deserted —it was not the first time.

A far more serious matter for future generations arose when it appeared that the Prussians were threatening to seize Schleswig, which belonged to Denmark. In 1864 the Germans attacked. The French, sore at the failure of England to assist them in Poland, were supine. Russell wished for a naval demonstration to impress the Germans, but Bismarck and his Austrian allies were not to be intimidated. The Danes, unsupported, were defeated; the Germans had tasted the first fruit of that success in the Bismarckian policy of force which was to culminate in the great German wars of the twentieth century.

At the time, however, the British people as a whole were indifferent. They had begun to realize that England had not the power to do more on the Continent than protest. The period of Palmerstonian bluff was over. The Prussians were beginning to organize themselves into a great military machine. Not Goethe and Kant, but Moltke and Bismarck became their exemplars.

The behaviour of the Germans at this period was prophetical. They had been a party to the possession of the Duchies of Schleswig and Holstein by Denmark in 1852. They now alleged the insufferable wrongs of Germans in those provinces! The Liberals in Germany supported Bismarck. They with the Austrians, soon themselves to be routed, decided to crush the Danes while the rest of Europe stood by. In the end Prussia obtained the deep-water port of Kiel which, in truth, had always been the purpose of the whole campaign. Next year it was the turn of Austria to be defeated at Sadowa; and Hanover, helpless, was incorporated into Prussia—the beginning of the era of conscious German chicanery and aggression may confidently be dated from this time. Never till now were politics to be free from a perpetual Teutonic menace to the peace of Europe and the World.

The War Party, according to Gladstone, were Palmerston, Russell, Lord Stanley of Alderney and the Lord Chancellor, but the majority were against intervention. In the House, Disraeli taunted the Government with failure to uphold the independence and integrity of Denmark; Cobden asserted that England had encouraged the Danes to fight and then had deserted them. Gladstone was put up to reply. The reality was that England had not 20,000 men to put in the field against the Germanic hordes and there was little opportunity of naval demonstration. The refusal of the French to move made intervention impracticable, and the Government accepted an amendment which was carried by eighteen votes in favour of inaction; it was a great decline from the earlier days of Palmerston.

In July, 1865, there was a General Election; resulting in a gain of some twenty seats for the Government, and thus encouraged, with a majority of about sixty, on the death of Palmerston in October, a new era of Liberalism, specifically "Gladstonian", started with "Peace, Retrenchment and Reform" for its watchwords. Until the close of his life Palmerston had continued to demand more defences and national expenditure, though, curiously, the rapidly mounting power of Germany did not seem to trouble him.

"Gladstone will soon have it all his own way", he remarked; "whenever he gets my place, we shall have some strange doings"—as clearly as any one, he saw that the day of chauvinistic Whiggery was over.

And now to speak of the new man whose actual leadership might be delayed, but whose coming power was inevitable. What manner of person was he? It is remarkable that no biographer has ever succeeded in making the character of the founder of Liberalism really intelligible. G. W. E. Russell is probably the nearest the mark when he wrote that "Gladstone was essentially and above all, a Christian—it was this religiousness of character which won him the affectionate reverence of great masses of his countrymen, who had never seen his face". (*Gladstone*, Russell, p. 8.) He goes on: "This keen sense of the religious bearing of political questions determined Gladstone's action in not a few of the crises of his parliamentary life. It was the exacting vigour of a religious theory that drove him out of the Cabinet in 1845. It was his belief that marriage is a sacred and indissoluble union which dictated his pertinacious opposition to the Divorce Bill in 1857. Ten years later he felt that the Irish Establishment could no longer be maintained, because it could plead neither practical utility nor 'the seal of and signature of ecclesiastical descent'". He gives many other instances and concludes, "the administration of Government was in Gladstone's hands a religious act".

But unlike the Saints, Gladstone loved power. Though polite in manner, he was imperious and would not readily listen to criticism. With all his reformative zeal, he was at heart an institutionalist and was ever moved by precedent. He had, even in his later Radical years, though much obstructed by the Queen, a great respect for the Crown. He revered the Constitution almost in the manner of Burke, but also to the profit-making economic system which current finance and business supported he gave unquestioning allegiance. His method of helping the labouring classes was to remove restrictions and exchange commodities —"remove the obstacles of taxation and regulation", he wrote (*Musings for the good of Man*)—in all this he was an uncritical disciple of the old Utilitarians. In theology he admired St. Thomas Aquinas, but that Doctor's attitude towards usury and stewardship would have found little appeal in Gladstone's commercial mind. In his later years he detected a desire among the younger Liberals "To take into the hands of the State the business of the individual man—this idea", he said, "estranged him and had done so for many, many years". (*Letter to Lord Acton*, Feb. 2, 1885.) Morley points out his tendency to over-refine language, which won for him the reputation of being sophistical, yet, at the same time, abstract metaphysical discussion did not attract him; he escaped the reproaches levelled at Balfour and Haldane that they were in some way unfit for public confidence because they were philosophers. He had an overwhelming power of persuasive eloquence; even when his hearers could not understand half his argument, they came away with the feeling that they had heard something very great. His fury at cruelty and oppression, particularly where the victim was a foreigner and a Christian, was unappeasable and gave an unquenchable fire to his denunciations. More than once in his life he would retire from public life only to return to expose some atrocity and ruffle the complacency of the comfortable and the opportunist.

"His essence", says Strachey, "eludes the hand which seems to grasp it—one is baffled as his opponents were baffled fifty years ago. Compared with Disraeli, his attitude towards life strikes one as that of an ingenuous child." (*Eminent Victorians*, p. 273.) Yet in this paradoxical compound of Evangelicism and ritual, authority and freedom, national emancipation and industrial servitude, ambiguity and lucid logic, the recipient of consuming hatreds and unexampled political adoration, the Liberal Party found its basic inspiration.

CHAPTER VI

THE ADVENT OF DEMOCRACY

ON the death of Palmerston the Queen sent for Lord Russell, who resigned the Foreign Office to Clarendon, Gladstone continuing to be Chancellor of the Exchequer.   A new appointment, that of Goschen, who was connected with a wealthy financial firm in the City, aroused some feeling, more particularly when he was admitted to the Cabinet in January, 1866. His presence there proved useful; in the late spring there had developed one of many periodical financial crises which seemed inescapable in those days of hectic speculative commercial exploitation.   For the first time an important railway, the London Chatham and Dover line, failed, and in May came the collapse of the great banking firm of Overend Gurney with £19,000,000 liabilities.   As in 1848 and 1857 the Bank Charter Act had to be suspended—the whole crisis was due to faulty finance, for the trade of the country generally remained good.

It is curious that the obvious incapacity of the controllers of money operations to prevent these recurrent disasters did not shake the almost universal acceptance of the prevailing banking system, but little or no criticism is to be detected, even in socialistic circles which at that time were more concerned to attack the landlord and the manufacturer than the men of high finance.

The way was now clearer than it had been for a long time for reform of the franchise.   With the passing of Palmerston, the chief opponent of electoral advance had gone.   Gladstone, by his defeat at Oxford and acceptance by an urban constituency, had now a free hand.   Russell having been in the Lords since 1861, he was now leader of the House of Commons and had acquired strong Radical support in such talented members as Professor Fawcett, Hughes and J. S. Mill.

On March 12th, 1866, the Government Bill was introduced; it purported to give a borough qualification of £7 occupation and a county one of £14; this was higher than the £6 and £10 of the earlier Russell proposals and was designed to appease the Whigs; the accompanying lodger franchise had already been contemplated in a Tory Bill.

Nevertheless, despite the propaganda of the National Reform Union and League there was great opposition even from some Liberals. Lowe, himself representing the very small borough of Calne, led from the Government side a general attack upon democracy.   The result was rather to stir the working classes to demand their rights than to help the obstruction of Reform.   Lowe spoke of the manual workers as being guilty of "venality, ignorance, drunkenness and intimidation", and contrasted them unfavourably with the middle class £10 householder who had hitherto constituted the majority of the electors.

Encouraged by this Governmental division, the Tories took heart. Lord Grosvenor, a Whig, was supported by Stanley in a motion to postpone franchise reform until a scheme for redistribution was announced, an old device which had often before served as a dilatory tactic.   This time it was defeated by only five votes, and a promise was given directly the Bill had a second reading to bring forward the redistribution scheme. In committee, however, after a motion from a malcontent Liberal to substitute rating for rental in the borough qualification was carried by eleven votes, the Government gave up the struggle and Russell resigned —for the third time Lord Derby became Prime Minister.

In order that the contentions on parliamentary franchise which occupied the years 1866 and 1867 may adequately be understood, it is necessary to realize that, apart from the Radicals, no responsible states-man yet accepted the view that the existence of a Government should depend upon the decision of a numerical majority of the whole people. Whig reformers, equally with Tories, were insistent that all that was required was an adequate representation of the third estate of the realm in Parliament, where, as Disraeli said, "they sat by proxies".

That the other estates, the Lords Spiritual and Temporal, should lose their right to legislate—a privilege far more ancient than the right of the Commons to agree to taxation—despite Parliament Acts, has not been conceded to this day. In mid-Victorian times the notion would have been considered revolutionary.

The issue which had formerly divided Tories from Whigs had relation to the powers of the Crown; that matter had at last been settled in favour of the Constitutionalists, but the position of the Commons House was not yet clearly determined. The threat to create peers to carry out their will had been used so sparingly as to show the exceptional nature of the power—once only, at the time of the treaty of Utrecht, had the Queen actually been persuaded to use her prerogative in this way. The Peerage, probably appointed for life in very early times, had long been hereditary. Since the Reformation the estate of the Church, represented by the Bishops, had been in effect absorbed into the lay House of Lords; indeed, being appointed as individuals, the Bishops were often more pledged to a political view, at any rate in the eighteenth century, than were the lay peers.

The concern of Parliament, both in 1832 and again in 1866, was to give the Commonalty proper representation, and that, emphatically, all save Radicals agreed was not to be achieved by counting heads of the male adult population, but by giving to each social class its due weight and proportion. So, also, in the distribution of seats, the old mediæval idea of representation of areas according to their significance rather than their population still lingered. The University representation is the last surviving example of such representation by "Liberties" or "Peculiars".

The matter is well illustrated by the speeches of leading men made about this time. Said a great lawyer, Cairns, "Parliament must be a mirror—a representation of every class—not according to numbers, but according to everything which gives weight and importance in the world without". "The object we have in view is to represent all classes and give no class a preponderating influence." (Gathorne-Hardy.)

"It is important that the working class should not have a prepon-derating influence", declared Spencer Walpole; in the words of Lord Stanley, "no class should be excluded and no one should overbear the rest".

The first of the Liberals openly to criticize this view was Gladstone. In his debate with Lowe, the anti-reformer, who had said: "If you want impulsive, unreflecting violent people—where do you look for them? Do you go to the bottom or the top?" the Chancellor of the Exchequer had replied: "The persons to whom the remarks apply are our fellow-Christians, our own flesh and blood". The denunciation of these words as "sentimental rant" by Lord Cranborne was applauded by many; it indicated the great distaste for what is now called democracy existent at the time.

The real issue before the House in 1866 and 1867 was thus simply, how to readjust representation so as not to exclude any class entitled to be represented without conceding the full claims of democracy. The whole dispute was as to extent and method.

In these circumstances, the history of what happened is the more amazing. In the face of growing Continental anxieties and perils caused by the new intransigence of Prussia led by Bismarck (conditions which after the war with Austria culminated in the defeat of France in 1870), the Russell Government was forced to resign on a clause in the Franchise Bill which the Conservatives subsequently introduced and passed almost in the same form. The facts were these: on March 12th, 1866, Gladstone introduced the Liberal Reform Bill—for the moment he did not raise distribution questions. Reform Bills had been introduced by five Governments since 1849. Bright had produced one in 1858, and the Tory Government in 1859—this was the one which did not really extend the franchise at all, but Gladstone had voted for it. In 1860 Russell had suggested a £6 occupation limit for boroughs, £10 for counties; now what was proposed was a £7 town and a £14 county on rental, together with a lodger franchise (which was in the defeated Tory Bill), and the addition of copy and leaseholders in the counties. This was denounced by Cranborne the Tory and Lowe the Whig as Democracy. On this issue a fortnight was spent in debate. Thirty Liberals voted against the second reading; the majority was only five. A redistribution Bill followed and the measures were joined.

At length a proposal to substitute rating for rental as the test of eligibility was carried against the Government, who then resigned. It is well to remember that—apart from this trivial matter—all the Bill did was to reduce the county franchise from £50 qualification to £14 and add people not freeholders; and, in the towns, to lower the franchise from £10 to £7; this was the abhorred democracy!

Since the achievement of Free Trade and the failure of Chartism, there had been little public organization of opinion in the country, but Bright and his friends had come to see that it was only possible to create a demand for reform by such means. The times were propitious; the avoidance of all domestic questions had died with Palmerston—instead, under the earnest influence of John Stuart Mill and the new humanistic movement—Carlyle also had his influence from quite a different angle—people had become discontented with the old order. Notions of a society based upon reason and forethought, such as had possessed Bentham and Mills' father, were again in the ascendant, and, as a product of this, there arose a claim that all citizens should, directly or indirectly, participate in Government.

One of the first to be moved was Gladstone. As early as 1863—to the alarm of the Court and gentry—he had declared that "every person, not presumably incapacitated by some consideration of personal unfitness or political danger, is morally entitled to come within the pale of the constitution". The context shows that he was not speaking of that equality before the law for which Wilkes had contended, but of the right to vote at an election.

Reform, it was said, "was in the air". Popular demonstrations, organized openly or in secret by the Reform Associations, were taken up by the trade unions. The National Reform League and the National Reform Union (the latter Bright's especial care) were increasingly active throughout the country. The Secretary of the League, Howell, succeeded in interesting many working-class organizations to demand the suffrage, as did others later when permeating them with Socialism. At this time individualistic notions were still strong; the International Working Men's Association, formed to support the recent pronouncements of Karl Marx, made as yet but a small appeal, yet the Socialists supported the Radical and Liberal demand for electoral rights. A ferment such as had not been known since 1832 was developing.

A great conference and public demonstration and a deputation to the Prime Minister, Russell, heralded the opening of Parliament in 1866. In 1865, at the General Election, as has been said, John Stuart Mill, Tom Hughes and Professor Fawcett, all advanced Radicals, had been returned to Parliament, and Gladstone, defeated at Oxford, had thereby increased his popularity, for he had found a more democratic seat in Lancashire. On the defeat of the Russell Government he became a national hero. The crowd surged round his house shouting for "Gladstone and Liberty".

By the upper classes he was rapidly being ostracized. He was a revolutionary—another Wilkes or perhaps even a ritualistic Lord George Gordon: his hegira from the old system had begun.

In these circumstances it was necessary for the new Tory Government to act, but what were they to do? They had defeated the very moderate proposals of Russell and Gladstone, there was no new road down which they could travel; they must either stand still or go the same way as their predecessors.

In April an attempt had been made to ban Reform meetings in Hyde Park; nevertheless, under the plea of the doubtful legality of the prohibition, on May 6th a huge mass meeting was held there. Meanwhile the middle-class Reform Union, having its headquarters in Manchester, stood behind Gladstone. On June 1st it organized processions to London from all the greater towns, fifty-eight deputations in all, which were joined by the Trade Unions and the Reform League. In July the crowd broke down the railings of Hyde Park, a meeting having again been prohibited, and further agitation went on in Birmingham, Manchester, Leeds, Glasgow, and Dublin. In the result, Derby—writing to Disraeli—in September had said: "I am coming to the conclusion, reluctantly, that we shall have to deal with the question of Reform". For the moment Disraeli disagreed, but the Queen took a part in the matter, insisting that the question should be put at rest. She was prepared to work to obtain a measure by general consent.

Remembering the success of the settlement by resolution of the Indian Government problem, the Tories thought the same device might be utilized again. Instead of a limitation by rating or rental, Derby in December, 1866, had suggested Household Suffrage—a Radical proposal emanating from Hume and supported by Bright. By this time Disraeli had been converted to the idea that the public demand for immediate action was real, and declared that Household Suffrage on a rating principle could be supported on Tory principles.

There are two matters difficult to explain in relation to the introduction, after some false starts, of a Bill which, in substance, differed not at all from that for which Russell's Government had been defeated—the attitude of the dissentient Tories and that of Gladstone himself.

As to this policy, the objections were twofold; first, that the Tory measure was in fact a democratic Radical one; and, secondly, that it was not honourable to commend a measure which the promoters had just defeated when introduced by their opponents. Both these considerations moved Lord Cranborne (soon to pass to the Lords as Lord Salisbury), to resign in angry protest. He was remote in responsibility, for he had taken the office of India Secretary, but in the Cabinet, on studying the implications of Household Suffrage, he had come to the conclusion that the safeguards were useless and that in fact if he consented to the scheme he "could not look in the face those whom I urged last year to oppose Mr. Gladstone". At first, many other Conservatives were critical—it looked as if about fifty would desert. An assurance by Disraeli that "the Government would never introduce Household Suffrage pure and simple" soothed many, but Lord Cranborne remained obdurate—it was "a simple proposition of political morality", he said; "the party which behaved in opposition as ours did last year is not the party to propose Household Suffrage".

The position of Gladstone was more invidious. If it were true that the new Bill in principle was not different from his, it would appear to have been his duty to support it; but the indignation which he felt at the trickery which had been practised on him got the better of his judgment. His objections were petty and unconvincing; his party as a whole refused to follow him in an opposition such as the Tories had organized the year before. When he sought to remove the payment of rates as a qualification for voting he was taking a Radical position; at other times he said the Bill was too wide. The Radicals and many Conservative doubters very sensibly declared that the Bill should go to Committee. There many amendments were made, nearly all in a Radical direction. Residence was reduced to one year, and the Bill finally adopted in Bright's words was "the precise franchise I recommended in 1858–59". On July 15th he was able to note, "Bill passed with cheers from our side". A proposal to include women, moved by Mill, was defeated by 196 to 73. The troublesome case of the compounder for rates was met, temporarily, by the abolition of compounding.

Despite all apologies, when the matter is considered in that state of unprejudice which three-quarters of a century may bring, it cannot be denied that the attitude of Derby and Disraeli was morally indefensible. Either they should have allowed the Liberals to take responsibility for their own proposals, or they should have resigned rather than place themselves in so ambiguous a position. The criticisms of Lord Cranborne are just: "If," he declared, "no matter what a man has supported in opposition, the moment he gets into office it shall be open to him to reverse and repudiate it all, you practically destroy the whole basis on which our form of government rests, and you make the House of Commons a mere scrambling place for office." Moneypenny and Buckle (the biographers of Disraeli) have called the passage of the Reform Act "Disraeli's Parliamentary Triumph", but the ironic words of Lord Salisbury have gone unanswered.

On March 5th, 1868, Gladstone, who had succeeded Russell as leader of the Liberal Party, started his campaign in Parliament for the disestablishment of the Irish Church. It was already under examination by Royal Commission, but Gladstone would not await the report.

Already in May, 1867, he had said that the position of that body would have to be fairly and fully looked in the face. As Manning had declared: "The Irish establishment is a great wrong", and there were many grounds on which he could support his utterance. Three-quarters of the people were Roman Catholics, and of the remaining quarter at least a half were Presbyterian. Indeed, broadly, it was only the governing class who could be called Anglican. Liberals, Radicals and Irish, all agreed to support the Leader's resolutions. The first, that the Church in Ireland should cease to be established, was promptly carried by a majority of sixty-five, the others were not challenged. There was little serious opposition, as Manning did not hesitate to point out. Lowe, so long a dissentient, was reconciled; Bright supported with enthusiasm. To all other Irish proposals, Gladstone insisted on the priority of the Church question. The Queen was perturbed, Cranborne suggested that Disraeli would again betray the Tory Party by surrender, for Lord Stanley, showing considerable sympathy with disestablishment, was suspected of being the Tory leader's mouthpiece.

High Churchmen, who were fearful of State interference with religion, trusted Gladstone (himself of their opinion in ecclesiastical matters) more on this subject than on many others. The Coronation Oath, which had perturbed at least two of the Georges, weighed upon the mind of the Queen. Disraeli formulated the objections of the Government under three heads: "It would destroy conciliation, shake property to the centre, and dissolve for the first time the connection between Government and Religion". He suggested a Dissolution to test public opinion or, alternatively, advised resignation. It was suggested that the Prime Minister had unfairly enlisted the Sovereign on his side and the resulting acrimony was great. Gladstone carried a Bill through the Commons to suspend the creation of new interests in the Irish Church, but it was rejected in the Lords. So matters stood until the General Election on the new reformed register.

Before the Conservative Government resigned, as the result of a heavy defeat at the hands of the new electorate, they had taken their first step in Collectivism by acquiring the new electric telegraph, though the purchase was at an outrageous price. Election petitions had been transferred to the Judges; a new registration law and a measure against Corruption passed, but all these counted for nothing in withstanding the new Radical enthusiasm. In Birmingham, in particular, a local party organization had taken much influence out of the hands of the Reform Club in selecting candidates and promoting their return. Gladstone, it is true, lost his seat in Lancashire owing to Church opposition, to be returned for Greenwich. In all, over two million people voted. The Liberal majority was over five hundred thousand, and Gladstone became the first real Liberal Prime Minister.

He had been warned by Dean Wellesley that the Queen "differs from you on the question of disestablishment and will tell you so frankly", otherwise she had no objection even to "advanced Liberals". This, doubtless, was a reference to Bright, who had become President of the Board of Trade. In the Cabinet, however, there were still many peers: Argyll, Clarendon, Granville, Kimberley and De Grey; Hartington, afterwards Duke of Devonshire, was also included. The Radicals in the Government were Bright, Ayrton, Stansfeld, Trevelyan and Otway. It was a compound, but the advanced members were far greater in proportion than ever before.

The Irish Disestablishment Bill was introduced on March 1st, 1869—the incumbents were to be compensated and all churches and cathedrals retained—£1,000,000 was to be taken to cancel Maynooth liabilities to Catholics and certain obligations to Presbyterians. The rest Gladstone proposed to use for general pious uses "in Ireland and for charities". The Tories decided to oppose. The Lords asked for further concessions in money to the episcopalians, but, in the end, after many differences between the Houses, mostly about finance, the Bill became law.

Whatever merits from a Liberal point of view the disestablishment had, it did little to placate Irish discontent. Agrarian crime increased notably in 1869. Landlords were attacked and shot, farmers, bailiffs and the police constantly in danger of sudden assassination, and houses were destroyed. Gladstone's reply was to endeavour to give some security to the tenant. He was to receive a limited estate in the land, so that if he improved it he would have compensation. Disraeli relied upon the old principle of freedom of contract—he prophesied that the tenant would now refuse to pay rent and, on consequent eviction, more disorder would break out. Unfortunately his forecast proved later to be correct. Bright alone saw that the remedy lay in abolishing tenancy altogether and giving the Irish a peasantry owning their own land. To this solution Parliament was later to come.

The introduction of an Education Act by Forster in February, 1869, disclosed that less than half the children of England went to school—of those who went, half were at schools which were uninspected. Of the non-attending half it was said that forty per cent were not at work and were "running wild".

A national Education League was pressing these matters on Parliament and the public when Forster produced his measure. It did not in any way provide for universal education, but only enacted that School Boards might take power to compel attendance if the denominational bodies did not deal adequately with deficiencies in accommodation. As to religious education, where there were School Boards they could provide it if they pleased, with a right of individual exemption at a parent's request.

Joseph Chamberlain was now first heard of outside Birmingham as leading the opposition to the Bill. He and his fellow Dissenters objected to the opportunities it gave to Churchmen to fill up their schools in areas where there was no nonconformist place of education. He thought the optional powers of the School Boards would make the measure useless, but neither Lord de Grey (Lord Ripon), who subsequently became a Roman Catholic, nor the Prime Minister had any sympathy with non-sectarian schools—they adhered to their own plan.

But Chamberlain and his friends were not to be over-awed; the young "screw-maker", as he was derisively called, was fearless. On March 9th for the first time he met Mr. Gladstone face to face. He admitted that the proposal was in many respects "a noble measure", but urged that it would have the effect of handing over the education of the country to the Church of England—especially in agricultural districts—and that a mere conscience clause would not meet the matter.

The Conservatives not unnaturally supported the Bill, and the famous clause of Cowper-Temple, excluding from all rate-built schools "every catechism and formulary distinctive of denomination or creed" was accepted; the denominational schools were deprived of aid from the rates and the Government were driven to augment the State grants in order to help them. In the result Liberalism, to quote Garvin, "was split to pieces". (*Life of Chamberlain*, I, p. 115.) Sixty Liberals voted against the Government. On June 30th, the feeling among Dissenters had so increased that a majority of Liberals voted against their leaders, who were only saved by Conservative support.

It was in this debate that Harcourt first opposed his chief. He was a member of the Birmingham League and stood for national, free, compulsory education with the sectarian influence eliminated. Dilke also opposed the Bill, but he desired an entirely secular solution. It was in part because of Harcourt's thesis that the State "is absolutely indifferent to all forms of religious teaching" and "as regards any funds raised by the State, one form of religious opinion has as full a right to share in the appropriation of such funds as another", that the Cowper-Temple clause was accepted; Harcourt's proposal had been that in rate-aided schools the instruction should only be in the Bible and undenominational.

Subject to this amendment, the Bill went through substantially as it had been introduced. The principle of supplementing, rather than superseding, the voluntary schools had won acceptance. Compulsion was only to be applied in Board Schools, and they were only to come into being where the voluntary schools could not be adequately maintained—even then the School Boards need not enforce the clause for compulsion unless they wished.

In the opinion of Morley, "from the point of view of party strategy, the policy of this great statute was fatal. The Church of England was quickened into active antagonism by Irish disestablishment and the nonconformists were estranged by the treatment of endowed schools". (*Gladstone*, I, p. 941.)

The quarrel continued. In 1872 a conference of eight hundred nonconformist churches met in protest at Manchester; of four hundred and twenty-five Liberal candidates, three hundred were pledged to the repeal of that section of the 1870 Act which enabled School Boards to pay fees in certain cases for denominational schools, meanwhile, all consideration of the real purpose and method of education generally was forgotten in a sectarian struggle.

The decision in 1870 to enforce the obligation on parents, to a very limited extent, to provide their children with elementary education was a repudiation of Benthamite individualistic principles, though not so recognized at the time. The then existing law did no more than authorize State grants, not more than £20,000 in all, to be administered by a committee of the Privy Council. The possibility of a strong central authority, a Board of Education, was not considered until 1899—it was never before the minds of Forster or Gladstone. The power to control not only the service but the nature of juvenile instruction, enabling the State in effect to decide what ideas should, or should not, be presented to the young in their most formative period, had never been envisaged. In 1876 the duty of parents to cause their children to receive efficient elementary instruction in reading, writing and arithmetic was enforced by Statute, and, if we may anticipate, in 1880 the compulsory attendance of children at school was made universal. Finally, in 1891, the obligation to pay fees was abolished.

Thereafter, the overriding control of a Central Authority became inevitable; the use to which this may be put has been exemplified in authoritarian States. In England the power is exercised chiefly through the seductive agency of grants paid conditionally upon the local authority, *inter alia*, complying with the requirements of the Board relating to education. Higher education grants and State scholarships are also the subject of central regulation.

The grant regulations in elementary schools must be in accordance with a suitable curriculum. The non-provided schools are also in receipt of grants, except for religious education, and they also in effect are under the ultimate control of the Minister. His inspectors (called in courtesy "His Majesty's") are the means by which he can inform himself how far his principles and the statutory duties are carried out.

It is thus not too much to say that, by degrees, the State has acquired an immense control over the education of its young citizens, nor have the Liberal Party since 1870 ever objected. The matter is cited as an early example of the decay of the old principles and practices of individualism in the matter of parental right.

Soon the attention of all parties was distracted from domestic affairs by the war which France declared on Germany on July 15th. On the 19th France refused the good offices of England to preserve the peace; though it has been said that in fact Bismarck had tempted the French into war. These are questions which do not call for elucidation in this political history. In twenty-eight days ten battles were fought, the Emperor of the French was made prisoner and deposed. In February, 1871, Great Britain recognized the French Republic. In all this affray Gladstone and Granville stood aloof. The neutrality of Belgium, which had been guaranteed in 1839, in fact was not menaced; if it had been, it was apparent that this country was seriously deficient in armament to enforce it. No military preparations were made after the outbreak— apparently neither Gladstone nor Granville, the Foreign Secretary, at first realized their obligations to Belgium; Parliament was equally supine.

In the event practically nothing was done. Disraeli pointed out that we had only "skeleton battalions, attenuated squadrons, batteries without sufficient guns and yet more guns than gunners; a nation without a military reserve; a nation, moreover, which had left off shipbuilding, reduced its crews and its stores, and failed to furnish artillery for its men-of-war". "The balance of power has been completely destroyed," that far-seeing statesman declared. "You have a new world, new influences at work, new and unknown dangers with which to cope."

As if to illustrate his contention, Russia proceeded to denounce the treaty of 1856, which had neutralized the Black Sea, and the Italian Government occupied Rome, restricting the Pope to the Vatican. In all these matters, after protests and discussion, the Liberal Government stood aside and let matters take their course; the days of Palmerston were truly over.

Other matters to be noted at home in 1870 were the granting by the Universities to degrees without religious tests, a serious sacrifice of Gladstone's own prejudice to the public good; the full opening of the civil service to public competition; the reform of the Army by abolishing the dual control of Commander-in-Chief and War Office, and the ending of the purchase of commissions—this latter by royal warrant.

At last, also, the long fight for a secret ballot was won. Why this elementary necessity for the proper recording of opinion should so long have been opposed it is difficult to understand. It had been advocated by the Westminster Committee as early as 1783. Over twenty-five resolutions had been moved by Radicals in its favour before it received a majority of Liberal votes in 1838 on Grote's annual motion. It had formed an important item in the Charter; yet nothing was done. Fawcett complained of the want of enthusiasm of the Government, Gladstone confessed a "lingering reluctance", but helped to carry it with a majority of over ninety. In the Lords it was rejected, but being reintroduced in 1872 the Lords yielded. Voting was at last made secret.

The machinery of registration which accompanied the secret ballot did much to encourage the growth of party organization, in which political activity the Liberals were first in the field. So far such bodies had been for the most part, as it has been said, constituted *ad hoc* to obtain particular measures such as the repeal of the Corn Law or National Education. Now, however, they were coming to be attached permanently to political parties, and their work, therefore, was no longer limited to the achievement of a specific object.

Party associations had started with the Reform Act, primarily to maintain adequate registration of particular supporters. "The battle of the constitution," Sir Robert Peel had said, "will be fought out in the registration courts." On the Liberal side they were called Liberal Registration Societies or, more shortly, Liberal Associations. A Central Office in London took to sending them down names of suitable candidates. The Committees of the Associations varied in power, but as a rule they represented the most powerful influences on their side. Canvassing, a very ancient practice, fell often into the hands of the Central Committee of the Association, who relieved the candidate of much of his work; but it was not until 1867 that the full Caucus system, as it was derisively called, developed in Birmingham. In that year Birmingham received thirty thousand new voters. It was suggested that the City should be divided into wards, and the Central Committee be made up of elected ward representatives. They took upon themselves, more particularly where the minority clause was in operation, to tell the electors for whom to vote; each elector receiving a ticket with two names on it.

By the last Act, Birmingham had received three members, but the elector had only two votes. By a skilful allocation of the votes in each ward, the total votes in the City could collectively produce a majority for each Liberal candidate, and the machinery for ensuring minority representation was thus defeated. This device was very largely the work of Chamberlain—it depended, of course, for its success on the voters obeying the directions of the Caucus. They did so loyally, and the result was three Liberal members for Birmingham. The Caucus had justified itself.

A similar device was tried in Birmingham to defeat the cumulative vote at the first School Board election, but here the results were less successful. In 1873 Chamberlain was elected Mayor of Birmingham, with him was associated Schnadhorst, the Secretary of the Liberal Association, and between them they organized an all-powerful organization. They felt none of the qualms of John Stuart Mill with regard to minorities. They were advanced Radicals of the new collectivist type; their purpose was to capture the Municipality and the State in order to use them directly for social betterment and in the former case they were triumphant. Public works to improve the sanitation and buildings of Birmingham were begun, no timid fear of interference with vested rights deterred them. Slums were demolished, new streets built, libraries, public baths and hospitals opened, and the town acquired its own water and gas. There was a local social revolution; *laissez-faire* was overthrown—all this was made possible by the astuteness of Chamberlain and his Liberal Association.

Party membership was now open to every burgess, whether elector or not. The ward committees were reorganized, they elected an executive committee for the town to which thirty members were added, elected at a public meeting from the general committee. There were nearly six hundred in all, the cream of Birmingham democracy, needless to say, all devoted to their mayor. Many of them were on the Town Council and engaged in active public work.

After the Liberal defeat in 1874 (when Gladstone retired from the leadership), it was generally considered that the Birmingham principle should be universally adopted. A National Federation of Liberal Associations came into being and the great Gladstone himself came to Birmingham to bless it. The excitement was great—a new portent had arisen. It was Disraeli who gave to the new national organization the American name of Caucus. After deliberation the Federation at Birmingham thought that it would be "better to accept the word while trusting to time and experience to attach new and more attractive meanings to it".

It would appear to be the Nemesis of progressive governments that they are as likely to fall by disappointing their advanced supporters as by the attacks of opposition. In no other way is it possible to explain the failure of the Liberal Party in 1874.

The republican movement in France, and the continued seclusion of the Queen at home, had made the monarchy unpopular—on the proposal to give the Princess Louise a marriage dowry of £30,000, Fawcett, Dilke and Taylor had dissented. The Duke of Cambridge, as Commander-in-Chief, was attacked by Trevelyan, a member of the Government, and eighty-three members supported his views with their votes. In 1873 a "republican" conference met in Birmingham, but the Prime Minister was horrified at such disloyalty; this new attitude towards the Crown perplexed him and the older Liberals, they did everything to discourage the Radical elements. There arose a general disintegration. Both on the Budget and in liquor licensing, the Government showed they had no coherent policy. Harcourt, who was one of the most important of the younger Liberals, frequently attacked the Government, and in particular its leader. He moved against them a resolution paraphrastically borrowed from Dunning, that the national expenditure had increased, was increasing and ought to be diminished. He denounced the Home Secretary's Licensing Act, which limited the hours during which public-houses might be open, on the ground that it was an interference with liberty. Emphatically he was not a member of the new collectivist school! "I don't admire a grand maternal government which ties night-caps on a grown-up nation by Act of Parliament," he said. "The policy of the Liberal Party has been for generations a policy of emancipation from restriction, and is it now to begin to forge fresh fetters for the free?" That, indeed, was the question.

On March 12th, 1873, Gladstone had been defeated by three votes on an Irish University scheme, the Irish Catholics opposing. He resigned, but on Disraeli refusing office, resumed a few days after; the incident did nothing to rehabilitate the Government. Not long after, he was inveigled into a speech against disestablishment in England which increased his disfavour with the Nonconformists. On the resignation of Lowe, he himself took over the office of Chancellor of the Exchequer. The question was raised, must he resign his seat? It was a technical point but, like the cases of Sir John Collier's appointment to the Judicial Committee and the Ewelme rectory qualification, it was used to annoy and discredit him, the object being to represent him to the country as "Jesuitical".

The adverse judicial interpretation of the Conspiracy Law as relating to Trade Disputes produced a declaratory Bill which Harcourt piloted through the Commons, only to be defeated in the Lords. Next year it was carried by Disraeli.

Yet, while politically the Government was sinking, the country was prosperous and not indisposed to progressive measures. The Trade Unionists, little placated by a Bill in 1871 legalizing their funds (which was coupled with another which imposed great liabilities in Trade Disputes) had found that it was easier to obtain shorter hours by threatening strikes than by political methods. Wage increases had been secured through the organization of the agriculture labourers, remuneration pitifully small as judged by modern standards. The Trade Union Congress, representing nearly all the Unions, was increasing in power and endeavouring through its Parliamentary Committee to put pressure upon the Government, more particularly to amend restrictive Trade Union laws. The Radicals and workers generally were becoming restless, they had ceased to have confidence in the Government. Radical measures —a Burials Bill to enable dissenters to officiate in parish churchyards, a Bill to carry a much-needed reform of local government in London, a Bill to abolish the government of counties by Justices and to set up County Boards—were all rejected by a ministry fearful of antagonizing the House of Lords and the powerful landowning classes; "Exhausted Volcanoes" was Disraeli's description of an administration bankrupt of initiative. Moreover, the Queen had turned against Gladstone. His attitude towards the High Church offended her—"Protestant to the heart's core," as she described herself. The royal suggestion that the War Office administration should be chosen to please the Duke of Cambridge as well as the Secretary of State was difficult of acceptance. In the end she did not hesitate to show herself pleased when Gladstone asked for dissolution.

By 1874 the Tories had followed the Liberals in devising a national organization, planned by Eldon Gorst. In January that astute electioneerer had estimated a Conservative majority of three. When the seats were counted their majority was found to be fifty. In reality the situation from a Liberal point of view was even worse, for the Irish came back as an independent organization, fifty-eight strong, under the name of Home Rulers; there were only about a dozen Irish Liberals. In the counties and in the boroughs alike the Conservatives were victorious. In Great Britain alone it was estimated their majority was eighty-three, but the uncertainty of Irish distribution led to a net estimate of fifty; in reality, to quote Gladstone, "it was of much greater strength". The era of Disraelian Imperialism had begun.

One of the most noticeable social features which marked the middle of the nineteenth century had been the growth of organized societies of every kind; some recognized expressly by law (as in the case of limited liability companies first constituted under the Act of 1855; Trade Unions in 1871 and the earlier Friendly Societies), others incorporated by Charter for scientific and philanthropic purposes, and yet others, such as political associations, constituted on an entirely voluntary basis.

These last so completely entered into political activity as to produce a revolution in the method of parliamentary and local government representation, a transformation of power which at the time passed almost unnoticed.

The discipline of the contending forces, now drilled for battle, was greatly increased; individual resignations and hostile votes against party became far more rare. Programmes were prepared for the acceptance of the candidate and legislator, and individual initiative in all party issues regarded as disloyal. In the House the Whips assumed a coercive tone. Agents, acting under an agent-general, reported opinion in the provinces, the machinery of propaganda by poster and by Press was strengthened. In all this we see the beginnings of a great machine, unknown to the constitutional lawyer, but which, in fact, in the hands of a few competent controllers governed the party and thus, if successful, ultimately controlled the nation.

B

At Birmingham, so powerful had the association become that Conservatives (now openly called the "enemy") were practically driven out of public affairs; even the holding by them of public meetings became difficult. The Liberal victory in 1868 had been largely due to the adoption in other constituencies of the "Birmingham Plan". Schnadhorst went about the country hawking model associations and Mr. Gladstone himself praised them. "It is Liberal," he said. But he went on, significantly: "At Birmingham they are tolerably advanced, but they don't attempt to exclude the most moderate". (*Speech at Nottingham*, September 27th, 1877.)

There still existed, however, the old Central Liberal Association, controlled by the Parliamentary Leaders and Whips—it was Whig through and through, and regarded the new Federation with undisguised alarm. Lord Hartington, who had temporarily succeeded Gladstone as leader in opposition, was of the old school; Bright, now daily becoming more moderate, supported him.

When Gladstone reappeared in 1876 to fight the case for the eastern Christians against the Turk, the Federation stood behind him—no less than thirty thousand people were organized to hear the orator denounce Disraeli and the Turk at Birmingham. Hartington, on the other hand, unwisely declined to address the first annual meeting of the Federation. He attacked the organization as "American"; he declared it to be solely Radical, which Chamberlain would not admit; the meeting was held without him—again the official party was defeated.

In 1876 Chamberlain had been returned to Parliament at a by-election. On Gladstone's motions demanding that no material or moral support be given to Turkey, but that local government in the disturbed (that is, Christian) provinces be accorded, he found Chamberlain on his side. But the attempt of the Whigs to whittle down the Liberal attack to the denial of arms or a declaration that Turkey had forfeited all claim to British support induced Gladstone, to Chamberlain's disgust, to limit his resolution.

Gladstone's sentiments, however, embodied in pamphlet form and in great meetings was transparently clear. The Turks should be "cleared out from the provinces they have desolated and profaned, bag and baggage". For the moment he and the Radicals, save a few who hated Russia even more than Turkey, were as one.

The Constantinople conference, where Salisbury represented the Government, had failed to stop war between Russia and Turkey—it was then that the famous resolution was tabled. Gladstone, after his speech, was defeated by one hundred and thirty votes. In 1878 Russia entered Adrianople, and was drawing in on Constantinople. The Cabinet asked for a special vote of money, the British fleet passed the Dardanelles. The Russians replied by approaching to within thirty miles of the Turkish capital. Patriotic sentiment in London was intense—Gladstone's windows were broken, the "Imperial country" which Disraeli had proclaimed was reverting to a Palmerstonian condition. The purchase of the Suez Canal shares in 1875, the proclamation of the Queen as Empress of India, and Disraeli's general success in converting the Tories to the "vision of Empire" had roused the people to an excitement against Russia comparable to that which produced the Crimean War.

The Russians had freed Bulgaria from the Turks, but the Tories and the "Jingoes", as they came to be called, regarded that Christian province as merely under Russian vassalage. Austrians and Russians were in competition for the south-east of Europe. The German Chancellor had it in mind to destroy France first; that failing, he worked to help Austrian power in the Balkans, the policy being that the loose federation should become his dependant. It suited him to side with Disraeli and call a halt to Slavonic ambition.

There followed the Treaty of Berlin, which, though hailed in England as "Peace with honour", in fact aggrandized the Germans. Not for many years, however, was this realized. Russia had been held, Constantinople was still Turkish; that was all that concerned the British patriot. Even Gladstone was satisfied; Rumania, Servia, Montenegro and southern Bulgaria were free; it was for a later generation, at Serajevo, to realize how greatly Teutonic ambitions had been served by this inappeasable British fear of Russia. While Germany was increasingly menacing Europe, England persisted in regarding the distant Russia as her foe. To the Tories, her claims in the Balkans affronted patriotic sentiment; to the Liberals, Russian despotism was an iniquity.

As the time for the General Election drew near it was clear that Gladstone must again return, but still the Radicals under Chamberlain and Dilke had their many contentions with their nominal chief in the Commons, the Whiggish Hartington. On flogging in the army, Bright, Forster and Trevelyan all regretted the Whig complacency with existing discipline; it was evident that Hartington could not count on the support of the live elements in the Liberal Party. If Beaconsfield were defeated, Gladstone would have to be the Leader again.

Yet in matters economic the Radicals were almost as loath to advance as were the Whigs. Chamberlain alone protested against the Government Bill which restricted the borrowing powers of municipalities—the Liberals as a whole were still fast bound to *laissez-faire*. Indeed it was on the Conservative side that a recognition of the "condition of the people" questions was chiefly to be found; the Artisans' Dwellings Bill of Cross, the Home Secretary, inaugurated housing legislation. It sought to do for the country as a whole what Chamberlain had achieved in Birmingham—to enable local authorities to remove insanitary buildings and erect new ones. Fawcett, the Radical, characteristically opposed this invasion of proprietary right, and he was not the only one. Next, Friendly Societies received attention, their solvency being made capable of investigation by the State. A new Conspiracy Act removed doubts which were still held about the effect in the criminal law of Gladstone's Act of 1871 dealing with trade disputes. For this measure the Government was thanked by the Trade Union Congress. The one "Labour" member, MacDonald, nominally a Liberal, must ruefully have compared the failure of his own party to deal with social injustice contrasted with the activity of the more enlightened Tories.

Agricultural tenants now received that compensation for removal which Gladstone had only conceded to Ireland. In the same year, 1875, a great Public Health Act was passed, and in 1878 Lord Shaftesbury had the satisfaction of seeing a consolidating Factory Act enacted by which the hours of labour for women and young persons were reduced to fifty-

six a week or ten-and-a-half a day—this also was opposed by Fawcett
and no less than seventy-nine Liberals! In 1876 merchant shipping
was protected by statute and the lives of the sailors made more
safe.

Thus the great change over from Individualism to Collective Action,
of which so many publicists have written, took place under Conservative
auspices. In the face of history it is vain for the Liberals, other than the
followers of Chamberlain, to claim the credit; yet, once the Rubicon was
crossed, we do not find that there was any longer any notable cleavage
between the two parties on this issue—both were now prepared to
ameliorate conditions by public action, while at the same time neither
desired to interfere with the processes of profit-making and capitalist
finance. But already John Stuart Mill, in his later writings, had passed
over to a collectivist position; the Socialist criticism of monopoly in land
and capital was slowly seeping into the minds of the working people and
the less conventional intellectual classes. The Trade Union Congress,
which had been founded in 1869, afforded a platform for the new idea.
Even the less revolutionary Trade Unionists now demanded laws for
compensation in case of industrial accidents and an increase in the number
of factory inspectors.

The congress were active in obtaining the 1875 legislation, free-
ing Trade Unionists from fear of criminal prosecution in combining
in trade disputes, being advised in particular by Professor Beesly and
Frederick Harrison the Positivist, and they were much concerned to
assist to promote the Employer's Liability Act of 1880. Later, they came
actually to participate in government in the person of Broadhurst (once
Secretary of the Congress Parliamentary Committee), and Mundella, the
President of the Board of Trade, who had for so long advised the Congress.
But this was not achieved until 1886. About this time Herschell, the
Lord Chancellor, and Trevelyan, in the Duchy of Lancaster, first
appointed "workmen magistrates".

For the time being, however, active Liberal sympathy with Labour
was conspicuously absent. The excitement shown by Gladstone at the
introduction of the Public Worship Regulation Act to "put down
Ritualism", though important to the ecclesiastical mind, merely
bewildered the mass of the people on whom the Liberals relied or, if they
were Low Church or Nonconformist, annoyed them. His campaign against
"Vaticanism" did nothing to allay the suspicion which most Progressives
felt (and feel) towards those who hold sacerdotal or sacramental principles.
All this was before his whirling campaign in support of the Balkan
Peoples. In that enthusiasm, his foibles (as the people saw the deepest
part of his convictions) were overlooked.

But the most serious innovation in political life of the time has still
to be mentioned; for now there appeared a party in Parliament who
asked, not so much for the redress of grievances or the maintenance of
rights, as to be allowed to depart altogether—the Irish Home Rule
Nationalists.

Gradually, it will be found, all other divergencies between parties
come to be aligned according to their treatment of this matter. That a
small and depopulated island should throw the whole machinery of
British government and the prospects of social progress into confusion

may now be considered absurd—nevertheless, it so happened. It is not too much to say that for fifty years from this time Parliament and politics were dominated by what came to be called "The Irish Question".

CHAPTER VII

THE GREAT SCHISM

THE inability of the Queen to appreciate the forces which had united to produce the great Liberal majority in 1880 was never more clearly shown than in her endeavours to exclude the organizers of victory, Gladstone and Chamberlain, from the direction of affairs. In April the Queen saw Lord Hartington and asked him to form a Government; actually the Leader of the Party at the time was Granville.

The Whig statesman replied that he did not think that a Government could satisfactorily be formed without Gladstone, who would only come in as First Minister. On April 23rd Hartington saw Gladstone and stated that he and Granville had advised the Queen that Gladstone should be sent for—they both agreed to serve under him, Granville to return to the Foreign Office. After the Queen had stated that "some expressions of his had caused her concern", he kissed her hands and prepared to form a Government.

At the outset there were difficulties over Radical participation, for Forster had quarrelled with the progressive wing over Education and another advanced man was needed. The Prime Minister sent for Dilke, who refused to serve unless Chamberlain was in the Cabinet. After much protest, Gladstone surrendered; he was as loath to have the great democrat as the Queen was to have himself. A Cabinet half composed of Whig peers was scarcely such as the new Liberal Federation could approve. From the outset Chamberlain found himself in suspicious, if not hostile, company; in the past he had fought nearly all of them. Dilke, his particular friend, had been excluded from the Cabinet. Bright was fast becoming an uncritical Gladstonian, Harcourt was Chamberlain's only ally—and he was not very dependable.

Outside Downing Street, however, the social reformer had both Press and political machinery on his side. The *Daily News*, the *Pall Mall Gazette* (with John Morley as Editor) supported him; the *Birmingham Daily Post* was his, the *Manchester Guardian* sympathetic. In the outer government, Dilke had great popularity among the intellectual forces of Progress. But above all, the great Trade Unions were behind Chamberlain. He was a powerful man to tackle, more particularly now that he was inside the citadel. Meanwhile there was nothing to be done but to wait upon events.

The House now consisted of three hundred and forty-seven Liberals of various shades, two hundred and forty Conservatives and the new independent Irish Nationalist Party, some sixty-five in all. In personnel, the Radicals were powerful; Labouchere and Bradlaugh had been returned for Northampton. Firth (the advocate of a general Municipal Council for all London), Thorold Rogers, the economist (who did so much to break down the narrow views of the classical writers and draw attention to economic justice as a part of democracy), Jesse Collings, the friend of Chamberlain; and two specifically working-class members, Burt and Broadhurst, were all in the House, yet, counting heads, the majority of the Liberals were rich industrialists, bankers, brewers, shipowners, together with the remnant of the old Whig families and the inevitable lawyers. Both in the Government and in the House it was a most unstable coalition.

The only Bills passed in 1880 of any real value emanated from Chamberlain's department or owed their passage to his support. He safeguarded seamen's wages and legislated for their safety in his Grain Cargoes Bill. The juridical doctrine that, as workmen elected to go into danger by working with negligent fellow-men, they could not get damages from their employers—the principle of Common Employment, "a most unfortunate example of judicial legislation"—was partly overthrown by the Employers' Liability Act of 1880: it started a movement which finally resulted in the Workmen's Compensation Acts. This, as has been said, was one of the measures which had been demanded by the Trade Union Congress and was an instance of the utility of its Parliamentary Committee. The usual protest that the Bill would interfere with freedom of contract, rights of property and the like came as much from the Ministerial as from the Opposition side of the House. It was evident that they were far from accepting Chamberlain's notion of making the Country as reformable as Birmingham. A Burials Act, to enable Dissenting ministers to bury their people in churchyards, won far more general Liberal assent, though probably it was distasteful to the ecclesiastical layman who led them.

The Bradlaugh agitation may be shortly dismissed; his claim to affirm, instead of talking an oath, was rejected by a majority of one in a committee appointed to enquire into the matter. Thereafter, in the House, by 275 to 230 it was decided that Bradlaugh should not be allowed either to affirm or swear. Though Gladstone made a great speech for toleration, declaring that he had no fear of atheism in the House, the Affirmation Bill was rejected by three votes; it was not until 1885 that Bradlaugh was allowed to take the oath—in 1891 the record of 1881 was struck out and the Affirmation Bill finally passed in 1888.

In Imperial affairs this pacific Government was also unfortunate. The Conservatives had reversed the Liberal renunciation of the Transvaal (which had been accorded in 1852) by annexing it to the Crown, and though Gladstone had criticized this act of aggression he did nothing to reverse it, for he, Bright and Chamberlain had been overruled by the Liberal Imperialists. In 1881 the Boers revolted, defeating the British at Laings Neck and Majuba. In the end, a vague assertion of British supremacy was made, later in 1884, to be abandoned; the Boers thus resumed their independence. The prestige and honour of the Government and the Country had suffered a severe loss. At the northern end of the

African continent, Gladstone, contrary to all his principles, allowed himself, under financial pressure and commitments of the previous Government, to refuse recognition to the first Egyptian Nationalists. It was said that the Khedive must not be deserted. In 1883, the French refusing to use armed force, the British appointed a monetary adviser, and by 1885 they had obtained control over the finances of the country. That year, after the Gordon disaster, the Government barely escaped censure by fourteen votes. Only in Afghanistan, where they had made friends with the Ameer, was a withdrawal consistent with Gladstonian principles possible—for the rest, throughout this uneasy period it was Ireland that held the stage.

In May, 1870, partly as the result of disestablishment which had enraged the Irish Protestants, there had been founded an Irish "Home Government Association". Its purpose was to gain for Ireland the management of internal matters, leaving Imperial affairs to Westminster. Its name was soon changed to the Home Rule League, and an association for the same purpose was set up in England. The sixty-odd members, of whom mention has been made, were returned in 1874, pledged to the programme of the League. Its leader was Isaac Butt, an erstwhile Conservative lawyer, but under him were Fenians, advocates of Tenant-Right and even Orangemen! He himself, unlike many of his followers, was urbane and conciliatory. Every year he presented his Bills to give tenant right and to institute Home Rule, but without any success. It was not, however, until 1879 that the people in England took any active interest in Irish affairs. In that year Davitt, who had been imprisoned as a Fenian, returned to Ireland, passionately concerned for the amelioration of the Irish tenant. Famine was increasing and, under his guidance, a Tenants' Defence Association was formed to press for a general reduction of rents. In October a conference of Nationalist politicians and land reformers met, and an Irish Land League formed with Parnell at its head.

The Fenians did not believe in parliamentary action; some were for the use of physical force, but to this recourse Parnell was always opposed —many, however, were prepared to tolerate the obstructive tactics which he, following Biggar, had introduced at Westminster; a device to talk at great length on every sort of measure so as to make legislation difficult, if not impossible. These tactics had been used by the advanced Nationalists as early as 1877, when, on a protracted obstruction of the Mutiny Bill, Butt was foolish enough to reprove the younger men.

In Ireland it was his ruin, Parnell became a hero; he had worsted the British Lion! In May, 1880, he was elected Chairman of the Irish Party in Parliament.

A promise was made by Forster, the Irish Secretary for the new Government, that a Commission should be appointed to enquire into the working of the 1870 Land Act; meanwhile a Bill, authorizing compensation for disturbance, was thrown out in the Lords, a number of Whig Peers being in the majority. Dillon advised the tenants to pay no more rent till "justice was done". By September fifteen thousand persons were threatened with eviction. Parnell advised "Boycotting"—Captain Boycott to be the first to be "sent to Coventry". An agrarian conflict had started. It did not stop at boycotting; murder became frequent. At last Parnell was tried for conspiracy, but acquitted; the ordinary processes of law had proved useless.

In the result, the Government introduced a Coercion Bill. After a debate of forty-one hours, the Speaker, of his own authority, put the question. At the beginning of March it passed into law. The measure was disliked by many Liberals—as in the case of foreign affairs, once more Gladstone had been forced to deny his own principles. The support of Lord Salisbury, the Conservative Leader, did not increase its popularity with the Radicals. Conciliation, he said, to which the fortunes of the Irish landlords had been sacrificed, had failed.

The Land Bill, soon afterwards introduced, found more favour. The measure set up a Court to decide what was a fair rent, free sale and fixity of tenure, the "three F's" were all conceded by Gladstone to be necessary—in 1870 he had objected to them as an invasion of private proprietary rights. The Irish were gratified, but would not admit it. They now declared that they required complete peasant proprietorship. Parnell had half accepted the Bill, the Fenians would accept nothing. On October 2nd, 1881, Forster, pressing for that act of authority, again decided to arrest Parnell. When, in the following May, the suspects were released—even Tories had argued for this—Forster resigned, and Lord Frederick Cavendish was appointed Chief Secretary.

A few days afterwards he and the Under-Secretary, Burke, were murdered in Phœnix Park. Parnell, who was horrified, offered to resign. Gladstone, believing Parnell to be "sincerely anxious for the pacification of Ireland", refused to countenance the offer. A further Coercion Act was passed in 1882, and Spencer and Trevelyan, as Viceroy and Secretary, proceeded to Ireland. Ireland, to quote a well-informed contemporary, "seemed literally to be a society on the eve of dissolution". Even the Constabulary were disaffected.

To Chamberlain it appeared that the Irish "want to destroy their Government. . . . They also want to make all Government of Ireland by England impossible; all our people", he declared, "Radicals included, will resist them to the death". "They have great practical wrongs and grievances and one sentimental one, the Union." "The latter is one on which we cannot and will not yield." In these words, written to Morley in December, 1881, we hear the first murmurings of a storm which was eventually to wreck the Liberal Party.

The New Crimes Bill, as the Coercion Act was called, suspended juries and gave to the police complete powers of search and arrest on suspicion. Three judges could deal with murder, treason and crimes of violence whenever the Lord-Lieutenant thought that an impartial trial could not be obtained by ordinary law. There was a right of appeal. The Bill was not popular, but Harcourt, who was in charge, persisted. Gladstone, he suspected, was lukewarm, but the Home Secretary threatened to resign if the Bill were altered in principle. Chamberlain, then in touch with Parnell, also objected to Harcourt's attitude, but Dillon's violence converted many waverers, and in the end the Bill became law, after much obstructive debate.

Parnell was now in comparative favour with Gladstone; an Arrears of Rent Bill became law, much in the form which the Irish Leader had suggested, and for the time being, whether because of the strong action of Lord Spencer, the operation of the Crimes Act, or because of a reaction after the Phœnix Park murders, things became quieter in Ireland. There were still some murders to chronicle and there was trouble in the police force, six hundred temporarily resigning in Dublin; but the Cabinet, exhausted, turned to other matters.

Agricultural Holdings Acts were passed, to compensate tenants for improvement and prevent "contracting out"; the Factory Acts were extended to cover those working in dangerous trades. After Dilke became President of the Local Government Board, women inspectors under the Poor Law were appointed; a Royal Commission sat on the Housing of the Working Classes. At the Board of Trade, Chamberlain had produced and carried a Bankruptcy Act which "distinguished between the judicial and administrative aspects of Bankruptcy"; a Bankruptcy department of the Board of Trade was constituted and Official Receivers appointed to act in the large towns. In addition, a new Patents Act was passed with a central office properly equipped with experts. Finally came the Merchant Shipping Bill, violently attacked by the shipowners, most of whom were Liberals. The Cabinet were embarrassed, they did not wish to offend their wealthy supporters—it was a test case, for the preventible death at sea was very great. Chamberlain was defeated, and his Railways Regulation Bill, designed to protect the workers, was withdrawn. It is not surprising that the more advanced of the Trade Unionists, seeing the power of independence in the case of the Irish to extort legislation, should be coming to the conclusion that the Liberal Party was the stronghold of wealthy interests, and begin to think of forming their own organization, but before the time for action had come Chamberlain had left the Liberal Party.

Nothing daunted, the National Liberal Federation prepared for a new Franchise Bill; they realized that the only way to menace plutocracy was to get a new type of member elected and that this could only be done by getting more of the workers on to the register.

A Radical programme appearing in the *Fortnightly* demanded adult suffrage, payment of members and equal electoral districts. A great conference at Leeds began to speak of schemes for Bills rejected more than once by the Lords becoming law in their despite. Their demands were rejected. On February 28th, 1884, Gladstone introduced a new Franchise Bill. It was said that an increase in the electorate of two millions was involved; on June 26th it obtained a third reading. The Conservative opposition had been very perfunctory. In the Lords the usual policy was adopted of threatening to hold up the Bill until a redistribution scheme was introduced by the Government. This was carried as an amendment, and a serious political crisis arose, Lord Salisbury describing the Lower House as Mr. Chamberlain's "registration machine". In one sense he was right, Chamberlain certainly was the spear-head of the Radical attack. As to the Peers—"Mend them or end them", cried John Morley.

The attack now fastened on the House of Lords; not an instance of their illiberal past, and there were many, was forgotten. The violence of the Radicals, now infuriated, alarmed both Mr. Gladstone and the ageing Queen. Chamberlain was notified of the Queen's displeasure:

"This was no true Liberal feeling", she wrote, "but destructive". She called on Gladstone "to restrain, as he can, some of his wild colleagues and followers".

A riot at Aston forced the Queen to even more active protest—she accused Gladstone of approving the "disgraceful riot at Birmingham". It had been caused by the Tories holding a great meeting in Aston Park, a sacred place, ordained for Radical assemblies. Two great crowds fought one another and Randolph Churchill had to flee. He used the occasion to move a vote of censure on Chamberlain. It was rejected by only thirty-six; it was evident that the Whigs also were becoming thoroughly frightened.

At last negotiations took place on redistribution; single-member constituencies were to be the rule and not the exception. Minority representation was to go. "Not bad for a Tory Bill", commented Chamberlain to Morley. He had reason to approve; all constituencies with under fifteen thousand electors were to be disfranchised, all two-seated places from fifteen thousand to fifty thousand to have but one member. There was to be no reduction in Irish representation.

The Conservatives gained nothing by their delay and compromise, but it did mean the final end of Whiggery, still ensconced in a certain number of small boroughs. Thereafter, had the Radicals stood together, their triumph would have been assured.

In its final form the new franchise reposed uniformly on a £10 yearly value of household, lodger or service qualification. Two million new electors were created and London obtained thirty-seven, Liverpool six, and Yorkshire and elsewhere, thirty-one new members.

One of the consequences (which the Conservative Party in the House of Lords had tried to prevent during the passage of the Franchise Act) was greatly to increase the power of Parnell and the Nationalist Party in Ireland. It will be recalled that the number of seats accorded to that country was not to be affected by redistribution, and the voting power now given to the agricultural poor ensured that Nationalism outside Ulster was without a rival. The General Election in 1885 resulted in the return, mostly unopposed, of no less than eighty-six Home Rulers.

Meanwhile, Parnell, dropping the Land agitation, conceived a new plan whereby to win Home Rule; he determined to tempt the two British parties to outbid one another for the Irish vote.

By the end of 1884, after years of sterile attempts at coercion, a feeling was growing that a solution did not lie that way. Chamberlain and Dilke were prepared to favour an Irish National Council which would govern Ireland in domestic affairs, it being understood that Imperial concerns should continue to be directed from Westminster—there must be no "separation". These proposals were regarded by Parnell as a mere instalment or, possibly, only as an offer, to be contrasted with whatever might come from the Conservative side. However this may be, the Radicals in the Cabinet presented them to Gladstone sincerely as a means of final settlement; owing principally to the unreliability of the go-between, O'Shea, the Irish and English reformers were really never *ad idem*.

Notwithstanding the approval of Gladstone, the peace proposals of

Chamberlain (which included a modification of the Crimes Act) met with scant approval from the Whigs. Spencer, the Viceroy, would not agree to a National Council; he would concede more Land Purchase, but insisted that the Crimes Act must be maintained in all its vigour. In April, 1885, the Viceroy declared that he now "leaned to some Central Board, but the difficulties are very great". Cardinal Manning said that the Catholic Church would support Parnell if he would accept a scheme of local government. In May, Harcourt gave the scheme his support, but Hartington and all the Peers in the Cabinet, except Granville, opposed— a deadlock had arisen.

Chamberlain and Dilke threatened to resign—at most they would not tolerate a new Crimes Act for more than a year; Land Purchase they regarded as mere "tinkering". In the end Gladstone introduced a Bill to renew the Coercion Law, saying that in that session it was not possible to proceed either with land purchase or local government. Dilke, and then Chamberlain, resigned, and Gladstone at last, without consulting them, introduced a Land Purchase Bill, to which, he said, he understood that the Radicals had agreed.

At this juncture, Lord Randolph Churchill declared that he also was opposed to coercion. Parnell, foolishly, placed more faith in him than in the Radicals—he forgot that the Conservative Party, from whom Churchill derived what little power he had, was far more hostile to Irish and even more concerned to maintain Imperial unity than any Whig. For the moment, however, Churchill was in opposition. In a debate the previous November about murders at Maamtrasna, where Lord Spencer had refused an enquiry, he had supported the Irish demand—Parnell jumped to the conclusion that it was time to try the Tories.

On an amendment to the Budget (in which on a question of beer duty the Cabinet were divided) the Nationalists cast their vote for the Opposition and the Government were defeated by twelve votes. This was on June 8th; on June 11th, after some correspondence with the Queen, the Prime Minister resigned and Lord Salisbury was called upon to form his first administration.

The declaration of the new Government's Irish Policy was left to the new Viceroy, Lord Carnarvon; he pointed out that Ireland had been under exceptional laws with few intervals since 1847, and said, amid general astonishment, that the Government were prepared to risk the dropping of the coercion laws. In the Commons, Spencer was denounced by Churchill, to the agitation of the Queen, for his severe administration. This alarmed the Tories generally; it was pointed out by one of them that Lord Spencer had risked his life in upholding the law, with the approval in particular of the Conservative Party. Chamberlain, while not dissociating himself, approved the abandonment of coercion. Lord Salisbury also, to mark his dissent from the attacks of Churchill, Gorst and others, eulogized Spencer.

But a greater difficulty to Lord Salisbury was the approval which Home Rule had won from his own Lord-Lieutenant, Carnarvon.

It is not easy to say what took place. When at length Carnarvon, in the summer of 1885, had an interview with Parnell, according to the Irishman the Viceroy had told him that the Conservatives would offer to Ireland a statutory legislature if they had the power. Carnarvon subsequently denied that he had spoken with the authority of the Government—certainly Salisbury was, in fact, always opposed to any concession.

Meanwhile, it was clear that Chamberlain and Dilke had been deceived. Manning refused an introduction to the Irish Bishops, and the Irish Press, controlled by Parnell, attacked them as mere users of Ireland for British Radical purposes. Finally, Parnell, on August 20th, openly stated that he would fight the election on legislative independence for Ireland—all question of National Councils was at an end.

In July, Herbert, Gladstone's son, declared at Leeds for full Home Rule, and in the middle of August, about the time of Parnell's declaration, Parliament was dissolved.

A new conception of democracy is noticeable in the Radical election appeals. "New conceptions of public duty, new developments of social enterprise, new estimates of the natural obligation of the members of the community to one another, have come into view and demand consideration", appeared in Chamberlain's preface to the "Radical Programme". Their proposals, written with Chamberlain's approval it was said, "sound the death-knell of the *laissez-faire* system".

The Radical Leader himself spoke of the "social evils which disgrace our civilization and the wrongs which have cried vainly for redress", and added significantly, "if we cannot convince our allies (the Liberals) of the justice and reasonableness of our cause, we must part company". From the Collectivists he had taken heart to say: "We have to account for, and to grapple with, the mass of misery and destitution in our midst, co-existent as it is with the evidence of abundant wealth—it is a problem put aside by references to the eternal laws of supply and demand, to the necessity of freedom of contract, and to the sanctity of every private right of property. These phrases are the convenient cant of selfish wealth".

But with these socialistic sentiments he remained resolute to defy Parnell, saying that he would not enter into a competition with the Tories to secure him an independent Parliament. "I will not allow that five million Irishmen have the right to govern themselves without regard to the rest of the United Kingdom, any more than five million inhabitants of the Metropolis." That was his case; for it he destroyed in the social field all hope of achieving his ambitions.

Although Chamberlain and his followers were denounced as Socialists, it is clear that in the 'eighties progressive public opinion was divided between those who had merely come to doubt the old idea that each individual should be free to work out his own destiny without State interference, the reformers who were not prepared to deny that there were occasions when the State might usefully protect the weak (taking the view expressed by Jevons in 1882 that "it is futile to attempt to uphold, in regard to social legislation, any theory of abstract rights, it is all a question of probability and degree"), and the avowed Socialists, who found representation in the Social Democratic Federation and the Fabian Society, and asked for the "Nationalization of the means of Production, Distribution and Exchange".

Of these the "Radical Programme" inclined to the more moderate view. Despite the denunciation of its Leader as "Jack Cade", "Dick Turpin" and the like, Chamberlain was only a Socialist in the sense that Harcourt had said "we are all Socialists now". He repudiated the dead hand of *laissez-faire*, it is true, but the Tories had never accepted it—all he asked was that there should be no prejudice against the employment of the State and Municipality to redress specific abuses. At the same time he and his school set no limit, save that of expediency, to possible collectivist activity.

In particular the Radicals sought to appeal to the new county electors, promising the labourer treatment such as had been given in Ireland— "Three acres and a cow", as a Conservative derisively said—and, for the wealthier country dweller, the benefit of a simplification of land transfer. Both sides seemed to think that the time had come when the Government of the counties should be taken from the magistrates and given to County Boards. On Ireland, Lord Salisbury was reticent, though Parnell campaigned actively on his behalf, or rather against the Liberals. The large Irish vote in the industrial towns was told to turn Tory, and to a great extent obeyed; Parnell was seeking to produce a situation in which he could conduct an auction. Yet Salisbury had declared unequivocally against Irish parliamentary independence; even in local government a hint was given by him of the peculiar dangers in Ireland where "the population is on several subjects deeply divided". This is almost the first reference to the Ulster problem which afterwards became so important.

The Irish, throwing their vote in with the Tories, did much outside Birmingham to weaken the Liberals in the towns; probably also the shopkeeping class were beginning to be alarmed at Chamberlain's appeal to the working people. In the result, in the boroughs the Conservatives had a majority, but the counties told a different tale—the final result was three hundred and thirty-five Liberals, two hundred and forty-nine Conservatives and eighty-six Home Rulers.

Parnell had succeeded in holding the balance. Whether his tactics had been wise, time was to show.

Gladstone now endeavoured to come to some understanding with Salisbury for an agreed measure; this would perhaps have defeated Parnell, saved England from much acrimony, and in the end trained the Irish to self-government. It might even have satisfied Chamberlain; but it was not to be.

While Balfour, Salisbury's trusted nephew, was at Eaton, staying with the Liberal Duke of Westminster, Gladstone came over from Hawarden; the old man said that if some concession were not made to Parnell the Irishman would possibly resort to violence in England. "We are to be blown up or stabbed if we do not grant Home Rule by the end of the next Session?" asked Balfour. "I understand", said Gladstone, "that the time is shorter than that." The younger statesman reported to his uncle that Hartington, Goschen, Chamberlain and Dilke were all anti-Parnellites. He adds in his letter to Salisbury, and this may explain much, "Chamberlain finds it impossible to forgive the Irish Party for the way in which they have treated him and his Radical following".

Lord Salisbury, undeterred, repudiated all idea of Home Rule and, while a fresh Coercion Bill was being secretly prepared, a rural reform motion opposed by eighteen Whigs and seventy-eight other Liberals was carried as an amendment to the address by seventy-nine votes, and Salisbury resigned.

Before this, however, Granville, Spencer, Hartington and Rosebery had all become acquainted with the desire of Gladstone to concede a statutory parliament to Ireland, "Union of Empire and the supremacy of the Imperial Parliament being maintained". The reaction of Chamberlain was to say, "Mr. Parnell has appealed to the Tories. Let him settle accounts with his new friends". In substance he favoured leaving the Tories in office; it was a suggestion not very different from that which Gladstone had made to Salisbury through Balfour.

Parnell now, at length, discovered that his plans had failed; the Conservatives would rather relinquish office than give him Home Rule —all his labour to put them in had proved futile. His sympathizer, Carnarvon, while the Conservatives were still in power, and the Chief Secretary, Hart Dyke, had both resigned; but this was not generally known until the middle of January, 1886. As has been said, a new Coercion Bill had been prepared on the 27th; when the new secretary, W. H. Smith, brought back his Bill from Dublin, the Government had already resigned.

Despite the sympathetic treatment which Chamberlain has received at the hand of Garvin, his biographer, it is not easy to believe that personal resentment did not take a large part in his subsequent attitude. Beyond all question he had been basely treated by Parnell, O'Shea, and the Irish Party generally. He had resigned from the Cabinet because they could not carry the most advanced proposal for a National Council with domestic supremacy which had yet been proposed, and he had refused to tolerate indefinite coercion; by way of gratitude he had been reviled by Parnell and the whole Irish vote thrown against him and the other Radicals. Undoubtedly he was full of indignation. Nevertheless, knowing Gladstone's views, he re-entered the Cabinet. He took the Local Government Board. Harcourt was Chancellor of the Exchequer; Rosebery Foreign Secretary, and Campbell-Bannerman Secretary for War. Most significant, Morley, who had always supported Irish government of a "colonial type", was made Irish Secretary. Hartington, Goschen and Derby declined to serve; the rumours of the intentions of Gladstone, ever since the statement on December 6th in the *Leeds Mercury* that he wished to establish a Parliament in Dublin for dealing with purely Irish affairs, though dismissed at the time as "merely a speculation", had alarmed them.

The relations between Chamberlain and the Prime Minister, always strained, had not been made the more easy by the offer to him of the Admiralty, Gladstone's objecting to making him Colonial Secretary, and by an abortive attempt to reduce the salary of his friend Collings.

Yet, in so far as Chamberlain was willing to take office, albeit with "unlimited liberty of judgment and rejection" of Irish proposals, he showed a desire to avoid a breach. The difficulty is to see in the difference between an acceptable National Council, such as he had suggested, and a local Parliament, such a divergence as would justify his subsequent conduct. "He was willing", says Garvin, "not to go beyond a subordinate legislature compatible with Home Rule all round." (*Life of Chamberlain*,

Vol. 2, p. 179.) "He would not go beyond a point" (*ibid.*, p. 180), but what was the point beyond which he would not go? This neither Garvin nor any other writer has made clear. Chamberlain's honesty is beyond question. He knew, as he told Morley, that he would be left almost alone for a time. "I cannot of course work with the Tories", he said, "and Hartington is quite as much hostile to my Radical views as to Mr. G's Irish plans."

The crisis came on a proposed scheme of the Prime Minister to buy out the landlords in Ireland for £120,000,000 at twenty years' purchase. Chamberlain insisted that before he agreed he should be told the contents of the Home Rule Bill—Harcourt apparently already knew them. Then it came out—a separate Parliament for Ireland with full powers to deal with the Irish affairs. This differed only from the National Council scheme by abolishing representation at Westminster, but for this double representation Chamberlain never before had pressed.

Chamberlain thereupon said he must resign, Trevelyan took the same course. A scheme comparable to the "States basis in the United States", Chamberlain said, could have been discussed. On March 26th, Gladstone replied to Chamberlain's questions: Irish representation at Westminster was to cease, taxation in Ireland would be given to the Irish Parliament, they were to appoint the Judges and have authority in matters not excluded. On this Chamberlain and Trevelyan withdrew. Had the second condition been called Local Taxation, Chamberlain had already agreed to it in his own scheme. The last was a mere matter of exclusion by Schedule, a drafting point. The appointment of Judges had not been considered in the Irish Council scheme; in any case, as there would be an appeal to the Privy Council, it does not seem a sufficient reason for the rupture.

Outside the Government, Randolph Churchill now abandoned his coquetting with Parnell, and stirred up the Ulstermen; rioting occurred in Belfast. "Ulster will fight and Ulster will be right", he cried. Not long before, the Ulstermen in Liverpool had forced him to abandon a meeting on account of his suspected alliance with Parnell! Finally, he invented a name for a new party, the "Unionist", and asked the dissentient Liberals to join it. He succeeded in working the country into a state of anxiety and alarm.

Chamberlain was now asked to join the Tories, or the Whigs; by the Radicals he was petitioned to save the Liberal Party. Under pressure he even went so far as to say there must be a legislative body or bodies in Ireland. The Prime Minister, to meet him, gave up the claim that Ireland should have control of Customs and Excise; but this did not content—there remained the cessation of Irish representation at Westminster and the appointment of Judges to divide him from Morley and the other Liberals. In the debate on introduction—April 8th—for almost the first time Chamberlain said "Ireland is not a homogeneous community—it comprises two races and two religions". It was Churchill's argument, but in the past it had not prevented either of them from seeking an understanding with Parnell, nor did Chamberlain's proposed National Council for all Ireland recognize the division as an insuperable difficulty.

"Even now", he writes to Gladstone, "the differences may be further reduced when the second reading is taken." On the debate on the Land Bill he contended that if there were to be a legislature in Dublin there would have to be another one in Belfast; yet he admitted that the Bill had been much modified to meet him. Friends and enemies alike were confused as what he really wanted or to what he took objection.

At Birmingham, after a fierce fight, he defeated Schnadhorst, and the Caucus supported its member; but later, in London, the general committee of the Federation carried a resolution expressing confidence in Gladstone. The motion of Birmingham, asking for Irish representation to remain at Westminster, was defeated, and Chamberlain resigned from the national body.

The vital matter, he now said, was to maintain the Irish at Westminster; if this were granted he would vote for the second reading. As the Bill now stood there would be an Irish Executive, with Law and Police under its powers, it would pay one-twelfth of the taxes collected to the Imperial Treasury. This provision alone showed that its autonomy was limited; establishment and endowment of religion was also excluded. Chamberlain raised the question of Irish control of the declaration of war and of the armed forces. Salisbury declared the Irish were incapable of self-government; it was the prevailing opinion in England.

At last Gladstone announced that he would compromise on the retention of Irish members at Westminster. How, after this, Chamberlain could continue his opposition- except upon Harcourt's supposition that "he has no thought but war to the knife", it is not easy to understand. Salisbury and Hartington appeared together at a great meeting, and Gladstone was socially ostracized. But Chamberlain had never been in Society; such exhibitions of bad manners in the ruling class meant nothing to him; he had won the concession, declared by him to be vital. He showed his teeth; refused to attend a meeting of the Liberal Party and summoned one for May 31st, the next day, of his own group. All depended upon him—if he abstained the Bill would get a second reading; if he voted against it, it meant defeat. Parnell, if he were capable of admitting error, must have regretted the day when he betrayed Chamberlain and was in his turn disowned by Churchill.

In the end, when his party meeting was held, Chamberlain refused to give them advice. He stated the case both ways, but concluded by reading a letter from Bright, saying that he would vote against the second reading. That decided them; the fifty agreed to oppose the Bill.

On June 1st Chamberlain spoke in the House. He denied inconsistency, but now declared that he could not see that the amendments suggested by the Prime Minister would meet his objections in any considerable measure; but the old statesmen had the last word—taking up Chamberlain's statement that a dissolution had no terrors for him he went on to say, "I do not wonder at it. He has trimmed his vessel and touched his rudder in such a masterly way that, whichever direction the winds of heaven may blow, they must fill his sails".

When the tellers came to the table it was seen that Home Rule had been defeated by thirty (343 to 313)—forty-six of the malcontents had followed Chamberlain, the remaining dissentient forty-seven Liberals were Whig.

A new organization, the National Radical Union, supplied Chamberlain with opportunities for meetings all over England. He spoke much of his conscience and his honour. He spoke of British courage and British pluck in a manner worthy of Randolph Churchill himself; he spoke of cowards quailing before the assassin and the dagger, but he did not explain how it was that, when terrorism was at its height in Ireland, he had been willing to hand over to the assassins or their friends the whole internal government of that country.

CHAPTER VIII

IN THE WILDERNESS

THE defection of Chamberlain, for reasons which must, it is suggested, having regard to the slender grounds of difference, be deemed insufficient, had the most far-reaching effects upon political development. It is at least possible, had he remained to lead the Radicals, that the Labour Party, which ultimately undermined the confidence of the working people in Liberalism, would never have come into being. The gradual absorption of the Whig elements into Conservatism was inevitable, but Chamberlain stood in quite a different position—indeed the departure of Hartington, Goschen and other territorial and city magnates could only have strengthened his control over the party at large. Almost certainly he would have succeeded Gladstone as Prime Minister. In that office, in control of the party machine, the first political leader in whom the trade unions and reformers generally had confidence, he might have proved irresistible. The academic shibboleths of Socialism would not have bound him, as later they did the Labour Leaders, nor would that doctrine have embarrassed him in soliciting the votes of such of the middle classes as were not wedded to materialist economics—instead, he came gradually to abandon his own programme. Apart from intermittent incursions into that province of social reform which he had made peculiarly his own, he sank back into the acceptance of a plutocratic imperialism, never more clearly indicated than in his acceptance of the Boer War.

Meanwhile, Home Rule was dead; not the Lords, but the people's House, had rejected it. If the interested Irish vote were deducted, the opinion against the proposal was irresistible. In the new Commons, after the General Election, the hostile majority was one hundred and eighteen. The Conservatives had a majority of over forty against Gladstone and Parnell; in the whole House they were in a minority of twenty. Thus they were driven to depend upon Chamberlain and Hartington.

There was, however, no real fear of defeat. Arrangements had already been made before the election for "Unionists" (as they were now called) not to oppose one another; on the other hand, Gladstonian Liberals had not hesitated to fight Chamberlain's candidates—the fissure was already complete.

A suggestion to make Hartington Prime Minister failed, and Salisbury, for the second time, became Premier, Churchill taking the Exchequer— there was to be no open coalition as yet. Soon a crucial test was offered. Chamberlain declared that he would not vote for an amendment "equivalent to a vote of censure on the Government". "I shall do nothing to turn out the Government, so long as the Government which would take its place is committed to a separate policy." Nevertheless, he still asked that the tenants of Ireland should be given land through State purchase.

A crisis nearly arose over the proposed new County Councils, a proposal which it was thought would remove the last power of the governing class as magistrates in quarter sessions to administer the counties. As so often is the case, their fears were entirely unfounded; apart from mining and similar industrial areas, the County Councils, when constituted, in nearly every case consisted of the same class of landed gentry who as Justices had formerly ruled the county—indeed their supremacy was even greater, it turned out, than before, for in time Labour men were nominated as Justices in many County areas; the expense of travel, the cost of contest and general inertia often had the result that no single member could be said by any reasonable interpretation directly to represent the working class on the new Councils.

All this, however, was not realized in 1887. It was reported to Chamberlain that the new Councils were to be filled in part by *ex officio* members. Salisbury was told that Chamberlain insisted as the price of his support that they should be wholly elective. The Government compromised, aldermen elected by the Council were to be created, following the borough tradition; the police to come under a joint committee of magistrates and councillors—in such form the Local Government Act of 1888 was passed. As time went on considerable powers and duties came to be entrusted to the Councils, and to County Boroughs who had the like powers. The advance towards collective action in matters of Health, Roads, Housing and the like increased yearly as more activities were entrusted to these local governing bodies. The staffs grew ever greater and more competent; alone in the personnel of the elected members there was practically no change. In the result the governing of most counties fell into the hands of the chairman and a few colleagues, but administration was controlled by officials to a far greater degree than it was in Parliament, for opposition in the Council Chamber was, in most cases, non-existent.

Nevertheless, though it was not then recognized, the establishment of County Councils was greatly to encourage socialistic experiment. The Fabian Society, under the skilful guidance of Sidney Webb, realized the opportunity. The Bill which became law on August 13th, 1888, made London into a new county, though the City retained many of its peculiar privileges. An advanced party, calling themselves Progressives, set out to rival Birmingham in municipal activity. The election of Lord Rosebery as first Chairman was carried, a few Radicals only objecting, and he certainly did much to give the new body a feeling of corporate dignity. The vigour of the London Progressives and the healthy state of Liberalism therein was in marked contrast to the confusion at Westminster, where Whigs and the followers of Chamberlain combined to force a feeling of inadequacy and frustration upon the followers of Mr. Gladstone.

The sudden resignation of Churchill on the most unconservative of issues—a complaint of the undue size of the service estimates—robbed Chamberlain of his most advanced Cabinet associate. It was at this time that he made a suggestion that a round-table conference between himself and the Gladstonians might even now end the discord: "A frank conference on the part of the members with him and those who disagreed with his line of action with reference to the Irish question". Harcourt agreed cordially—Gladstone concurred. Hartington, however, stood aloof; to him Chamberlain stated that he would never agree to a Parliament in Dublin with an executive dependent on it. On land and local government, he thought, there was room for compromise. The Conference met three times in January and February, 1887. Chamberlain declared that he would consider Home Rule on the Canadian basis, but Ulster must receive separate treatment. As to representation at Westminster, Harcourt was in favour, Morley against. In the end nothing resulted. "All hope of a reunion was abandoned" is the entry in Chamberlain's memorandum, made shortly after the February meeting.

In that year he supported by his vote the Tory address to the Crown, as did Hartington and Bright. He took no objection to the new Crimes Act which occupied Parliament from March until July. It was piloted by Arthur Balfour, the new Irish Secretary, with great skill amid constant Nationalist obstruction. To two matters the Liberal Unionists objected: the holding of trials for Irish offences in certain cases in England and the proclamation of the National League. In the latter case, though Hartington supported the Government, Chamberlain voted in opposition —the proscription of the League was carried, however, by seventy-seven votes.

The severity of Balfour's methods of coercion was greater than anything Harcourt had formerly countenanced. In the earlier days the eviction of tenants had not played a principal part in the disturbances, but now they could no longer pay the rents which had been fixed by the Land Courts, or would not. Chamberlain and Churchill demanded some concession and the Government surrendered, giving power to the Court to revise the rents originally fixed.

Parnell had introduced a Bill which would have halved all rents. On this being rejected, the tenants were advised by their leaders to pay only a part of their rents into a pool, which, if the landlord refused, was to be used for "defence", a term often including boycotting and terrorism, though to the latter method Parnell had always objected. This scheme was called the "Plan of Campaign"—the Liberals were ambiguous about it, some even went to speak in support. In the end there was a general consensus that the system of dual ownership was a failure, the only solution was to buy out the landlords; in effect this was the only matter on which all parties agreed. Prosecution and Proclamation failed to stop the Plan of Campaign, and murder and violence continued. Nevertheless, in 1889 Balfour introduced Irish Drainage Bills and, in 1890 (taking money from the disestablished Church surplus of £41,000 a year and £84,000 from the Fishery Loan Funds), he took over the Congested Areas (places where the land could not support its inhabitants), using the money for assistance and development: weaving, improving stock and implements, providing seed potatoes, and the like.

Another Conservative measure was the extension of land purchase—£33,000,000 to be guaranteed by the Government to support loans to enable the peasants to buy new land. Harcourt opposed on the ground that the Bill made the British taxpayer advance moneys on Irish land at a price that could not be obtained in the market and to receive on it a rent of 20 per cent less than it now yielded. Chamberlain, who had opposed Gladstone's Bill on the principle that British credit should not be pledged for Irish landlords, now supported Balfour who sought to do that very thing. Indeed, by now, as regards Ireland at any rate, personal rancour and political opportunism had excluded all consistent principle.

But an event more important than these squabbles had occurred. On November 27th, 1890, a fortnight after the O'Shea divorce had been granted in the Courts, only twenty-five of the Irish followed Parnell into the Opposition lobby. In the Judicial Commission, which among other things had inquired into his alleged approval of violence in Ireland and pronounced Piggot's letter (approving Burke's murder and imputed to Parnell) a forgery, he had obtained a great victory, but on his citation as co-respondent in the divorce case, Gladstone, after hesitation, wrote to Morley saying that Parnell's continuance as Leader of the Nationalists would render his own leadership of the Liberal Party almost a nullity.

Parnell refused to retire, and Gladstone's letter was published in the recess. The Irish were divided and acrimonious. In the end, forty-six with whom Gladstone continued to work deserted Parnell; twenty-six supported him. The effect was to break that power of the Nationalists in the House which Parnell had so laboriously built up with so little practical result.

On October 6th Parnell died and was succeeded by John Redmond—even then the two groups, though seeking precisely the same object, were not reconciled for several years, but the general improvement in parliamentary manners was marked. Balfour carried his land purchase schemes. As they finally emerged, if the landlord would sell, the whole purchase money would be advanced by the Exchequer up to £30,000 and after forty-nine years the tenant would become owner. On the death of W. H. Smith, Balfour became Leader of the House and First Lord. Hartington soon went to the Lords and Chamberlain became leader of the Liberal Unionists in the Commons.

Other measures which the Government sponsored were supported by the Liberals: a new Factory Act in 1891, limiting hours of labour for women to twelve a day with an hour and a half for meals, controlling of sub-contracting, and raising the minimum age of employment for children to eleven. Education became free and a Small Holding Act was passed. In all these measures, it is interesting to note, the old Liberal opposition on the ground of objection to State interference was notably absent.

It was evident that collective action, as such, was no longer regarded as objectionable in principle; a new Board of Agriculture testified to a growing interest of the State in that great industry. We already detect a feeling that the future problems of reform were likely to be more social than merely electoral. There was still a feeling among the masses that the Liberals rather than their opponents were likely to deal with these matters, though a dispassionate examination of the Statute Rolls would have shown them that the contrary was the case. In reality a new cleavage between Plutocracy and the masses was arising which threatened to overrride the old political divisions, but the time for the recognition of the fact was not yet come.

In 1891, before the General election, the advanced Liberals drew up a manifesto known as the Newcastle Programme. It included proposals for the taxation of land values, the abolition of entail, extension of small holdings, the building of rural cottages, payment of members, District Councils, Local Veto in the drink trade, disestablishment of the Church and reform of the House of Lords—a medley of proposals designed to satisfy different interests. The great dock strike of 1889 and the formation of socialistic Trade Unions alarmed the wealthier Liberals; the articles in the programme proposing still further to shorten hours of work and extend compensation for accidents seemed to be directed against their financial interests. The disestablishment proposals affronted some of the more Erastian Church people, the local option scheme enraged the publicans, who in any case were inclined to join the Church in supporting the Tories. Gladstone himself approved the programme, though in fact caring for little at this time but Irish Home Rule. When the election came the Liberals found that, even with Irish Nationalist support, they had a majority of only forty for Home Rule. It was at this election that Keir Hardie was returned as Independent Labour candidate for West Ham; the other fourteen working men returned were not prepared to assume such a position: they ranked as Liberals or Liberal-Labour.

In this Government the chief new-comer was Asquith. In 1889 he had declared himself in favour of Home Rule all round, with the unimpaired supremacy of the Imperial Parliament, a position not easily distinguishable from that of Chamberlain. He agreed with Rosebery in the now popular cry for supporting imperial expansion and the maintenance of the Egyptian protectorate. In domestic affairs he was associated with Haldane, Buxton, Ferguson and Acland; they tended to form a Radical element.

Salisbury decided to meet Parliament: the Liberal Unionists had fallen from ninety-four to forty-seven, and Asquith, in moving the amendment to the address, predicted their early extinction. He said that the Conservatives, to placate this little group, had inaugurated some Liberal measures in which they did not believe and he asked the House to reject the address, which they did, whereupon Salisbury resigned. Haldane was not found a place, but Grey became an under-secretary at the Foreign Office.

The second reading of the Home Rule Bill was taken on April 4th, 1893. Chamberlain was reminded how in 1885 and 1886 he had been prepared to hand over the government of Ireland to the Nationalists. It was said that the present Bill guaranteed imperial supremacy by

retaining eighty Irish members at Westminster and by inserting a clause
as to the Imperial Suzerainty in the preamble. The second reading was
carried by three hundred and forty-seven votes to three hundred and four.
In September the third reading was agreed by thirty-four. In the Lords
the voting for rejection was four hundred and nineteen to forty-one.

It had been said by Lord Kimberley, a Liberal, that there was "No
enthusiasm for Home Rule in the Party", and the indifference seemed to
have infected a large part of the Cabinet. Morley has declared that only
Asquith and he shared Gladstone's belief in Home Rule. Harcourt,
Gladstone said, "hated Home Rule as a Britisher hates those whom he has
ill used". At any rate the Cabinet would not agree to a dissolution on
the action of the Lords. Writing in 1897 in *Essays in Liberalism* six young
Liberals declared that: "A dissolution would have been the best course—
the Ministry had a real cry with which to go to the country". It was not
until March, 1894, that Gladstone finally retired, but before that he also
had come to the conclusion that dissolution on the rejection of the Home
Rule Bill would have been the right course. The Lords had so maimed
an Employers' Liability Bill as to force its abandonment, and they had
wrecked a Local Government Bill for parishes. On all these matters,
but particularly on the Home Rule Bill, Gladstone, aged eighty-five, was
prepared to go to the Country; he suggested dissolution in January, 1894,
but, to quote his own words, "received by telegraph" (he was in Biarritz)
a hopelessly adverse reply". In Asquith's words: "We all agree that this
is madness". Not until 1911 was the issue with the Lords faced; not
until 1912 was another Home Rule Bill to be introduced.

The real cause of Gladstone's resignation was a growing disagreement
with the majority of his colleagues on the question of armament. He
objected to the increase of three million pounds odd which Spencer and
his advisers thought necessary for the Navy; nevertheless, had his advice
been sought, he would have recommended Spencer as his successor. It
was not. The Queen offered Lord Rosebery the premiership. The new
Prime Minister startled the Radicals in his first speech by declaring that he
agreed with Salisbury that, before Home Rule was granted, "England, as
the predominant member of the partnership of the three kingdoms, would
have to be convinced of its justice". This presumably was a reference to
the fact that in England there was a hostile majority; it was a new
constitutional doctrine so to divide the United Kingdom, but Lord Rosebery did not explain how he came to remain a member of a Government
which had treated the three parts as one for the purpose of obtaining a
parliamentary decision.

In the Commons, however, great things were stirring. In the Budget
Harcourt sought to equalize the charges on personal and real property at
death—the duty was now to be paid on the whole estate at the selling
value in the market. It was to range from one to eight per cent. By a
majority of fourteen this was carried, the Lords not daring to interfere.
Without exaggeration, this duty may be said to have done more to
change the social complexion of England than almost any recent legislation. The need for the money had come through the demands of the
Navy. To Harcourt it was a good expedient, but upon the landed
aristocracy the cumulative effect of the taxation was to prove
disastrous.

The temptation to increase the yield was too much even for Conservative Chancellors of the Exchequer. In a quarter of a century the yield had risen from four to forty million. "The consequence of cutting off something like a third (in 1942 considerably more) of each big estate whenever the owner dies has reduced the aristocracy of England to the position which the remains of the ancient régime occupy in France", writes Hamilton Fyfe. (*Liberalism.*) It is to be marked how, with failing economic resources, the political power of the old families had died away. Yet if Harcourt had been told that his was the axe which felled the family tree, he would have been astounded.

Rosebery sent Harcourt "an elaborate memorandum directed against the Budget generally, and the graduated death duties in particular". The Chancellor pointed out that the fear of taxation of capital is out of date. "At present", he wrote, "capital is not in deficiency, but superabundant." As to the break-up of large properties, he predicts they will be kept together by the prudent. The Prime Minister's suggestion that properties should be held, irrespective of the character of their possessors, is denounced as "very fine old Tory doctrine". Rosebery withdrew his objection, but Goschen and Chaplin marshalled the City and landed interests in opposition. The publicans and brewers objected to a tax of 6d. per gallon on spirits and beer. Fortunately, the Irish were now divided, the Parnellites, as they were still called, voted in opposition, but the other Nationalists supported Harcourt. The principle then won has never since been disturbed.

The foreign issue between Harcourt and Rosebery has still to be considered; it was one which threatened the integrity of the whole party. There is no doubt that the prosperous classes were seeking for an outlet for their capital abroad—a spirit of gambling and speculation was afoot and the old respectable city merchant was giving way to the more modern type of financier. The game of manipulating shares and limited companies was found to be more remunerative than the manufacture of commodities, and the cautious instincts which moved the old Manchester School were fast disappearing. The discovery of gold and diamonds in South Africa brought into the powerful classes a very undesirable element. Murmurs were heard that the Jews were polluting public life. Of a section of that race whose restrictive pressure of environment had produced a marked concentration of character and purpose, not attractive to the easy-going English, it was true to say that they stimulated the worship of money—their interest in its expenditure on art and public benevolence did not wholly reconcile their competitors and neighbours. From the time of the Boer War it is perhaps true to say that anti-semitism, though not virulent, became a conscious force.

Apart, however, from the ambitions of the plutocrats, there were other influences at work which operated to end the dominion of that individualistic pacific outlook of which Gladstone, Harcourt and Morley were surviving representatives. The new conception of the Kingdom and Empire as an estate, new, that is, since the Industrial Revolution, had shown itself in the disappearance of objection to the use of the State in internal betterment, but this was only half the story—if the State was once more to be regarded as an entity in the domestic sphere, so also, figuring as the Nation, it had come to claim a new vigour in Foreign

Affairs. Disraeli was, perhaps, the first statesman to realize and encourage this fact—in Palmerston the external aspect had absorbed all his energy and interest, but by the time of the new *Imperium et Libertas* the two functions had become complementary.

The Germans under Bismarck had led the way; he foreshadowed a State strong within and without. Conscription demanded a healthy army. In England, where conscription was advocated only by a few enthusiasts, the same considerations were subconsciously at work. The day of Protection had not yet come, but it also ultimately arose out of the same influences. The Nation, as it is said, had "found itself"; whether in the process the individual has not been lost is still to be discovered.

Poets, romantics and adventurers swelled the imperialist enthusiasm; it was left for Will Crooks to point out in answer to the claim that on the British Empire the sun never sets, "in our alley it never rises".

To return to the situation which arose on the resignation of Gladstone, there is no doubt on which side Rosebery stood. He was an Imperialist. Why the pacific Gladstone had entrusted him with the conduct of Foreign matters it is not easy to understand. As early as 1874 he had spoken of the great stream of emigration from England being an "affluent of giant Commonwealths and peaceful Empires that shall perpetuate the best qualities of our race". As the years went by, his passion for Empire did not abate. It was dislike for Turkey which brought him on to Gladstone's side; for that reason he objected to the Treaty of Berlin which had saved that "impotent" country. He joined in the great Midlothian campaign and acted as host to the old leader, and in 1881 joined the Government as Under-Secretary to the Home Office, but in June, 1883, he had retired. In the Franchise fight, when Salisbury sought to hold up the Bill until redistribution had been effected, he fought in the Lords from the Liberal benches, attacking in particular the Whig Argylle; yet, from the Liberal view, his imperialist heresies were still about him. In 1884 he addressed the Trade Union Congress on Imperial Federation. He demanded a stronger Navy and opposed the evacuation of Egypt. He would not surrender that country to any other Power.

When the Liberals returned dependent upon the Irish vote, a crisis arose for Rosebery; he declared that "though they might kill Mr. Gladstone's Bill they could not kill its policy". He was not prepared to follow Chamberlain, but his real interest was not in the Irish question at all. In 1886, Granville, having patently failed in Foreign Affairs, Rosebery was appointed in his place. Unlike Granville he claimed much independence. Gladstone supported Russia against Turkey, with France he was not unfriendly; Salisbury feared Russia and desired an alliance with the new German Empire. The new minister admired the new Germany, the Russians he did not trust. As to France, he regarded their Government as dangerous and jealous, while Gladstone was almost entirely absorbed in Irish questions. Undoubtedly Rosebery altered the whole trend of Liberal foreign policy. He had a dispute with Russia over Batoum; he succeeded in settling the Afghan frontier and in pacifying the relations between Turkey and Greece. In the Lords he was congratulated by Salisbury, who uttered these momentous words: "The policy which this country is pursuing (in foreign affairs) is not that of one Party or Government, but of all Parties in the State".

When Rosebery returned to the Foreign Office, in 1892, he insisted that Egypt should not be evacuated, as Gladstone had promised during the election, and had his way; generally he refused to disturb the policy of his predecessors—in this policy Grey, his Under-Secretary, agreed. In time this departure from active parliamentary criticism of foreign affairs produced very far-reaching effects. For the moment even Radicals seemed to acquiesce in the withdrawal of this, the most important of all public functions from popular public information and control. At the end of 1892 the Foreign Office dictated to the young Khedive whom he was to choose to be his Prime Minister. The French protested, and Cromer demanded that the Egyptian garrison should be strengthened; then at length the French gave way.

The statement of Rosebery to Cromer that he was to "inform the Khedive in case of his refusing to take your advice, that he must be prepared to take the consequences of his act", and in his warning to Paris that "as long as the British flag was in Egypt and British forces in occupation, the whole Administration could not be reversed at the whim of the Khedive", was far more in the Palmerstonian tradition than in that of Gladstone. So also the declaration of a British Protectorate over Uganda in 1894 was proclaimed against the wish of Gladstone and Harcourt—it was evident that a real cleavage on foreign policy was arising.

His accession to the Premiership accentuated the differences—the unfortunate reference to the need for British approval of Home Rule has already been noted.

Although Harcourt was Leader in the House of Commons, Kimberley, who had succeeded Rosebery at the Foreign Office, failed to give him adequate information on international matters. Thus Harcourt protested in terms on the failure to communicate with him about the Anglo-Belgium treaty which transferred to Belgium a sphere of British influence on the Upper Nile, its object being to keep out the French. He declared to Kimberley that the matter had assumed a most serious aspect, for Harcourt opposed British intervention in foreign affairs; true to the Gladstonian tradition, he hated Jingoism and "prancing proconsuls".

Rosebery, on the other hand, was one of the promoters of the new Imperialism, but both men understood how everything else; finance, defence, domestic politics, all depended on our relations with foreign Powers. It was their methods of dealing with the problem which were irreconcilably divergent. Experiments such as the Belgium understanding, which antagonized both Germany and France, were wholly deplorable from Harcourt's standpoint.

Germany, which was now in alliance with Austria and Italy, disliked Gladstone's pro-Russian policy. The wealth of the British Empire was beginning to cause envy abroad, The claims now being made in Africa intensified the feeling. To the last, Harcourt deplored the developments he saw going on around him; to use modern jargon he was an "isolationist"—in his own time he would have been called a "little Englander".

In March, 1895, Grey had said in the Commons that the whole Nile was under British influence; he objected to French encroachments, and spoke of them, to Harcourt's disgust, as unfriendly actions. Harcourt did his best to save England from being involved in the growing European complications, for he was a good Liberal of the old type. "Is there no pie in the world out of which we can manage to keep our fingers?" he vainly asked.

The policy of Rosebery caused a demand for more expenditure on the armed forces. A reorganization of the War Office was effected, resulting in the resignation of the Duke of Cambridge from the office of Commander-in-Chief which he had held for nearly forty years. The megalomania shown by pan-German and pan-Slavonic movements, the notion of "Will to Power" and the horrible idea that "the good war justifies every cause", emanating from Nietzsche, the desire for a "greater Servia, a greater Bulgaria, a greater Greece" and other nationalist demands had reduced Europe to that condition of alternative armistice and war from which she has never since recovered. In this country the disease took a milder form. Dilke spoke of the "grandeur of our race, already girdling the earth, which it is destined, perhaps eventually, to overspread"—a "greater Britain". These words, it is to be noted, came from an advanced Radical. Chamberlain, increasingly, was of the same way of thinking, and Rosebery was not far behind. Kipling was their lyrist; the Diamond Jubilee their occasion.

In all these circumstances it is not surprising that when the Government were defeated—significantly on a War Office vote—and resigned in June, 1895, that the Conservatives should come back with the great majority of one hundred and fifty-two over Liberals and Nationalists combined.

This time Chamberlain, with little hesitation, joined the Government as Colonial Secretary. He was now an ardent Imperialist. Far more than Salisbury or Balfour (who had become Prime Minister), he guided the rising national vainglory until it was involved in war, the certain end of all such amoral ambition. It was his own choice; from henceforth Imperialism looked to him for guidance.

Balfour became First Lord, the Prime Minister took the Foreign Office, Hicks Beach the Exchequer. The other Liberal Unionists in the Cabinet were Whigs—Lansdowne at the War Office and James at the Duchy of Lancaster. Austen Chamberlain was Civil Lord of the Admiralty.

Chamberlain began with small things; the King of Ashanti was told to accept a British protectorate. He refused. His capital, Kumassi, was occupied, and Ashanti annexed, but trouble in Africa was not over —bigger problems soon arose.

It was the desire of the Boers in the Transvaal to obtain access to the sea, a reasonable ambition it would be thought. It had been said by Lord Ripon that for them to obtain a port was unfavourable to the interests of the paramount Power, a claim which the Boers would never admit. In the negotiations in 1884, in which Chamberlain had taken an active part, the title of South African Republic had been acknowledged to the Transvaal and the claim to British suzerainty removed from the preamble of the Treaty. It was clear that in law the claim of Ripon to

Imperial paramountcy was at least doubtful—but this was not all. The non-Boers in Africa had complained that they were excluded from public government (with perfect propriety according to international law if the Transvaal was to have its own independent government), and domestic autonomy on any view had been conceded without question in the treaty following Majuba. It was said that the Boers were unprogressive and that they needed the new blood of the "Outlanders" who already were busy extracting gold from the Rand.

Meanwhile, Kruger had obtained a seaport through the opening of the railway to Delagoa Bay from Pretoria. He unwisely proclaimed that the fords across the Vaal river would be closed to goods imported from Cape Colony; he negotiated with the Germans. All this made Rhodes, the pioneer of Empire development in South Africa, turn to revolutionary methods. Chamberlain pointed out that the closing of the fords was unfriendly and a breach of the London Convention of 1884. He notes in the autumn of 1895 that "the representatives of the Chartered Company (i.e. Rhodes and his friends) were convinced that unless the Transvaal Government made some concessions there would be a rising in Johannesburg". At this time, in fact, Rhodes was conspiring to bring about such a revolution. Rifles and guns were to be bought in England, the de Beers company was to smuggle them into the Transvaal capital.

Kruger had given way on the importation over the fords and the Outlanders were in a state of exultation. It appears probable that Chamberlain knew of the preparations for the raid, but he did not expect that Jameson, who was in command, would so soon act.

On December 28th, Jameson started to advance on Pretoria with a few hundred men; on January 2nd he surrendered—two days before Chamberlain had instructed Sir Hercules Robinson to denounce the raid as "an act of war, or rather filibustering". A proclamation was issued forbidding all British subjects to aid Jameson. Next day the Kaiser telegraphed to Kruger, congratulating him on having succeeded "in establishing peace against armed bands" without calling on the aid of friendly Powers. This fact of course saved Jameson and, perhaps, Chamberlain. Both became popular heroes. It remains to consider the action of the Liberal Party during this tumultuous time.

It must be remembered, in the first place, that England was in the throes of a gold fever, and that the suppression of the Boer Republic would, it was thought, increase the profits. Next, there was a bitter feeling among the older people arising out of the defeat of Majuba and Gladstone's consequent 'humiliation', as it was construed; a surrender in which Chamberlain, it was conveniently forgotten, had taken an active part. Austin, the poet-laureate, praised Jameson in a doggerel beginning: "There are girls in the gold-reef city", there was much other absurdity of the music-hall type, so easily in times of excitement to be mistaken for patriotism.

At this time, Harcourt writing to Bryce said: "I know that the South African directors have advised that they knew of the intention to organize an armed rising at Johannesburg, and that Jameson was at Mafeking with their knowledge and authority to take part in the rising when it occurred". Harcourt did not accept the view that Chamberlain was involved. The Chartered Company included as directors the Dukes of

Abercorn and Fife, and all Society held shares, which were now worth £9. They all turned on Harcourt, but he was not deterred. In the House he made a great speech. "Stock jobbing Imperialism" was his description of the Company's activities. The Government were forced to concede an inquiry, but Chamberlain would not agree that Rhodes should retire. He was at that time both Prime Minister at the Cape and Chairman of the Chartered Company, and by far the most powerful Englishman in South Africa. "He was necessary to South Africa," declared Chamberlain, "for he had the confidence of the whole community."

The inquiry opened in the autumn of 1896 and continued during 1897. Meanwhile, the raiders were tried before the Lord Chief Justice and convicted, but their sentences were light; the real question was the responsibility of Rhodes, and, indeed, of Chamberlain. As to the first, he was proved to have consented to everything except the exact hour for Jameson's action. Nevertheless, nothing was done. He remained a member of the Privy Council, and Chamberlain went so far as to say that there exists nothing which affected Mr. Rhodes' personal honour. "If a man goes into a revolution, it follows as a matter of course that he must deceive other people." With this example of the decay of moral judgment in this acquisitive period we may leave the matter. From that time, war became inevitable.

The conflict, when it happened, is here only to be considered in so far as it affected the fortunes of the Liberal Party. Before it came, Rosebery had resigned the leadership on the ground that he could not follow the veteran Gladstone in a crusade against the Turk after the Armenian massacres. He feared, and with reason, a general European conflagration. Gladstone proposed that England should at least withdraw her ambassador. Most naïvely Rosebery replied that the British Empire had increased by 2,600,000 square miles in twelve years, and that with this mass of "undigested Empire" peace was essential.

The Radicals were infuriated; they saw an affront to the beloved Grand Old Man in Rosebery's refusal, and possibly also some electoral advantage lost. On October 8th, 1896, Rosebery wrote to his chief Whip saying: "The leadership of the Party, so far as I am concerned, is vacant". On September 24th, Gladstone had urged independent action on England's part against the "infamous Turk", but Rosebery would not take the responsibility of fighting one who, he said, "so long as he lives will always be the real leader of the Liberal Party".

At this time the division among Liberals as to Imperialism was growing wider; Harcourt was content to remain Leader in the Commons, but Rosebery had already expressed to Asquith a hope that "you very soon will replace me". There was reason in this; as the biographers of Lord Oxford and Asquith wrote: "His leaning in this and similar conjunctures were on the whole Roseberyite." (*Life*, I, p. 115.)

In 1898 Kitchener conquered the Soudan, and the dispute with France at Fashoda produced a diplomatic crisis. The Liberal Imperialists joined with the Government in demanding the withdrawal of France. Harcourt expressed the hope that we should all abstain from language "of vulgar swagger or provocation or menace which might embarrass their conduct or precipitate their action". It was a wise caution, having regard to the marked increase in Jingoism which was now so universally rampant.

That the party was "rent by sectional disputes" was the reason why Harcourt declined any longer to attempt to lead—this was in December, 1898. In January of the next year Morley also resigned his official position—he would not "sponge off the slate all the lessons Mr. Gladstone has taught us". Next month, Campbell-Bannerman, who then occupied a central position between the disputants, was elected Leader without opposition.

By May, Rosebery had suggested the formation of a new party to include "the factor of the larger patriotism which I have called Imperialism". Harcourt replied: "What is this Imperialism which, in the slang of the day, is paraded as the highest form of patriotism?"—"If it was to relieve distress and raise the standards of comfort for all the subjects of the King, he was an Imperialist", he declared; but, "there is another and exactly opposite view of imperial policy—it is to postpone and subordinate all these objects to vanity, to the acquisition of fresh populations, the adoption of additional burdens. To these ends social reforms are neglected—to talk of social reforms is ' parochial' and that what we ought to occupy ourselves with is this inflated Imperialism".

So far, therefore, from Rosebery's retirement easing the position, as Harcourt had hoped, it accentuated the divergence. Asquith, Grey, Haldane and Fowler were all sympathetic in varying degrees to the Rosebery policy. E. T. Cook, the editor of the *Daily News*, was an enthusiastic supporter of Liberal Imperialism. In the country the Jameson raid, so far from disgusting people with the 'new order', had increased their patriotic zeal, nor was the benevolent treatment of Rhodes, the prime conspirator, by the Government anything but popular. What the Liberal Imperialists failed to understand was, that if the nation wished for a swashbuckling Government, they would look for it on the Conservative and not on the Opposition side of the House.

In South Africa the position became ever more acute. Milner, who had succeeded Robinson as High Commissioner, was truculent. In May, 1899, he telegraphed to Chamberlain of "thousands of British subjects kept permanently in the position of helots". He demanded action. In a conference, Kruger offered the franchise after seven years' residence. This was refused. Campbell-Bannerman deprecated military preparations on this side, but by July the Government had already started to mobilize their forces. Kruger then offered a five-year qualification—by this time the seven-year condition was law—if Britain would no longer interfere in the affairs of the Transvaal and abandon her claim to suzerainty, further disputes to go to arbitration—a most reasonable demand. Chamberlain, who in earlier years had agreed that the suzerainty claim should be dropped—though this was before the days of the Kaffir-market and gold interest—insisted on it. Now that the franchise had been granted it was the only issue outstanding. In October, fifty thousand Outlanders left the Rand. England moved troops up to the Transvaal border. The Boers then sent an Ultimatum, demanding the withdrawal of the British army from the frontier, and a stop to be put to the landing of troops from England. This was refused, and on October 11th they crossed into Natal and surrounded Mafeking and Kimberley. The War had begun.

The effect upon the Liberal Party was disastrous. Harcourt had said that the Boers were right on the suzerainty dispute; Sir Edward Clarke, another considerable lawyer, though Conservative, took the same view. Morley declared against the yellow Press that "you may give greater buoyancy to the South African Stock and Share Market. You may send up the price of Mr. Rhodes' Chartered. Even then it will be wrong". This was on the eve of war. Asquith, with Grey and Haldane, was on the Government side.

Bryce and Reid agreed with Harcourt and Morley, as also did the young Lloyd George. In the end one hundred and thirty-five Liberals voted on an amendment "disapproving the conduct of the negotiations which had involved us in hostilities with the South African Republic". Campbell-Bannerman's position was intermediate between the Imperialists and those who came to be called "pro-Boers". He thought the Ultimatum had made war certain, but believed that Chamberlain, by nominating a friend of Rhodes as High Commissioner, by exonerating Rhodes for the raid itself, and by harping on suzerainty was at least *particeps criminis*. His constant criticism of the past action of the Government soon made him associate with the Harcourt side; indeed, apart from his laudable desire to preserve the party from further disruption, that was obviously where his heart lay.

In reality, it made little difference. The Country and the Government, smarting under early military defeats, abused all Liberals indiscriminately as traitors. The Imperialists asserted their patriotism, the pro-Boers declared that the party must stand aloof from Jingoism. Still the leader tried to keep a middle course. He refused to attack the Boers as evil men; on the other hand, on the question of annexation, he disagreed with Asquith who had spoken against it—he saw that annexation must follow victory in war.

At home, the institution of London Borough Councils was opposed to some extent by Liberals, more particularly as it left the ancient rights of the City unaffected. An Act to relieve the Clergy of rates on tithe, costing £87,000 a year, angered the Nonconformists, and Sir William Robson, afterwards Liberal Attorney-General, obtained an Act raising the school age to 12 years.

An amendment of censure on the King's speech, when Parliament met early in 1900, regretting "want of foresight in the conduct of South African affairs since 1895 and in their preparations for the war", was officially moved by the Liberals. The Imperialists and "pro-Boers" again disclosed their differences; the Leader taking a middle course. In the end there were abstentions, but no serious cleavage was as yet exhibited. The question of annexation now came to the fore, for the military position was improving. Campbell-Bannerman from the outset took the view that the proper course was to annex and then give a Liberal constitution to united South Africa. This, in 1906, he was able to achieve; it was his greatest work.

During the election of 1900 the Liberal Imperialists suffered more than their party opponents. The whole party had been attacked with equal violence. Just before the election the Government had put through the Commonwealth of Australia Bill, which had generally been approved. From now on Australia had the same dominion status as Canada; even the anti-Imperialists could not deny that this measure was unobjectionable. By the nation as a whole it was regarded as Chamberlain's personal triumph.

Circumstances had made him by far the most important person in the Cabinet, yet, notwithstanding his abusive speeches, the Government only gained four seats—the remark of Chamberlain that "every seat lost to the Government was a seat gained by the Boers" was an example of his manner—the result was to infuriate the Imperialist Liberals and to make the prospects of Liberal reunion the brighter.

Milner now wished to suspend the Constitution at the Cape, though the Colonial Secretary had announced for the Government that the Republics would be incorporated into Her Majesty's dominions. The time seemed not far off—in May the British were in Johannesburg To the gratification of the Liberals, Chamberlain hinted at an ultimate constitution leading to self-government. Campbell-Bannerman was surprised at a speech "very much more favourable to our object than I had anticipated". But he was premature; in answer to his speech on the address in the new Parliament that the Boers should be told that "by and by, when things have settled down and there is safety, they will have their share in the full rights of self-government", Balfour, the Prime Minister, replied that "he knew not how long the delay might be, it might be years, it might even be generations". It soon emerged that the Unionist policy towards the Boers was unconditional surrender.

In truth, despite the assurance at the election that the war was practically over, guerrilla warfare was still universal in the Transvaal. The military decided upon more punitive methods. They put the women in concentration camps, and burned the farms which were often centres of resistance. It appeared that both Kitchener and Milner had objected to the method of conciliation, and the proclamation promising the Transvaal self-government was not issued. Thousands of women had been driven out on to the veldt, and an unfortunate proclamation made, though afterwards withdrawn, that "the Boer women should apply to the Boer commandant for food", enraged Campbell-Bannerman and the "left" Liberals. In June, 1901, he denounced such proceedings as "methods of barbarism". In the House he repeated his accusation, to be at once reproved by Haldane. On a motion for adjournment by Lloyd George to call attention to the whole punitive system, fifty Liberal Imperialists, including Asquith and Haldane, abstained from voting. The temporary truce was again broken.

In June, the Leader called a meeting of the Party and received a unanimous vote of confidence from Liberal Peers and Commons. Thereupon Rosebery declared that he would "never voluntarily return to the arena of party politics", he would "plough his own furrow alone".

Rosebery had gone too far, the other Imperialists did not follow him; indeed Asquith shortly afterwards, while claiming the right of his opinions that the war "was neither intended nor desired by the Government or the people of Great Britain, but that it was forced upon us", went on to say that he desired "the fabric of a free, federated self-governing South African Dominion".

Next, Rosebery delivered himself at Chesterfield. In his speech Liberals were exhorted to "put away their fly-blown phylacteries", though what was to be discarded was not very clear. At any rate, he meant to insult the past traditions of Liberalism, presumably in their dislike of foreign commitment and Imperial expansion. Fowler, Grey and Asquith were all upon his platform. "The efficiency" which he recommended was something other than Liberalism as it had so far been understood. Campbell-Bannerman went to see him; all that emerges was that they could not co-operate. Grey demanded, as the price of his allegiance, that the Leader should accept Rosebery's views on the war; this the genial Campbell-Bannerman described in a letter to one of his friends as "damned egoism and impertinence". It was clear that the Imperialists wished the Leader to abdicate or surrender, but the skilful Scotsman was not to be intimidated. Soon Rosebery became more lucid; he said he was opposed to Home Rule for Ireland, though favouring devolution. "I am outside the tabernacle," he declared a little later. The followers of Rosebery treated Campbell-Bannerman with contumely; when he spoke in the House, the author has been informed by a Radical member then in Parliament, it was the habit of the Imperialists on the front bench to withdraw.

They were evidently scheming to make his position intolerable. The Liberals in the country, however, were quite of another opinion. On February 19th, when Campbell-Bannerman repudiated the Rosebery "clean slate" and declared his belief in Home Rule, he received from the National Liberal Federation a call on all Liberals to support him.

Thereupon the Rosebery faction formed a Liberal (Imperial) League with that nobleman as President; Grey, Asquith and Fowler were vice-presidents. Harcourt alone stood behind the Leader. The journalist, Harmsworth, daily attacked him and tried to persuade Liberals to put back Rosebery. Still the bulk of Liberal opinion in the country trusted him rather than the brilliant nobleman and lawyers who were busy reconstructing Liberalism on an Imperial basis.

All this, however, became very stale once the War was over. New interests arose which united Liberals once more; the League and its President were alike soon forgotten.

This unifying influence came in the first place from opposition to the Government's Education Bill of 1902. In July, 1902, Salisbury had resigned and Balfour became Prime Minister. He it was who insisted upon rate-aid for Voluntary Schools against the advice of Chamberlain and the wise old Lord Salisbury, but the Cabinet was persuaded. The trouble had arisen from a legal decision that, under the existing law, School Boards could not use rates outside the very restricted definition of elementary education in the earlier Acts. The vast majority of the Voluntary Schools were Anglican, and any final assistance to them out of the rates was objectionable to the Nonconformists. In country districts, "single school areas" as they were called, where the school had often been built by the Squire and the pupils taught by the priest, though a Wesleyan child might be withdrawn from the religious teaching, it would be at the cost of being left without any religious education. Money, however, was the difficulty; the Church school did not receive the assistance of the local rates, but only a small grant. Unless fresh subscriptions could be

raised, the Church people could not always maintain their buildings or furniture or pay proper salaries to teachers. They were in constant fear of condemnation by the inspector.

The promotion of Welsh disestablishment by the Liberal Party in 1892–95 had made most parsons Tory agents, they now asked for their reward. But times had changed—dogmatic religion was rapidly losing its hold, particularly on the urban population. Not one-fifth of the people of Birmingham, said Cadbury, entered any church or chapel. The same was true of other towns. It followed that a Bill which would take State money to satisfy Church people must antagonize not only Nonconformists but also the immense hosts of voters who were without any religion at all.

In 1896 the Duke of Devonshire, who was then President of th Council and so, indirectly, Minister of Education (for there was no spec department at that time), and his representative in the Commons, John Gorst, sought to make each county the supreme education auth for its area. The Government was to stimulate secondary educati grants and the founding of new institutions and also to give gr School Boards and to Voluntary schools, where attendance w pulsory, in single school areas. Thus the Church would b receiving rate aid, while the Radicals were to be pleased by school age to twelve, and the increase in staff.

The Bill was withdrawn, but many of its proposals four in the measure of 1902. In 1899 the Board of Educat established; the old Education Department and the Sc Departments were absorbed into it, and also the educa of the Charity Commission. To all this there was no increasing interest in education generally, stimulated German rivalry, was arising. Then came the decisic that the grants from the Central Authority were technical education. It was at this point that Society raised the cry that in each district of conve be only one education authority. They attack special School Boards. The contention was no what had been accepted in the 1896 Bill. In 190 to clear up the whole muddle. Gorst was Devonshire lugubrious. Sir Robert Moran Gorst, was an intimate friend of the leadi Sidney Webb, who combined with his Socialism" practical experience of local County Council, where he sat as a Pro knowledge of the history of the subject.

Sir William Anson had taken the expert, a fellow of All Souls, and a me as it passed, abolished the School the county councils and county bor certain larger urban districts were the objection was expert and tech that which dealt with the Vo in opposition and in the Government.

F

The Voluntary Schools, now for the first time were to receive assistance from the rates. They had to set up a Board of Managers (on which sat representatives of the foundation trust and of the local education authority). The Board were to see that the religion taught agreed with the views of the founders.

From March till December the Bill was fought in the Commons. The abolition of the School Boards was called an attack on the people's rights, the presence of co-opted members on the Education Committee of the Council being the justification for their indignation. All were united: Imperialists, little Englanders and Nonconformists agreed that it was an outrage.

The Nonconformists, led by Dr. Clifford, denounced the financing of Church Schools out of public funds; that they had long received State grants, though not rating assistance, was generally overlooked. The cry, "the Church on the rates", the passive resistance of several thousand people, including in Wales a County Council, added to the excitement. Campbell-Bannerman addressed the National Free Churches Union, describing the measure as a Church Bill in disguise. Even Rosebery came out of his solitude to condemn it, yet, to-day, no impartial person can deny that the educational work of the Councils has been one of the most successful of their enterprises. The new secondary education proved invaluable. In the school year before the passing of the Act there were but three hundred and forty-one secondary schools; in five years the number had risen to six hundred and eighty-nine, and the increase, both in numbers and efficiency, has continued ever since: never were the Liberals less justified than in their attack upon this measure as doing nothing for education. The truth is that the Dissenter had largely secured the old School Boards and the Anglicans controlled the majority of the county Voluntary schools. By-elections were being won on the

was, in part, the fear that they would lose their power in urban which caused the Liberals to lament the extinction of the School —in reality their abolition was but one instance of the general cy to eradicate special *ad hoc* authorities, to "use a convenient sm" as Sir William Anson, in his academic manner, had said in ing the Education Bill. When Government intervention was al and irregular, as in the earlier portion of the nineteenth it was natural that Parliament should appoint specific Boards with particular difficulties; now that the notion of collective the social sphere was coming to be accepted, the multiplication ies would make the further specific endowment of powers for poses impracticable. Gradually they were absorbed into one erning body. The Highway, Sanitary and Burial Boards gone; there was everything to be said from a constructive w for the elimination of the School Board also—the Liberal this occasion was in reality obscurantist and unimaginative. the sectarian objection to endowed Church schools, the without substance. Already, as has been said, the State em. Whether their assistance was to come out of taxes matter which could raise no sort of principle. In fact the cils to take them over or supplant them was greatly

increased by the 1902 act. Regarding the whole matter dispassionately, it must be confessed that the Liberal agitation was unfortunate.

In May, 1903, however, a far greater excitement arose out of the declaration of Chamberlain at Birmingham in favour of preference in import duties for Colonies, and in his more or less overt advocacy of a return to Protection.

The matter had been touched upon in the Imperial Conference resolutions in 1897, and in a more marked form in 1902. Among the latter appeared a specific request for preferential treatment for the Colonies, either by exemption from or reduction of duties. At that time there existed a very slight Corn Tax, and Chamberlain, who was visiting South Africa, desired an assurance that the existing shilling duty on corn should no longer apply to the Empire. According to the Prime Minister, this was agreed to in the Cabinet. Nevertheless in the Budget, Ritchie, the Chancellor, an irreconcilable free-trader, decided to repeal the whole tax. Hicks Beach supported its abolition, and a "Free Food League" was instituted on the Conservative side to fight food taxes. In September the Free Trade ministers, Ritchie, Lord George Hamilton, and Lord Balfour, resigned, and shortly afterwards the Duke of Devonshire joined them. On the other side Chamberlain also went, but his son Austen, who was a Protectionist, remained, and the Prime Minister tardily declared himself in favour of "safeguarding industry but using tariffs only for purposes of negotiation". Clearly he was prepared to go further if the country would support him.

That the old Liberals should fight was intelligible, but few people at the time saw the anomaly of the Imperialist Opposition taking up the same position. From an Imperial point of view the argument of Chamberlain that preferences would have pleased the people overseas and strengthened the bonds of the Empire was strong. Why Lord Rosebery, Grey, or Asquith, remained such inflexible advocates of Free Trade is not clear; was it not one of the "fly-blown phylacteries" which Rosebery had denounced?

The attitude of Campbell-Bannerman and his school was logical and consistent. They saw that the growth of aggressive nationalism was bound to lead to a demand for economic autarchy such as is now seen in its extreme form in Fascist countries. In a sense it was a military rather than an economic requirement which condemned free importation and general unfettered trade between nations. It was a necessary part of the Cobdenite conception of nations and their peoples as trading entities peacefully exchanging goods and services for the benefit of the whole world—a "bag-man's millennium", as that early Fascist, Carlyle, called it. But the new Liberalism had pledged itself under the name of Empire to Nationalism; such an ideal was bound sooner or later to lead to a demand for the re-introduction of Protection.

Much contention ranged whether the consumer was to bear the duty, but this was a minor point; the real question was whether the abandonment by England of Free Trade would increase the isolation and bellicosity of nations or help towards international comity. That issue was never fairly stated by either side, perhaps it was not yet understood.

Yet international matters were approaching a crisis. One of the last acts of the Tory Government, accomplished with Liberal approval, was in effect to make an alliance with France. That country was clearly falling into weakness, her population was declining; conversely, her neighbour, Germany, was daily increasing in numbers, power and truculence. The creation of the Committee of Imperial Defence in 1904 showed how little confidence was felt in the stability of Europe. The alliance with Japan was made to safeguard the eastern position. King Edward, who disliked his nephew, the Kaiser, insistently urged an understanding with the French. There is now little doubt that secretly, at this time, 'conversations' between the military staffs of England and the French Army were started. It was with reluctance that Balfour abandoned the Salisbury tradition of regarding Russia as the potential enemy and began to watch the Kaiser. The defeat of Russia by the Japanese in 1905 weakened Britain's fear of that country. Undoubtedly the Germans were becoming very unpopular in England. Ever since the Kaiser's telegram to Kruger relations had been precarious. The doubling of the German Navy, following a failure of the attempt to come to an understanding, helped on the undefined French alliance.

Nevertheless, the understanding with France, as has been noticed, was welcomed by the Liberals, Lord Rosebery alone dissenting. He urged the Opposition to be more cautious in agreeing with the new policy; he spoke of "violent polemics with Germany"; he protested that cordial relations with France should not mean animosity with her neighbour—yet all informed persons knew that it was fear of the Teuton which had forced France to come to terms with her ancient enemy, England.

At home there passed a Licensing Act, providing that licences should not be refused to public-houses except for misconduct or other special reasons and setting up a Compensation Fund, all of which greatly increased the value of the public-houses by practically giving them a freehold; and an Irish Land Purchase Bill, easing the rental for the tenant and giving him a fee simple subject to a small rent-charge—a Bill approved by the Liberals as a whole. After disputes among the Conservatives as to what part Tariff Reform should take in the election, Londonderry saying it was moribund and Austen Chamberlain describing it as a foremost issue, the Prime Minister equivocating as he had done in the House for a long time, on December 4th, 1905, Balfour resigned. Not until 1922 was a Conservative ministry again in office.

CHAPTER IX

THE LAST LIBERAL ADMINISTRATION

DESPITE a number of attempts, no very convincing explanation has ever been given to account for the very great turn-over of votes which took place at the General Election of January, 1906. The Liberals returned three hundred and seventy-seven members, the Conservatives were but one hundred and fifty-seven, of which about a dozen were free-traders. Some thirty Labour members pledged to independence, and the odd eighty Irish Nationalists completed the tale.

From the Conservative side, Mrs. Dugdale, the biographer of Balfour, suggests as causes of defeat the Education Act and the Food Tax cry. She adds the agitation against "Chinese slavery". The Liberals certainly used all these matters as arguments against their opponents. On the other hand, their commitments to the Irish (now at the height of their unpopularity owing to their dubious loyalty in the Boer War), an obligation denounced on the eve of the election by Rosebery; the almost universal antagonism of the landed and commercial classes, and the great weakness of support in the Press must all have told in favour of the outgoing Government. The Liberals themselves expected no more than a working majority. It is suggested that the reasons for their unique victory are to be sought in more profound sociological changes than most political historians have been willing to suggest.

Since the Liberals were in power in the 'nineties there had been a constant movement, more particularly in municipal activity, in a collectivist direction. Apart from those who held that, ultimately, all industry should be socialized, there were many who saw no objection to State activity to deal with specific social ills, or even, in certain cases, to embark upon direct trading. The rich and self-interested objected to anything approaching commercial competition from a civic source; they opposed the increase of rates which might follow the development of non-productive corporate activity, but their objection, though often pushed to extreme lengths by ratepayers' associations, was now frankly opportunist. The old Benthamite objection to State action as such (of which Herbert Spencer had been the last forceful exponent) was dead.

It followed that the electors now looked for a political party who would utilize the machinery of government for their advantage. Judged from this standpoint, the record both of Tory and Liberals in the past had been woefully insufficient; even old age pensions, long promised, had not been forthcoming; the compensation laws were still inadequate—the Statute Roll had been shrinking to very meagre dimensions. There was much to be accomplished, and it could only be achieved by a party which had no objection to use the machinery of legislation for social betterment.

This view, in its extreme form, accounts perhaps for the appearance and return of independent Labour members. Their power and significance have been much exaggerated. A few were conscious Socialists, but the majority were leaders of Trade Unions, who did not object in theory to the broad collectivist resolutions which were passed by Congress, but had little practical interest in them. Indeed, the structure of the Trade Unions which they administered assumed a continuance of capitalism and collective bargaining between employer and workman.

Moreover, nearly all of them were, in part, returned on Liberal votes in two-membered constituencies or crept in through a three-cornered contest—it is doubtful, outside the coalfields, if half a dozen held their seats by absolute majorities.

There were, it is true, among all the Liberals, some old-fashioned

Individualists who deplored all collective action. The Prime Minister was not one of them. His sympathy with the Labour leaders was strong. Keir Hardie, one of the least easily reconcilable, declared that "Sir Henry deserves all the praise that has been heaped upon him; where the Liberal Party falls short of its promises, the blame will not rest with C.B." The attempt of the Liberal Imperialists, led by Grey, to force the new Premier into the Lords, had it succeeded would have been most unpopular. It was the weakness of this little group of highly intellectual gentlemen, Grey, Haldane, and Asquith at their head, that they failed to recognize that the days of Whiggery were over, and that select government by a small clique had become as objectionable if it emanated from Oxford, as if it were limited to large land-holders.

The circumstances of Grey's action have been so frequently recounted that they do not need repetition. His behaviour to Campbell-Bannerman at the time of the Cabinet construction was entirely inexcusable. The demand of Asquith that Haldane should be Chancellor also showed that the Imperialist Liberal believed they possessed a power which was far from existent.

There is little doubt that the Prime Minister, had he been a vindictive man, could easily have formed a government from his loyal friends, and abandoned the whole of the Leaguers, as in fact he did in the case of Rosebery, where the gulf was unbridgable; but his noble character inclined always to the healing of differences rather than to the hardening of them. In the matter of the Woolsack, however, he was obdurate. Reid, his old friend, not Haldane, whom he had never trusted, was to be Lord Chancellor.

On December 21st, 1905, the Cabinet being formed, the Prime Minister laid down his programme in the Albert Hall. If the views here expressed are correct—that the electors were waiting for a bold programme of reform—that speech contributed very largely to the subsequent Liberal success at the election. He declared the country to be tired of 'tactics'; he said that "we desired to develop our undeveloped estates, to colonize our own country". Already the researches of Booth and Rowntree had disclosed the frightful poverty which had followed unregulated commercial competition. There followed these memorable words: "We wish to make the world less of a pleasure ground for the rich and more of a treasure-house for the nation". The land system and the rating system should be reformed, so also the poor law. He warned his hearers that we are fighting "powers, privileges, injustices and monopolies which are unalterably opposed to the triumph of the democratic system". It was on this broad issue, rather than Chinese labour, trade union law, or even education, that the ordinary elector responded to the Government's appeal.

Abroad, the situation rapidly worsened. Again the Germans were the disturbers of the peace. In 1904 Germany had not overtly objected to the Anglo-French arrangements in Morocco. In 1905, however, the Kaiser intervened. He landed in person at Tangier and declared that he would never permit any power to step between him and the Sultan of Morocco. Delcassé, the French Foreign Minister, who had settled the *entente* with England, was forced by threat of war with Germany to resign—a most disgraceful French humiliation. The German Navy increased in power, and Teutonic threats both to England and France became very gross. Up to now the Germans had been restrained by fear of Russia, but Russia was now prostrate, and they felt they could safely resume their old policy of hectoring aggression.

The Balfour Government had already pledged England to help the French against German claims in Morocco. Grey was asked by the French where he stood. He replied that he had no hesitation in affirming Lansdowne's policy of *entente*. He did not dissent from the Gallic proposal that "unofficial communications between our Admiralty and the War Office and the French Naval and Military attachés should take place". On January 31st the French Ambassador asked Grey in terms: "Whether France could count upon the assistance of England in the event of an attack upon her by Germany"; he answered that, as a personal opinion, in the event of an attack by Germany on France, "public opinion in England would be so strong that no British Government could remain neutral". Grey also stated that if a defensive alliance was formed, though it could be concluded without the consent of Parliament, it would have to be published afterwards!

These words illustrate very clearly the way in which the Foreign Office—even under a Liberal minister—was seeking to escape from parliamentary control. Grey certainly did not commit the Government, but equally he made it clear that if they wished to do so, they could make treaties without previously consulting Parliament. In the end a settlement was effected at Algeciras, and the Kaiser accused the French of 'nerves', but those in the centre of things realized how nearly both countries had been to war; thereafter, until 1914, the peril of hostilities was never absent from the minds of men responsible for the ordering of the foreign relations of this country.

But even now, hopes of an understanding with Germany were not abandoned. Haldane, as Secretary for War, visited Berlin; Campbell-Bannerman, despite the laudation of militarism by the Kaiser, was never inclined to abandon a hope of understanding with that imperious neurotic.

In Russia a democratic movement, centering round the new Duma, complicated foreign relations. The Liberals in England naturally supported the Russian developments. At the same time a fear that the Czar might make an alliance with Germany made them fearful of offending him. The Czar dissolved the Duma, and the hatred of him by Radicals and Labour Party members increased. The Prime Minister's speech, "The Duma is dead, long live the Duma", while pleasing them, was considered in St. Petersburg to be a censure on the Czar. The Germans, fishing as usual in troubled waters, stirred up the Turks to come to the Suez Canal from the east; doubtless the German General Staff were behind them. A British ultimatum was sent to Turkey and they withdrew. Nevertheless, it was clear that the new Government could no longer say, as had the Prime Minister at the Albert Hall, that "the outlook abroad was most pleasing".

From the outset of their legislative career it was evident that a great conflict between the two Houses could not be avoided. With the breakdown of territorial aristocracy, the House of Lords had increasingly become the stronghold of the new wealthy class, who, if they succeeded in acquiring a great amount of capital, were almost always ennobled.

Brewers and bankers had long been there, but now the proprietors of cheap newspapers were given seats. Moreover, now that nearly all rich men were on the Conservative side, it lay in their power to kill any Liberal Bill they disliked. If they allowed some legislation, like the Trade Disputes Act and the Workman's Compensation Acts, to pass, it was because, as a matter of party tactics, they deemed it expedient not to quarrel with organized labour. Their behaviour was quite without principle; if there ever was a measure which might reasonably have been rejected, it was the Trade Disputes Act, which gave a complete immunity to Trade Unions for all wrongs committed by them, not even limited to those done during a Trade Dispute: it was not even a Government Bill, yet the Conservatives, despite the protests of their lawyers, let it pass. The Education Bill (which would have transferred the non-provided schools to the local authority with provision for special religious teaching, the local authority to take over the fabric—a most sensible solution of the problem of inefficient non provided schools) the Lords so fundamentally amended, conceding even in council schools the option to give full denominational teaching, that the Government declared they would not go on with the measure—as amended, it was indeed almost exactly the contrary of their own in its effect.

The King was concerned at the signs of coming conflict. The Lords passed the third reading of the amended Bill; time was spent in conference between Lords Lansdowne and Cawdor on the one side and the Minister, Mr. Birrell, and Lord Crewe on the other. In the end Lansdowne moved that his House insist on its amendments, which was carried by one hundred and forty-two to fifty-three. The minority vote was about representative of the strength of the Government in the Lords. The Prime Minister declared it intolerable that a "second chamber when one party is in power, should be its willing servant, and when that party has received condemnation in the country, be able to thwart the policy of which the electors show they approve". He went on in minatory manner to say: "The resources of the House of Commons are not exhausted".

Next, the Lords destroyed the Plural Voting Bill. The Liberals, on the whole, were against dissolution, but they demanded some reform whereby, it was said, "the will of the people as expressed through the House of Commons must be made to prevail".

The recognition of an "expeditionary force" in the Army Bill of 1907 pointed the way in which the Government saw the foreign situation. Haldane's reforms, generally, were carried, though the "patriots" on the Conservative side, Brodrick, Arnold, Forster and Wyndham, did not hesitate to obstruct his work so far as they were able. Behind the scenes, the Committee of Imperial Defence was considering the whole position on the assumption that war was not unlikely in the near future. The Prime Minister had hoped that some limitation of armaments might arise from the Hague conference, an international congress originally summoned at the suggestion of the Czar, but the Germans were determined that the question should not arise. They professed to see in its advocacy, coupled with the reorganization of the English Army, some subtle conspiracy, though in their own interest, they were very willing to have declared the immunity of private property at sea. In view of their later record in destroying neutral shipping it seemed a cynical request. England, as a great maritime power, refused to concede the demand.

In May, 1907, at length the inescapable question of Home Rule was once more raised. Mr. Birrell, the Irish Secretary, introduced a Bill for a representative Irish Council. As it was promptly opposed by a National Convention in Ireland, this method of conciliation by stages had to be abandoned; it was clear that Redmond, like Butt before him, who had been willing to give the measure consideration, was being overborne by a more intransigent policy.

In South Africa, Home Rule had a happier passage. At the end of 1905 a form of Crown Colony government had been suggested for the Transvaal. There were to be both nominated and elected members, the Governor to have great powers of rejection of Bills. The Executive would still be under the Governor—this was all the Conservatives would concede, but the Liberal Cabinet, by February, 1906, had decided in favour of complete self-government. When the proposals were known they were violently attacked; "Dangerous, audacious and reckless" was Balfour's description of the experiment. Lansdowne and Milner predicted a Boer Government which would evict the whole British civil service. If the matter had depended on legislation, the Lords would probably have rejected it, but the new constitution was issued under Crown Patent, it was to inaugurate "immediate responsible government for the Transvaal". On December 17th the House of Commons, by resolution, approved the new democratic charter. It was the crowning achievement of Campbell-Bannerman's career.

There remained the scheme for dealing with the Lords. A Bill passed three times in the Commons was to become law after six months (afterwards in the Parliament Act, two years were to elapse between the first rejection and legislation). There was no such provision as to Money Bills as appeared later, for no one then conceived the possibility of the Lords rejecting such measures. A long debate followed the introduction of the proposals. The Labour Party moved that the House of Lords ought to be abolished, but this, of course, was not at the time a serious suggestion.

The resolution approving the scheme was carried in the Commons by four hundred and thirty-two votes to one hundred and forty-seven. It was clear that Irish support would also be forthcoming. They saw in the Liberal proposals the only way to Home Rule.

This was almost the last public work of the Prime Minister; he continued to preside at the Cabinet until February of the next year. On April 22nd, 1908, he died. He was the first leader, since Fox, in whom advanced Liberals could expect to find full understanding, sympathy and confidence.

The passing of the great Radical statesman at a comparatively early age had consequences, it would seem, decisive for the future of the Liberal Party. Asquith, his successor, educated in the formal atmosphere of classical Oxford and the Inns of Court, though possessed of an eminently honest and judicial mind, lacked that foreseeing genius which is the endowment of so few politicians. That the commercial assumptions of Victorian England had resulted in the subordination of life to the pursuit of profit was not to him a distasteful notion. The accumulation of so

F*

large a share of national wealth in the hands of a very few people (and
they often of an undesirable kind) gave him, it would seem, very little
concern; in his view the diversion of the employment of surplus wealth
from public necessities to luxury was inevitable. Retrenchment, the old
panacea, the lifting of taxation from the capitalist, seemed, save in case
of urgent necessity, to be the prime purpose of financial administration.
The social services must be curtailed rather than taxes should unduly rise.
He did not discriminate between the growing monopolies and price-fixing
combinations of his time and the old, small, competitive businesses which
Liberalism, through a perverted reading of the fashionable doctrine
of the survival of the fittest, had thought to be inevitable, and indeed
excellent.

All this was to say that, in essentials, he repudiated his predecessor's
dictum that England had become a pleasure-ground for the rich.
He had little sympathy with the now active and popular socialistic
opinion.

Although the Labour Party had been blamed by their adherents for
their constant support of Campbell-Bannerman, it might at least be
urged on their behalf that they knew instinctively that he was on their
side; the same could not be said of the new Prime Minister.

For the time (still being Chancellor of Exchequer), he made himself
popular by introducing an Old Age Pension scheme giving 5s. a week
to persons over seventy who had no more than 8s. a week of their own.
The Tory Lords and Rosebery opposed it, the latter declaring that "it
would deal a blow at the Empire which might be almost mortal"—a
form of Imperialism which the most ardent must have found disquieting.
The Opposition attempted to amend the Bill in Committee, but the
Speaker ruled their efforts out of order, and the Lords submitted. It
was an indication what they would be likely to do with a distasteful
budget.

A further attempt to solve the education impasse was made. A
second Bill, which would have stopped the rate grant to denominational
schools, while permitting specific religious teaching to be given in council
ones, at one time seemed to offer hopes of conciliation, but, again, theological acrimonies prevented all chances of legislation by consent. Looking
back, as the Council schools were continually encroaching on the non-
provided, it would seem that the Church were very ill advised in
refusing the right of entry into the public schools which the Bill gave
them.

In June, 1908, Austria formally annexed Bosnia and Herzegovina,
which she had controlled since the Treaty of Berlin, and the Russians
took umbrage at the act. It became clear that the Germans were behind
Austria in their action. The Russians by now had an alliance with
France, and the alignment of forces, which some years after made peace
impossible, was already ominously apparent. The Turks, who had been
affronted by the annexation, received from Austria the Sandjak of Novi-
Bazar and certain financial compensation. Germany threatened Russia
that if she did not recognize the annexation she would allow Austria a
free hand. The Serbians, who had claimed access to the sea, were reluctantly abandoned by Russia; she was ill-prepared for war and, in the end,
the Teutonic powers undoubtedly increased their influence over Eastern

Europe. What is more significant is that they had achieved this by little-disguised threats of war. The Kaiser was evidently intending to use force, or the fear of it, as his prime method of diplomatic action. Thus the seeds were sown of which the full harvest has not yet been gathered.

All this necessarily meant an increase in the service estimates which the Admiralty very properly demanded. Curiously, in the light of subsequent history, Winston Churchill was found to be supporting Lloyd George, now Chancellor, in his demand for economy; but in the end, largely owing to public agitation, the Admiralty won, getting eight new capital ships. It is to be noted that the German menace was now very clearly recognized by the whole nation.

To raise this extra sum and, generally, to implement Liberal pledges, Lloyd George, in his famous Budget, introduced a scheme for the taxation of land values with duties on undeveloped land and increment. For years the land round great cities had passed from agricultural to building-site value, and the owners had thus reaped immense capital gains through the necessity of the community to acquire more houses near their work. Even Asquith, supposed in his own language to be "a financier of a respectable and more or less conservative type", thought the taxation of the added value to be consistent with natural justice that "the State should from time to time levy toll"; a guarded defence—it was evident that his approval of the Budget was not enthusiastic.

A Budget Protest League was formed by the Conservatives. They seemed to have lost all sense of proportion, and Lloyd George, by very offensive remarks about Dukes and Peers, exasperated them still further. Regarding the matter with the soothing tranquillity of time, the whole dispute seemed a little absurd. On the Progressive side the tax did really almost nothing to cope with the fast accumulating and surplus wealth of the rich; the uncontrolled language of the Opposition, which daily described the proposed taxes as confiscation and robbery, helped only the growth of opinion that the Lords were utterly self-regarding and that the abolition or the curtailment of their powers was essential to the national interest.

The other taxes (apart from the 20 per cent unearned increment on land payable on sale or death) were a larger income and a new supertax, and increased duties on spirits and tobacco. The biographer of Lord Balfour says, somewhat naïvely, that the Conservative decision to oppose the land taxes "sprang from the irresistible instinct of self-preservation in the class from which the Party derived its tradition and much of its strength. The land taxes and the land valuation clauses were a death blow to the landed gentry". (*Balfour*, Vol. 2, p. 55.) Whether they or the speculative builder were most affected may be disputed, perhaps by then they were indistinguishable. On November 16th Lord Lansdowne moved in the Lords that: "This House is not justified in giving its consent to the Bill until it has been submitted to the judgment of the people". Balfour, next day, approved this action; on the 30th Lansdowne's motion was carried by three hundred and fifty to seventy-five votes.

This division showed the growing contempt of constitutional propriety and usage which was steadily growing in the Conservative Party, soon to be exemplified in Ulster. It was very many years since the House of Lords had tampered with finance, the raising of which is constitutionally the principal reason for the summoning of the Commons. In the King's speech this is recognized when he directs the financial part to the House of Commons alone. The Conservative Party had inaugurated a constitutional revolution.

On December 3rd Parliament was dissolved; the Peers had for the moment succeeded, but their victory was to prove a costly one.

The issue at the election was expressed in the resolution, carried in the expiring House of Commons by 349 to 134 votes, that "the action of the House of Lords" in refusing to pass into law the financial provision made by this House for the service of the year is a breach of the Constitution and an usurpation of the rights of the Commons. During the election Lord Rosebery took occasion to say that he had "long since ceased to be in communication with the Liberal Party". It was the end of the Liberal League.

The outgoing Parliament had much legislation to show to its credit; among other things the establishment of the Union of South Africa. On one matter, the exclusion of the negroes from the franchise, Asquith reluctantly had to give way. At this time he was approving more of votes for the African natives than for women at home—so inscrutable are the processes of the human mind that no explanation for this outlook will be here attempted; it is sufficient to record the fact. Milner and the Opposition generally had been hostile, their Imperialism seemed to stop short at the African continent; but Balfour, in the House, generously admitted that the South African Act was a "wonderful issue out of the horrors of war. I do not believe the world shows anything like it in its history", he concluded.

It appeared that the Tariff Reformers and Chamberlain had incited the Lords to throw out the Budget; for the reason, said Asquith, that it provided a sound substitute for their schemes, rather than because it was socialistic; it was evident that Socialism, whatever it had meant to Harcourt, was most distasteful to the Prime Minister.

The Government majority after the election was only one hundred and twenty-four; without the Irish and Labour Party they could not have survived. It was uncertain what line the Irish would take. Redmond was suspicious, the Irish had objected to the spirits duty in the last Budget and, if they again opposed, the Government might fall. The Government refused to withdraw these duties, and at the end of April the Irish voted for the same Budget as the rejected one; the next day, the 28th, it was accepted by the Lords—they had won the first, but lost the second round.

Meanwhile, in March, resolutions, afterwards embodied in the Parliament Bill, had been passed. Save that it contained the clause that a Bill certified to be a Money Bill by the Speaker was one with which the Lords could not interfere, it followed the Campbell-Bannerman scheme, extending only, as has been said, the period for which the Lords could delay the measure. Further, the life of Parliament was to be limited to five years.

In June, King Edward VII had died, and a Conference with the Conservative leaders to discuss the relations between the two Houses was inaugurated. The Labour Party were not represented and, apparently, made no protest. Home Rule and other constitutional matters were sought to be excluded from the Parliament Bill, but this was 'tactics' again—of course with such a concession the Irish would vote against the Government—in any case it was impossible to draw any such distinction. The Conference broke up and the Prime Minister saw the new King, who promised, that if the election supported the Government he would "use the constitutional last resort to prevent it being stultified in the subsequent Parliament". This was to be kept secret, and even the Opposition leaders did not know of the royal assurance until the following July.

In the event, the election made practically no change in the balance of parties; owing to the foolish manœuvres of the Conservative leaders the curtailment of the powers of the House of Lords could no longer be avoided.

When, on July 18th, Lloyd George told the Conservative leaders that the King had agreed to create peers sufficient if need be to carry the Parliament Act, great differences of opinion were expressed among them as to what course they ought to take. With these disputes a history of Liberalism is not directly concerned. It appears that in 1910 Lloyd George had approached Balfour in view of the danger of war to form a coalition. The proposal was laid before the inner Cabinet—it included suggestions for a settlement on the questions of Second Chamber reform, Home Rule and National training for defence, together with an impartial enquiry into the fiscal system. How far the further proposal that Asquith should go to the Lords (which would have meant his withdrawal from the office of Prime Minister) was known to him and his friends it is not possible to say—it certainly did not appear in Lloyd George's memorandum. The authority for it is Mrs. Dugdale in her *Life of Balfour* (Vol. 2, p. 79), where she quotes J. Hill's diary to that effect. In the obituary notice of Lord Balfour in *The Times* of March 20th, 1930, it is said that "a common programme was laid down, Mr. Asquith being excluded." Balfour, however, declined participation in the intrigue". If Asquith knew of this, he behaved subsequently, during the Marconi troubles, with extraordinary forbearance and loyalty—in any case, whatever discussions there were came to nothing. The position of Balfour himself was not strong; the Tory Party was enraged at the counsel of submission given by its elder statesmen, for both Lansdowne and Balfour were in favour of surrender. A violent campaign was launched against their philosophic leader, and in November, 1911, he resigned, his place being take by Bonar Law.

The most important legislation of that year was the National Health and Unemployment Insurance Act introduced by Lloyd George. It contained features which have left a lasting mark upon the policy of this country; in the first place, in order to carry out its provisions it gave to the Minister great powers of a novel order, to legislate by order and regulation, under the Statute, without further consultation with Parliament —a power found so attractive to the Bureaucracy and so speedy in its operation that nearly every Government Department exercising administrative functions is now endowed with similar authority. In the end it may operate to displace parliamentary control of the executive. It was not content with administrative regulation; the Bill also in effect excluded the Courts from nearly all jurisdiction to decide whether a particular person was or was not entitled as a matter of law to receive benefit.

The third new feature was that the measure imposed obligations on limited classes of persons not arising out of their occupational function, as does, say, the Army Act, but the extent of its operation was solely dependent upon income—broadly, only the poor were affected. This exclusive compulsion on the humble, said Belloc, was the institution of the "servile state"—the argument was too philosophic, perhaps too inconvenient, to be understood by politicians. The Labour Party, who, as a whole, supported the Bill, had a minority who objected to the scheme being contributory, but no one took the point in the House that it was only compulsory on the poor. Lloyd George subsequently spoke of the staunchness and loyalty of the Liberal members—no thanks were accorded to the Labour Party for taking their share in the considerable obloquy which followed the passage of the Bill. Attacked by their own following for their subservience to the Liberals, by the Liberals they were treated with contempt. The time was to come when Liberals would vainly seek an alliance with the then despised forces of Labour.

The year 1912 witnessed the last Home Rule Bill before Parliament. No one foresaw that when the Irish question was eventually settled the representatives of that country would appear as Plenipotentiaries, speaking of treaties as between independent nations. It may have passed the minds of some old Conservatives of long memories, with the example of South Africa before them, that they would have been wiser to have compromised with Gladstone; certainly from an Imperial point of view, nothing sort of complete secession could have been worse than the settlement to which the English Government was ultimately driven, but for that the Liberal Party was not responsible.

Indeed their days of responsibility were rapidly drawing to a close, perhaps for ever. Meanwhile, Home Rule and Welsh Disestablishment still awaited consideration.

It was decided to include all Ireland in a Bill, allowing that Ulster's case might be met by amendment. The measure was welcomed by a National Convention in Dublin. Peace and war, treaties and customs, were reserved for the Imperial Parliament, where forty-two Irish members were still to sit. There were transitional provisions affecting the Irish constabulary, and restrictions on the imposition of religious disabilities.

In January, 1913, the Bill had its third reading in the Commons; to be rejected in the Upper House by a majority of two hundred and fifty-seven.

Meanwhile, under the stimulus of Sir Edward Carson, a so-called "Provisional Government", with armed forces, was established in Ireland. Another lawyer, F. E. Smith, joined him as aide-de-camp. The Government did nothing to prevent these flagrant illegalities. Whether they were wise or not in the action they took is questionable. Discontent was general. In 1911 no less than nine hundred and three big strikes and lock-outs were raging. In 1913 the number had risen to an average of one hundred and fifty a month. Tom Mann, the revolutionary trade union leader, was treated less leniently than Carson—he was imprisoned for inciting the troops to mutiny. The contrast between them should have given the Labour Party its opportunity, but under the hesitant leadership of MacDonald nothing was done, and a supine support was given to the Government in nearly all its doings and omissions, though Henderson in 1910, speaking generally, had gone so far as to say: "The Labour Party is not always treated with that consideration and fair play to which it is entitled".

Women's suffrage was another issue. The Labour Party were pledged to it, the Liberals were not. Prices were rising, for gold was becoming cheap; the pound of 1900 was now worth only sixteen shillings. The miners were demanding a minimum wage for workers in bad places, which rapidly spread to a movement for an all-round minimum.

The railways had a dispute as to the recognition of their unions, which in the end reluctantly was accorded. In March, 1912, Asquith very hesitantly agreed to the fixing of the miner's minimum wage. The principle had already been recognized in the case of sweated industries, yet to the old *laissex-faire* mind of the Prime Minister, to fix wages by statute was almost heretical.

The failure both of the Government and the Labour Party to meet the industrial crisis with any more resolution than they had shown in the case of Ulster, led to the growth of Syndicalism and a clamour for striking, not merely to obtain better conditions in a particular trade, but as a means of reconstituting the whole social fabric and destroying Capitalism. The activities of Mr. Osborne to prevent trade union funds being spent on parliamentary candidates, though successful in the Courts, by putting further obstacles in the way of parliamentary representation, actually strengthened the hands of the Syndicalists.

A compromise in 1913, not disturbed until 1927, enabled individual trade unionists to withhold their subscriptions from political objects. It was no great victory for the Labour Party, but it was almost the only one to be recorded before the Great War.

The Irish position became worse; attempts at settlement were made by the King and by direct contact between the Leaders (Labour, as usual, being omitted from all consideration). They allowed these great decisions to be taken without any recognition being made of their existence. This is not a history of the Labour Party, and it is not directly relevant to trace that sense of inferiority which prevented any degree of self-assertion. It was useless for them constantly to proclaim their independence; in Parliament they behaved in a manner far more subservient than did the old Radicals. The selection of MacDonald as leader, in place of Keir Hardie, accentuated their feebleness. What is important is to note that few in the Liberal Party had the imagination to realize that, nervous and fumbling as the Labour leaders were, the working-class movement who sent them to Parliament was rapidly coming into its own heritage. In the industrial field it had taken the offensive; if Liberalism was to become anything but an outmoded middle-class and Nonconformist coterie, it behoved its adherents to be generous to those who were at least prepared to support any reformist proposal which went in the direction of social democracy.

In the result, as is known, the new movement of Labour was ignored and its aspirations mocked at by the old-fashioned Liberals. The error of underestimating the forces behind Labour, subservient as might be its political behaviour at the moment, was in the end to destroy Liberalism as a potent political force.

From the problems of Ulster and industrial dispute the country passed to that of war. In July, 1914, an attempt by non-party conference to define the area to be excluded from the Home Rule Bill had failed. In September, the Home Rule Bill and that dealing with Welsh disestablishment which had passed the Commons in 1912 were to be placed under the Parliament Act, but with a suspensory clause providing that they should not come into force for twelve months, or, if the war still continued, until a date to be fixed by Order in Council.

In the case of Ireland, Parliament was to be given power to pass an amending Bill excluding Ulster. Bonar Law and his party took the occasion of the debate to insult the Prime Minister, comparing his conduct with that of the Germans in entering Belgium—they walked out of the House, though the war was then at a most critical stage. The failure to settle the Irish measure may well have assisted the revolutionaries in 1916; in any case it was a poor return for that Nationalist loyalty to England which later caused the political ruin of Redmond and his followers.

As the war developed, the impatience of the Conservatives at being kept out of office, where they might hope to participate in and influence the control of the war, increased. They suspected a shortage of munitions, and were very uneasy at the resignation of Fisher from the office of First Sea Lord. It was Lloyd George who forced the matter—Bonar Law and he had been in contact. He knew that the shell shortage was known to the leaders of the Opposition and he believed that the only way out to avoid recrimination in public and to fortify the future was a national coalition. He threatened to resign unless Bonar Law could come to Downing Street. Of all this Balfour knew nothing, but soon all was settled; a coalition government was formed, Balfour became First Lord of the Admiralty, McKenna Chancellor of the Exchequer, and Lloyd George went to the new Ministry of Munitions. The Liberal Government was at an end. It is only necessary to add that Labour was contemptuously thrown a sop in the appointment of Arthur Henderson as Minister of Education, an office which, by common consent, beyond the barest routine administration, scarcely functioned in war-time.

This was in May, 1915; after much dissension about conscription, during which dispute Lloyd George threatened to resign, compulsory service was imposed. But divergences still existed in the coalition; they culminated in a demand by Lloyd George, now Secretary for War, that the Prime Minister should cease to be President of the War Committee. According to Churchill (*The World Crisis*, 1916–1918, Part I, p. 249), Asquith was at first prepared to agree, but later refused, whereupon Lloyd George did actually resign. This act brought down the Government; the Prime Minister, in his turn, proffered his resignation, and Lloyd George became Prime Minister. Henderson still represented Labour in this, the second coalition.

. . . .

It is now nearly thirty years since Asquith ceased to be Prime Minister in a Liberal Government; from that time the Liberals have never comprised a quarter of the House. In 1918, after the election, when Lloyd

George and his followers and the Conservatives went to the country as one, the independent Liberal representation fell to thirty-three, that of Labour was just over sixty. Asquith himself lost his seat. An offer by him to assist at the Peace Conference was not accepted by the then omnipotent Lloyd George. When he, in his turn, was overthrown by a Carlton Club 'palace revolution', some of the 'National Liberals', as they called themselves, being without an organization and attacked by the Conservatives, tried to return to orthodox Liberalism, but most of the local independent associations decided to oppose them. In the result, sixty-four Independent and fifty-three 'National Liberals' were returned. Together they were outnumbered by Labour, who were now one hundred and forty-two strong.

The Conservative Government lasted but a short time; in November, 1922, Baldwin again went to the country—Protection being the issue. Now was the time for the Free Traders to come to some accommodation. Lloyd George and Asquith issued a joint manifesto which had the result of raising the total Liberal membership to one hundred and fifty-eight; Labour was one hundred and ninety-one and still officially pledged to Free Trade, though many of its younger members no longer held passionate convictions about that ancient dogma. In the event MacDonald took office, depending on the Liberals for his majority.

The author of this book was a member of the MacDonald Government, and it is his opinion that the Liberals were prepared to consider a joint programme which might have led to great social benefit for the poorer classes. Although some of the Labour Party were committed to Socialist theories (some, like the writer, inclining more to the method of the mediæval guild), there was a great amount of legislation on which they and the advanced Liberals could have agreed. There was suspicion on the part of some of the Labour politicians of any "fraternising" with Liberals, but such an adroit politician as MacDonald could, perfectly honourably, have come to a private understanding as to the promotion of selected measures, by methods known to every member of Parliament, without any overt proclamation of alliance.

In fact he did no such thing; from the outset he held himself markedly aloof from those on whom he depended for his power. This was an impossible situation; had he not wished to work with the Liberals, he should not have taken office. To expect support without some degree of concession was ridiculous. As is said by the biographies of Lord Asquith, for "lack of touch between the two parties, the life of the Government seemed always to be in danger".

A Housing Act was passed with Liberal support, but on Asquith suggesting a committee of enquiry into the "Campbell case" (a withdrawn Communist prosecution), MacDonald, though there was ample precedent for a government remaining in office in such circumstances, very impetuously resigned. At that election, at which a proposed treaty with Bolshevik Russia was used to alarm the voters, the Liberal representation fell to forty; Labour, although its number of seats was less than before, actually increased its total vote by over a million.

Asquith was defeated at Paisley, and shortly afterwards took a peerage. It was evident that the leadership in progressive politics had passed away from the Liberal Party.

Even then, small as they were in numbers, they were divided; there was, as ever, a Radical and a Whig wing. The divergence came out very clearly at the time of the General Strike in 1926, roundly condemned by Asquith and Simon, but sympathetically treated by Lloyd George in the sense that he realized that there were grievances to be redressed and that the Government was not free from blame.

The same cleavage was witnessed when, next year, the Government introduced their Trade Union Bill to make large-scale striking, affecting the community, illegal. On the whole, Sir John Simon lent the weight of his authority in support of the Government. Lloyd George and Mr. Harney, a K.C., supported the Labour Party in opposition. Moreover, Lloyd George insisted on keeping his party fund distinct from that of the Chief Whip, which was held in trust for the whole organization. The National Liberal Federation sought to raise a new revenue from a "Million Fund Appeal", but the results were not enough adequately to finance a general election. Liberal reunion, to quote Lord Oxford, "has turned out to be a fiction, if not a farce". Lloyd George insisted that his fund was at his personal disposal; Asquith was unwilling to wrangle with him about money—in October, 1926, he resigned the leadership of the Party.

Poor as was the representation of the Liberal Party in Parliament, their condition was even worse than their numbers would disclose. Broadly speaking, the rural and suburban areas were Conservative, the industrial ones inclined to be Labour; it was only on the "Celtic fringe", as it was called; in Wales, Scotland and Cornwall, that an old-fashioned type of Nonconformist Radicalism held its own, and even there the growth of collectivist assumptions was at last penetrating even into the agricultural industry. The labourers' trade unions and minimum wage, the application of scientific methods to farming and the urbanizing influences of the cinema, the etherial activities of the broadcasting corporation and, above all, the motor omnibus, were fast breaking up an age-long rural self-sufficiency.

Dogmatic theological politics were ceasing to attract the young, who, conveyed in their childhood to neighbouring towns for education under the Hadow scheme, were becoming secular in outlook. Gradually the country, like the towns, was becoming ranged as Conservative or Labour, the latter slowly winning the labourers' assent. The Liberal farmer, in perplexity, taking refuge in pluto-conservatism, the modern substitute for old Tory.

But another reason, even more deadly, was sapping the last strongholds of Liberalism. By 1930 it was recognized that the hope of a Liberal Government being returned within the lifetime of its remaining supporters was very slender. No one joining it could hope to receive the fruits of patronage in Government, Church or Law. To adhere to the Party entailed an abnegation which few would care to accept. Even the laudable desire to serve the State in office would be frustrated. The Party retired to the fastnesses of Summer Schools and Universities—there they prepared schemes for the regeneration of Society by Liberal principles. Their views obtained a hearing in the Press, who, having no real fear of Liberalism, hoped to embarrass Labour by causing disharmony as to ends and method by popularizing the rival schemes of other progressives. This gave to the Liberals an unreal importance. The electors as a whole did not read the reports of the young Liberal intellectuals; in the testing times of elections they proved impotent to sway votes.

Yet, at bottom, a great matter was at stake. In their several ways both Conservative and Labour were inclined to be authoritarian. They looked to the State and its power to control the individual citizen, whether in matters military or social. The necessity of war had brought about conscription, and it was then to be noted that academic Liberals, such as Sir John Simon, were more reluctant to introduce it than were the Trade Unionists who, at least, did not dislike a compulsion which, in theory at any rate, was to be imposed without distinction of persons.

The many Liberals who, after the first German War, drifted over into the Labour Party—Haldane, Ponsonby, Trevelyan, Lees Smith, Kenworthy, Benn and others—were all ready to accept Collectivism. The greatest of them all, Haldane, who became Labour Chancellor in 1924, had been offered the Board of Education by MacDonald. He was never a Socialist, but had no prejudices against collectivist activity. He was an Hegelian and looked upon the nation as a corporate entity—why he ever joined the old individualistic Liberal Party is more difficult to explain than his association with Labour. At the end he desired "a progressive party more wide in its scope than any we have seen".

He thought the old feud between Liberal and Labour could only end in futility—now that the Liberals were fast abandoning their individualistic prejudices, the hostility was not only absurd, but fatal to social advancement.

As Lord Haldane said in 1925: "The mistake Tories and Whigs alike made was in failing to see that as the franchise was extended, and as education permeated further and further, it became vital for any political party which desired to remain effective to be in the closest contact with the people. Labour is the only party that has so far succeeded in giving this faith to its supporters".

Despite these endeavours to promote reconciliation among Progressives, the Liberal Party went to the poll in 1929 in opposition to Labour, returning only fifty-eight strong, while the Labour Party became the largest in the House with two hundred and eighty-eight members; the Conservatives numbering but two hundred and sixty.

For two years the Liberals were reduced to the same position as Labour had sustained between 1906 and the War, supporting them in the lobbies without any real share in determining policy. During this time useful legislation in housing, road improvement and electrification was passed, but the real problem was unemployment—here all devices in the way of public works and relief proved utterly insufficient.

The Labour Party had never given serious consideration to the third element in their credal triad, the nationalization of the means of exchange. The Socialists, as a whole, had been most unwilling to study the more modern aspects of economics; Snowden proved himself in office to be an orthodox Gladstonian Chancellor—Banks and Credit were sacred, not to be touched by any collectivist principle. The notion that credit controlled industry, that mere nationalization did not touch the real problems of wealth production, was an idea which developed later than the time when Snowden, MacDonald and their contemporaries had come to their ideas, nor did the advanced Liberals take the problem of credit into their consideration. In a work entitled the *Liberal Way*, published in 1934, issued with the authority of the Liberal Federation, under the heading "Finance", all that is proposed is that the Board of Direction of the Bank of England should include representatives of Government, industry, trade and labour; otherwise the ancient refuge for the confused, the dilatory method of a Royal Commission, was suggested (p. 120). They admit that £463,000,000 was spent in 1930 on social services, which vast sum went mostly to poor people in the form of pensions, unemployment and sickness benefit and the cost of education. Nevertheless, they think that the only remedy for the "crippling weight" on industry is to "free trade from its shackles", which, if it mean anything, is but the old plea for free importation. For the rest, the demand of the workers for a share or the control of industry, as exhibited in the desire of the Miners' Federation to co-operate with the State in organizing their industry—a desire now fast spreading to other industries—is ignored. Poverty, insecurity of livelihood and unhealthy conditions of life are cited as the causes which most seriously restrict true liberty" (p. 187). The dissolution of the Poor Law and the distinction made in the Unemployment Acts of recent years, distinguishing between insurance and relief, is praised, but there is a complete lack of recognition of the fact that the immense wealth which plutocracy had gathered into its hands before the second great War had made cultural and social freedom for the dispossessed impossible. The danger to liberty of great State enterprises is emphasized, and the evils of the programme of the Labour Party in this direction exposed, but of the no less, and far more sinister, powers of uncontrolled trusts and combines, working for dividends, and not even in theory for Society, little is said.

Thus, until the Coalition of 1931, formed in the financial crisis of that year, when once again the Liberal Party was split asunder, the Party either grudgingly assisted Labour or aided the Conservatives. In either case the Liberals did little to revive that belief in the sanctity of individual right which is the fundamental justification for their continued existence.

Though many Liberals, such as Sir Herbert Samuel and Sir John Simon, had joined MacDonald's Coalition Government, the prevailing tendency of the administration to favour Protection produced much uneasiness. At the annual meeting of the National Liberal Federation in April, 1932, much disquiet with the position of the Liberal ministers with regard to Free Trade was expressed, but no action was taken. In January of that year, Samuel, Maclean and Sinclair had already declared themselves "inflexibly opposed to the imposition of a general tariff". The Cabinet, nevertheless, agreed to support the proposal of a committee for a 10 per cent duty on many imported goods, leaving the Free Trade dissentients at liberty to express their dissent by word or vote—a most extraordinary departure from the doctrine of collective ministerial responsibility; as a result Samuel, in February, attacked the proposals of his own Government, pointing out that they wished for general Protection. In September he and Sinclair; Foot, Hamilton and Lothian resigned; Simon, Hore-Belisha and Brown remained. The immediate cause of the resignation of the more orthodox Liberals was the Conference at Ottawa, whereat it was agreed to add to the existing preferences to Dominion products taxes on foreign meat and specified minerals. In return, the Dominions consented to lower their tariffs against certain British manufactured importations.

This was too much for the Free Trade Liberals, even under the "agreement to differ". Snowden associated himself with them in resignation. The remainder of the Liberals, constituted as National Liberals, continued in or in support of the Government, but their existence as an independent party was very precarious. Most of them depended upon Conservative benevolence for their continued existence, as was also the case with the so-called National Labour Group. Both these were now protesting that their continued existence was in the national interest, but many Conservatives and the impartial historian alike must confess doubts whether the country would not have been just as well off without them. They represented no real public opinon.

The total Opposition vote was now under ninety; the National Liberal and Labour sections but confused the issue—possibly this is why their services were retained in Government.

The Liberal Federation met on February 6th, 1933, when Samuel attacked the Government's policy on tariffs. Next day the Parliamentary Liberal Party decided to support a waiting policy, Major Nathan alone deciding to go into opposition; shortly afterwards he joined the Labour Party. By May, when the annual conference met, it was clear that the Party as a whole was no longer willing to abstain from opposing the Government particularly for failure to succour the unemployed or to utilize the League of Nations; again they deplored the official tariff policy. But in the end, Samuel was still allowed a free hand in Parliament; finally, however, in November, the Liberals decided to go into "full opposition". They were to resume the "fullest independence", but even now were not prepared to come to an understanding with the Labour Party.

The programme, set out in a book compiled by Mr. Ramsay Muir, called the *Liberal Way*, was declared to the Federation by Sir Archibald Sinclair on May 4th, 1934, to be "an authoritative exposition of the principles of Liberalism"—again it was decided not to come to an agreement with the Labour Party. In September, a suggestion by Sir Charles Hobhouse that at the next election the Liberal Party should only contest those constituencies "in which it had a reasonable hope of being successful", was rejected in favour of "fighting along the widest front". The more timorous proposal would have meant restricting candidature to about one hundred constituencies.

In November, 1935, MacDonald resigned the Premiership and a greater sense of reality in politics followed when Baldwin, the leader of the one and only party really in power, the Conservative, again became Prime Minister. The pretence of non-party government was over.

The formation of the Coalition Government of 1931 is not easy to explain; the Liberals in any case played a very minor part in it. On August 22nd of that year, MacDonald, though refusing to meet his colleagues on the financial situation, had been visited by Baldwin and Neville Chamberlain. The proposal to cut unemployment pay was refused by the Labour Government; whatever economies were sought it should not be there—at length MacDonald suggested that his colleagues should resign if the unemployment pay be cut—the Cabinet for the most part declined to follow him and he resigned to lead a new Ministry; it was in this manner the new National Government had been formed.

For all this plot and counter-plot, the Liberals, as such, bore no responsibility. The loss of all Labour seats but fifty-two in the election of 1931 did nothing to strengthen the Liberals; disguised as a national triumph, it was in fact a Conservative victory—Protection, among other things, was the natural outcome. In 1935, after the election, the Independent Liberals were still negligible in number, and the holding of a National Liberal Conference in June drew attention to the divided state of the Party. Sir John Simon and Runciman declared that they were remaining true to Liberal principles in supporting the Government and influencing it in a Liberal direction. To this the editor of the *Annual Register for 1936* comments: "Whatever measure of truth there may have been in that statement, there can be no doubt that the National Liberal ministers acquiesced in many things that were quite contrary to the spirit of Liberalism" (p. 55). Indeed, Baldwin prophesied that they would all soon become Conservatives.

The Independent Liberals, now organized in a Liberal Assembly in place of the Federation, declared that nobody supporting the Nationals could be in the Liberal Party organization; they condemned the withdrawal of sanctions against Italy, which policy had been defended by Sir John Simon in Parliament. So matters continued until the resignation of Chamberlain in May, 1940, when the whole Liberal Party agreed that their Leader, Sir Archibald Sinclair, should join the Government. Under the exigencies of war, the issue between them and the National Liberals as to the participation in a Coalition Government was ended.

In September 1942, notwithstanding their participation in the War Government, the Liberals at their Assembly carried a resolution endorsing a specific programme entitled "The Liberal Goal". It is very similar in scope and intention to the formulations of Mr. Ramsay Muir; while refusing to commit itself to anything like Socialism—there is no demand even for national control of monopolies or trusts—yet the Liberal Party wished to use the State "to do whatever is necessary to overcome the evils of ignorance, squalor, idleness and want". There is proposed an "Economic General Staff to advise the Cabinet on economic problems" —it will be observed that no direct powers are to be accorded to the State as such over the conduct of industry—indeed, anything like a "planned national economy" is "utterly opposed". For the rest, the programme supports a social order in which "there shall be neither poverty nor privilege". Believing that the paramount test of all policy must be a moral one, it repudiates "unbridled individualism and the tyranny of collectivism". It would appear that no specific remedies to cope with after-war confusion are envisaged.

This economy of detail may be wise, but at the same time it is likely that the electorate will demand some guidance other than that of abstract aspiration. Already a significant drift away from the Party has been disclosed in the departure of Sir Richard Acland to form his Common Wealth Party—one which directly attacks the holding of property for purposes of individual exploitation—and seats have been won for his cause which would scarcely have gone to Liberalism. Mr. Quintin Hogg and his school of young Tories have produced a policy which, while preserving the essential features of capitalism, is far more concrete in its specific remedies for social maladjustments. Indeed, compared with these pronouncements and the complementary ones of the Labour Party, there is an academic and aloof atmosphere about the current publications of Liberalism which make them appear to be more suited to study circles and places of ethical improvement than to those demands which the consequences of protracted modern warfare are likely to impose upon future government and administration.

Thus, while insistent upon the value of personal liberty, little is said about the very real menace of the supersession of the Law by bureaucratic ordinance and decree. The peril (from a Liberal point of view) of industrial conscription being continued in times of peace is not considered. The uncritical acceptance of the *Beveridge* proposals (themselves containing potential limitations of freedom) by modern Liberals must, to an old-fashioned individualist, prove disquieting, nor is there any recognition of the growing danger of central control of local authority by nationally appointed regional officers or otherwise.

Indeed, the modern Individualists, represented by their league under the guidance of Sir Ernest Benn, are no longer apt to look to the Liberal Party, as their predecessors in the days of the philosophic Radicals were wont to do, for the natural political expression of their views. It may be that the new dispute between Liberty and Authority—perennial, but now destined under modern mass conditions of production of goods and thoughts to be acute—will destroy the old party cleavages. The influence of a victorious Russia in Europe is incalculable; the future ideals of Europe are uncertain. It may well be that politics, as they have been understood for so many years, will cease to have meaning or interest for future generations—for the time being we have to note, reluctantly or not according to our temperament, that the days which were favourable to a middle class, petty commercialism are apparently over, and to recognize that it was in such a period of English history that Liberalism flourished.

●　　●　　●　　●　　●　　●　　●

Three reasons, perhaps incompatible, have been advanced to account for the disappearance of the Liberal Party as an effective force in politics. The first, and more superficial, is to assert that the purposes for which the Whigs and their successors stood have been fully achieved: the relations of Crown and Parliament have been finally determined, the rule of Law has been irrevocably established, and the Commons, under adult suffrage, have been finally accepted as the rulers of the nation, to govern according to the people's will; there is nothing more for Liberalism to do. They have perished of success; their work is done.

Another explanation for their failure to continue as a party with any reasonable prospect of power lies in the assertion that the ideal for which Liberalism contended is spent. Sociology, it is said, has exploded the notion of the free autonomous individual—man is but the creature of his race and environment; the exact influences of each may be a subject of dispute, but essentially he is but a unit in society—we are back with Plato and Hegel.

In this latter view, planning by competent authority must be the prime concern of governments and society. Irresponsible plutocrats are to be condemned as much as eccentric anarchs; both distract the community from its essential purpose, to breed, educate and sustain functionaries to serve and fight for the Nation—all else is futile and may be dangerous. Liberalism is negative, it relies upon the notion of Liberty; social purpose, not freedom, is the modern ideal; from this standpoint, Fascism and Communism are but extreme illustrations of the good life —even a religious sanction can be found in the notion of uncritical dedication to service.

Whether, therefore, a resurrection of Liberalism is probable may depend upon the possibility of the recapture of the vision of the basic invaluable quality of personality. If the present collective outlook persists or develops, the very notion may be incomprehensible to future generations. Recurrent war has done much to destroy Liberalism. It is not an accident that Asquith, the last Liberal Leader, was unable to weather the upheaval of 1914. As has been said, his prejudices against conscription and compulsory labour delayed the passing of the Military Service Acts.

As to the Common Law, for which the first Liberal parliamentarians contended, ever since the introduction of the National Insurance Acts, one civic function after another has been withdrawn from juridical determination. The decision of the House of Lords in a recent case, that a minister has but to state that he has reasonable grounds for the exercise of his powers under some statute or regulation to justify detentions without trial, opens up a possibility of autocracy which need not necessarily be confined to the exigencies of war.

The decay of party government may assist the progress of benevolent surveillance; in the Middle Ages, the cities of Italy won their freedom through the contending claims of Pope and Emperor—when all are agreed how to organize and educate the citizen, his prospects of independence are poor.

At the same time it must be confessed that the present programme of the Liberals, as exemplified in the publications of Ramsay Muir, their political philosopher, is very inconclusive.   In 1920, under the title, *Liberalism and Industry*, he wrote: "Real liberty is not mere absence of restraint, it is security in doing, by a man's free choice, all or any of the things that are worth doing and that are not harmful to his neighbours— first and foremost the Liberal concern is to preserve or increase human liberty—Liberalism attaches an infinite value to human personality" (p. 21).

This is very fine, no instructed civilized man could dissent from it. He goes on to point out how nineteenth-century Liberalism, in its limited advocacy of the mere removal of restriction in the economic sphere, meant that "the rich were left free to employ the power that their riches gave them over the unprotected poor" (p. 29).

"Liberals, nevertheless," he declares, "believe in a man being allowed to save what he earns" (p. 49). "Far from agreeing to the abolition of the ownership of capital, the Liberal would desire to extend it more widely. In the ideal Liberal State everybody would have the chance of creating capital by thrift (*Ibid*). This kind of capitalism, it appears, Liberals still defend. In conclusion, the author, not very convincingly, asserts that "modern Liberalism is not merely helpless and bewildered in face of the problems which surround us" (p. 193). Those not in the Liberal Assembly may be less sure.

Yet a third suggestion which has been advanced to account for the fact that in this present age few boys and girls are 'born little Liberals', (or become so) is that Liberalism has so converted the other two parties that the modern Conservative and supporter of Labour alike accept all Mr. Muir's assumptions. There is much to be said for this view. If it be correct, the fall of the Liberal Party is but an incident in the general acceptance of libertarian ideals; if it be false, the failure of Liberalism may prove to be an unqualified disaster.

INDEX

5 44